GOVERNANCE
& GRIEVANCE

To Istvan –
With the greatest apprecia-
tion for your many years of
support and encouragement.

GOVERNANCE
& GRIEVANCE

Habsburg Policy and Italian Tyrol
in the Eighteenth Century

Miriam J. Levy

Warmest best wishes &
thanks.

Miriam

Purdue University Press
West Lafayette, Indiana

Published in 1988
Printed in the United States of America

Library of Congress Cataloging-in-Publication Data

Levy, Miriam J., 1935–
    Governance & grievance.

    Bibliography: p.
    Includes index.
    1. Trentino-Alto Adige (Italy)—Politics and government. 2. Tyrol (Austrian)—Politics and government.
3. Austria—History—Leopold II, 1790–1792. 4. Austria—Politics and government—1740–1848. 5. Habsburg, House of. I. Title.
DG975.T792L48   1988   945'.3807   87-15189
ISBN 0-911198-86-5 (pbk.)

Book and cover designed by Anita Noble
Maps rendered by Timothy Gilbert

CONTENTS

TABLES

ACKNOWLEDGMENTS

So many people in so many places contributed their time, knowledge, and efforts to the successful conclusion of this study that to mention them all would require another essay. But some are owed special thanks.

In Rovereto to Dr. Ferruccio Trentini, President of the Academy of the Agiati; to the entire staff of the Biblioteca Civica Girolamo Tartarotti, especially to its late director, Dr. Pio Chiusole, and to Maria Rosa la Rovere who worked so hard to facilitate access to the library's extremely rich manuscript and book collection from the eighteenth century. In Trento to Dr. Annamaria Paissan Schlechter, director of the Biblioteca Comunale di Trento, to the library's entire staff, and especially to Luigi Compasso, whose knowledge of English acquired at a NATO naval base expedited the enormous amount of research done in this library. In Innsbruck to the staffs of the Tiroler Landesarchiv and the library of the Landesmuseum Ferdinandeum, especially Dr. Wolfram Wieser of the latter.

To the legion of historians and archivists in Vienna: at the library and Historisches Institut of the University of Vienna, the Nationalbibliothek, the Kriegsarchiv, the Allgemeinesverwaltungsarchiv, the Hofkammerarchiv, and especially the greatest of thanks, gratitude, and appreciation to everyone at the Haus-, Hof- und Staatsarchiv, where so much of the original work in this study was documented. To the many colleagues and friends in Vienna for their friendship, encouragement, and assistance in what was for only a very short time a strange city; especially to Dr. Adam Wandruszka of the University of Vienna; to Drs. Moritz and Eva Csáky, of the same University; to Dr. Grete Klingenstein-Walter at the University of Graz; and to Dr. Waltraud Heindl at the Österreichisches Ost- und Südosteuropa Institut.

To the many historians in New York City who assisted me: to Dr. Edith Link of Hunter College for sharing her knowledge and expertise in Habsburg history; to Professor Istvan Deak of Columbia University, who as my doctoral adviser first encouraged me in this research; to Professor Marc Raeff, also of Columbia, for his interest and support as he read, reread, and again reread the manuscript; and to Professor Harold Segel, director of Columbia's Institute on East Central Europe, for his advice and for making available the facilities of his institute.

ACKNOWLEDGMENTS

A note of particular thanks to Professor Karl Roider of Louisiana State University and Professor Charles Ingrao of Purdue University, for their long-standing encouragement, advice, and friendship begun during the Fulbright year in Vienna's archives.

A special thanks to the libraries of Columbia University—especially to the staffs of the reference desk and the Interlibrary Loan office in Butler Library—for their perseverence in helping track down obscure citations and in obtaining almost half the published works cited here plus microfilm of some unpublished sources.

Finally, my appreciation to the Fulbright–Hays Commission for the fellowship that made the original research in Vienna possible and to the Institute on East Central Europe for subsequent travel funds for follow-up research.

To all these people and organizations and to the many more whom I regrettably cannot name here, thank you for helping make this work possible and—equally as important—enjoyable to research and write.

Miriam J. Levy
JULY 1987

INTRODUCTION

Government policies often pit central against regional interests and some regional interests against one another. This was especially true in the Habsburg Monarchy of the eighteenth century as enlightened absolutists sought to centralize and modernize their realm. Dealing with the intensity and nature of the grievances that resulted from their efforts required able rulers willing to try solutions other than mere retrenchment.

From midcentury on the reforms were greater in number than ever before—or at least they seemed so to many Habsburg subjects—and reached avalanche proportions under Joseph II. Each succeeding ruler had to cope both with the need for change and with the new problems and reactions created by change. Each succeeding ruler also had his or her own style of government, and a close look at Habsburg policy for Italian Tyrol affords an interesting opportunity for a comparison of the different approaches used by Maria Theresa, her two sons Joseph and Leopold, and her grandson Francis II. While all these rulers attempted to deal with the problems of the Italians in Tyrol, the greatest activity occurred during the reign of Leopold II when an organized movement arose that sought a redress of grievances. But the Italians were not the only problems Leopold had to face.

In 1790 when Leopold II took over as head of the Habsburg *Hausmacht* in Vienna, he brought with him the experience of twenty-five years as Grand Duke of Tuscany and a reputation as one of the century's most enlightened, shrewdest, and most capable rulers. In almost all his new lands, he found unrest ranging from open grumbling to outright rebellion. The situation in the Princely County of Tyrol was one of the more serious— exceeded only by those in the Austrian Netherlands and Hungary and perhaps in Galicia. Although there were echoes of the more distant American Revolution and the much closer French Revolution, the Estates of Tyrol (and the other lands) were reacting above all to a half-century of reform that had gradually stripped them of a meaningful role in governing their land. In Tyrol the coup de grâce had been Joseph II's abolition of almost all Estate institutions.

To cope with the reaction to his predecessors' policies, Leopold ably used several strategies, including the traditional Habsburg one of divide and conquer. In Tyrol the Germans, who were predominant, were threatening

1

rebellion. Leopold therefore encouraged the province's Italians to come forward with their own list of grievances and supported them against both the local Germans and those reforms initiated from Vienna that had greatly disadvantaged them—such as the new language laws. Most of this occurred at the beginning of Leopold's reign, with activity spurred by the convocation of the Tyrolean Diet in 1790, the first Diet in seventy years. The 1790 Italian movement in Tyrol is therefore interesting as an example and a segment of Habsburg policy toward regional interests and toward national awakening of the many peoples of the Habsburg Monarchy at the end of the eighteenth century.

Until now there has been no full account of this 1790 Italian movement—its origins, growth, and achievements and how it became part of the struggle between centralization and regional rights. In Tyrol the struggle was three cornered, involving the monarch and his bureaucracy, the German Tyroleans, and the Italian Tyroleans. The actions and interactions of these three groups, although unique to Tyrol, were in many instances indicative of what was happening elsewhere. Tyrol's grievances, Italian and German, were shared at least in part by the Habsburgs' other lands and were in large measure the outgrowth of the same reform policies begun during Maria Theresa's reign (1740–80) and continued more vigorously during the reign of her son Joseph II (1780–90). These two rulers had in fact been building on the Habsburgs' long, at times unsteady but continuing, effort begun by Maximilian I in the sixteenth century to unify and centralize their many lands, that is, to create a *Gesammtmonarchie*.

In 1790 Tyrol's German Estates—the Italians were effectively excluded from Estate membership—were clamoring for restoration of their own historic rights and institutions while rejecting the quite fair aspirations of their Italian countrymen. Tyrol's Italians, after a century or so of economic, intellectual, and cultural flowering, were ready to seek an equitable share in the affairs of the princely county, to which they had been attached or incorporated in the early sixteenth century. Leopold supported the Italians because he saw their cause as fair and just and, as noted, because he knew that they could also serve as a counterweight to the problems created by Tyrol's German Estates, dominated by the wine interests of German southern Tyrol below the Brenner Pass. However, Leopold not only became the Italians' champion; probably with much less intent, he also became a factor in politicizing their national feeling. At the same time he also sought to lead, or at least control, the German Tyroleans and guide them into less troublesome paths. And all those involved, as they discussed strategy and decided on actions, were acutely aware of the revolution going on in France—none more so than the monarch.

Tyrol's Italians had four chief grievances in 1790. First, they asked for political equity in the form of seat and vote in the Tyrolean Diet and other Estate assemblies—or, now requested for the first time, separation from German Tyrol. Second, they wanted the right to import their wines freely into the rest of Tyrol. Third, they sought the right to use their own language in their schools, administration, and courts. And fourth, they wanted some control over what happened to property inherited by their daughters, especially when these daughters married "foreign" Italians.

Tyrol's Italians were economically far ahead of the Monarchy's other peoples. In a land where feudalism and the manorial system had never taken a firm hold, their silk industry had been able to profit enormously from the beginnings of the industrial revolution at the end of the seventeenth and in the early eighteenth centuries. Vienna's policies in chartering private individuals to run the enterprises (Vienna fostered silk manufacturing throughout the Monarchy but concentrated the cultivation of mulberry trees and silkworms in the southern areas) meant that no guilds hampered the private entrepreneurs. The technology was comparatively advanced for that era, the labor market was a free market, and the state was setting up schools to train the needed hands.

As Italian Tyrol's economic prosperity increased, its intellectual and cultural life became more vigorous. By the second half of the eighteenth century, Tyrol's Italians, like Italians elsewhere on the peninsula and indeed peoples elsewhere in Europe, were engaged in debates about the extent and effect of foreign influences on national histories and languages and about the more general questions that occupied eighteenth-century discussions. The Italian Enlightenment, from its major centers in several cities, gave shape and leadership to many of these intellectual currents. Two of these centers were in the Habsburg territories of Tuscany and Lombardy—the latter being Tyrol's next-door neighbor. The academies and *illuministi* of Florence and Milan exerted a strong influence on the princely county and especially on its Italian population. The greatest impact fell on the upper strata of the population, radiating outward through such channels as Tyrolean academies and Italian-language journals as well as among those who studied and traveled abroad and had the ability to read in German, French, or even English.

By the last quarter of the eighteenth century, therefore, the Italians in Tyrol were economically prosperous, culturally developed, and had a strong sense of their *italianità*. They were ready for the politicization that Leopold II encouraged. Leopold had not of course created the dissatisfactions and disadvantages that affected the Italians in Tyrol (or the other national groups in the Monarchy). But he did sympathize with their plight and helped shape their *domande*, and ultimately he took steps to remedy many of their grievances. As he did so, he used the pressure created by the Italians to help him calm Tyrol's rebellious German-dominated Estates. With Leopold's help, the 1790 Italian movement by and large succeeded, although some of the success came after his brief reign. Yet by politicizing national feeling, yielding to local language grievances, and increasing the role of local government, Leopold also removed some of the key pieces in the Habsburgs' centuries-long effort at state building. He also nurtured some of the forces that later would help bring down the Monarchy. In Tyrol especially, the aroused national feeling did not disappear when the problems of 1790 subsided, but remained and grew. After 1860 it became the full-blown *Italia irredenta* that ultimately took not only Italian-speaking Tyrol into the Kingdom of Italy in 1918, but a large piece of German-speaking Tyrol as well.

A third national group in Tyrol in the eighteenth century should also be noted. That group was the Ladins, a Romansch-speaking people who lived primarily in a coastal area known as Ampezzo (Haiden). This area too became part of Tyrol under Maximilian I and part of Italy in 1918.

Because of the geopolitical changes since 1790, some inevitable sources of confusion exist unless the reader is forewarned and careful. First is the problem of labeling, that is, what name to apply to a particular city, area, river, or other geographic feature. Where a widely accepted English term exists (for example, Vienna, Trent), it is used. Otherwise, the terms adopted here are the ones in administrative use at the time (1790), with alternative terms indicated in parentheses at the first mention. In practice, this has usually meant adopting the German name in the predominantly German-speaking areas and the Italian name in the Italian-speaking areas, with the dividing line at the Salurn-Salorno Gap. Where conflicts remain, the German name prevalent in the administrative documents has been adopted. The one exception is the river—Etsch in German and Adige in Italian—that runs through both areas. I have indicated both names but used the one appropriate to the area because I cannot bring myself to put the name "Etsch" in Italian mouths. Alternate geographical names are cross-listed in appendix B.

A further geographic-political problem stems from the same terms having one meaning in the eighteenth century and a different one today. The attempt throughout this work has been to make the meaning eminently clear in each case without overburdening the text with repetition and explanation. The following descriptive information should help clarify some of these differences.

Eighteenth-century Tyrol can be divided into three regions. Northernmost was the area north of the Brenner, which essentially comprises present-day Tyrol. The central region was German-speaking southern Tyrol, or the Etschland, now the Alto Adige Region in Italy, an area the Germans call Südtirol. And south of the Etschland was the area then known as the Welsch Confines (*Kreis am Welschen Confinen, Circolo ai Confini d'Italia*), which today is part of the Trentino Region of Italy. The other part of the Trentino is the area that before 1804 was the ecclesiastical Principality of Trent, an independent state of the Holy Roman Empire that at the same time was "confederated" with Tyrol. The maps preceding chapter 1 should be helpful in identifying these geographic areas. A distinction must also be made between the diocese of Trent and the principality. The Prince-Bishop of Trent's temporal power extended only to his own principality, but his ecclesiastical jurisdiction extended beyond these borders into the Welsch Confines of Tyrol. Italian Tyrol of the eighteenth century was therefore a different region from today's Italian or South Tyrol.

Another source of geographical confusion comes from two different territories being referred to as Upper Austria. Beginning with the reign of Maximilian I in the early sixteenth century and continuing at least through the end of the eighteenth century, Upper Austria was an administrative division with its seat in Innsbruck. This division included Tyrol, Vorarlberg, and at times the *Vorlande* (in the eighteenth century administered separately as Anterior Austria). Under Maria Theresa, Upper Austria became a *Gubernium* or *Regierung* (government of a province or land). The very different area that is the present-day state or *Bundesland* of Upper Austria was referred to through the end of the eighteenth century as Austria above the Enns. As used here, Upper Austria has the earlier meaning.

Another problem is what title to use when referring to the ruler. In Tyrol he was the princely count or land's prince; he was also emperor because Tyrol was part of the Holy Roman Empire. But Leopold II was technically not entitled to be called emperor until after his 30 September 1790 coronation. His contemporaries paid little attention to such technicalities, however, and the author has chosen to follow their example.

The translation of many German terms also presents certain problems, especially those eighteenth-century bureaucratic terms that have no reasonable or readily understandable English equivalents or that commonly appear in German in English language texts. Therefore, to avoid confusion, only a few of these institutional names have been translated; they are defined briefly when they are introduced and then explained in more detail in appendix A.

All translations in the text, unless otherwise noted, are the author's.

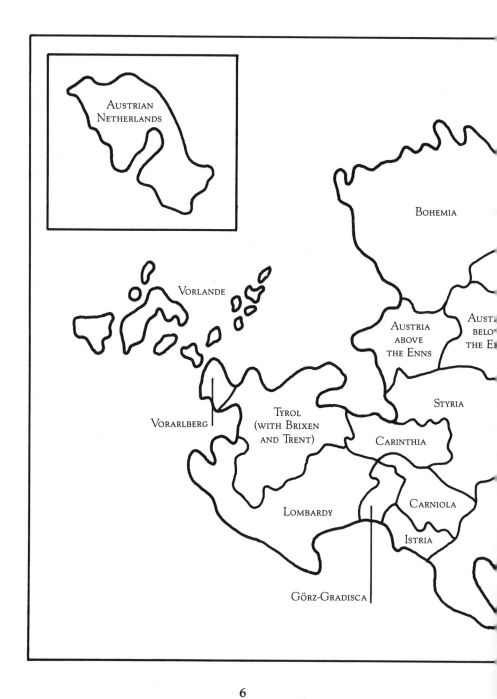

AUSTRIAN
NETHERLANDS

BOHEMIA

VORLANDE

AUSTRIA
ABOVE
THE ENNS

AUST
BELO
THE E

VORARLBERG

TYROL
(WITH BRIXEN
AND TRENT)

STYRIA

CARINTHIA

LOMBARDY

CARNIOLA

ISTRIA

GÖRZ-GRADISCA

The Habsburg Monarchy in the Late Eighteenth Century

SILESIA

GALICIA

MORAVIA

BUKOVINA

KINGDOM OF HUNGARY

TRANSYLVANIA

CROATIA

BANAT

MAPS

1790 Kreis and Principality Boundaries with Present-Day Austrian-Italian Border Superimposed

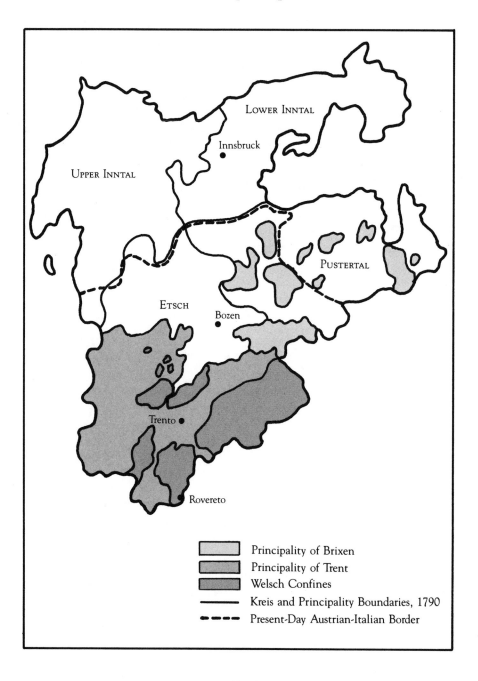

MAPS

Present-Day Tyrol (with East Tyrol), Alto Adige/Südtirol, and the Trentino

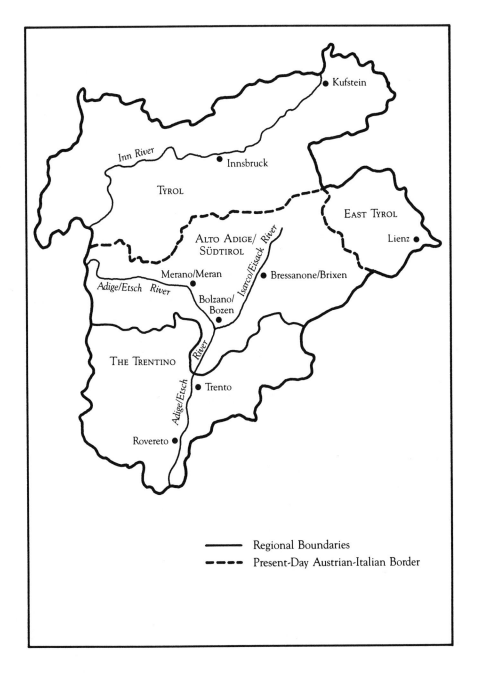

Regional Boundaries
Present-Day Austrian-Italian Border

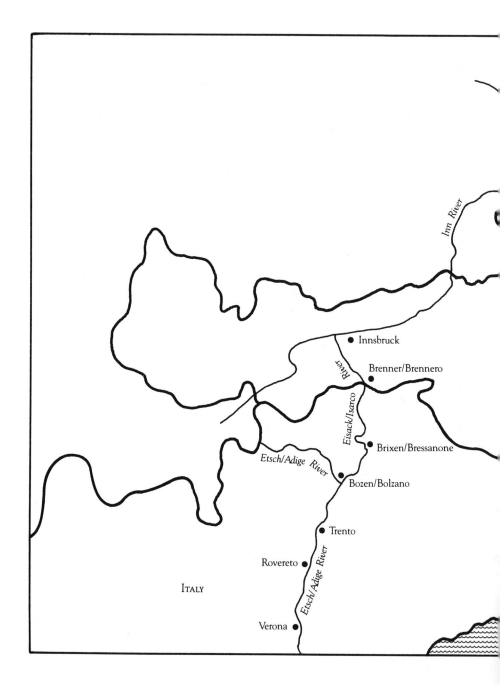

Present-Day Austria and
Part of Northern Italy

The Heart and Shield of the Habsburg Realm: Tyrol in the Eighteenth Century

Emperor Maximilian I (1493–1519), who made Innsbruck his capital, referred to the Princely County of Tyrol as the heart and shield of his empire. Tyrol, described by a modern-day Austrian as the Texas of Austria because of the people's intense regional feeling and identity, had been an independent state for several centuries, either with its own dynasty or with Habsburg cadet rulers, before it came under Vienna's permanent rule in 1665. The land's geography inevitably intertwined with its historical, political, and national development. From the sixteenth through the eighteenth centuries, the princely county had three primary geographical divisions: northern Tyrol, the area north of the Brenner Pass (approximately present-day Tyrol), which was culturally, linguistically, and historically German; southern German Tyrol, the area bounded by the Brenner Pass at the crest of the Alps in the north and the Salurn Gap just below Bozen (Bolzano) in the south (roughly the present-day Alto Adige Region in Italy, known to the Germans as *Südtirol*); and Welsch, or Italian, Tyrol, territorial enclaves that lay south of the Salurn Gap and extended almost to Verona, areas then known as the Welsch Confines (*Welsche Konfinen, Confini d'Italia,* now part of the Trentino Region of Italy).[1] (See maps preceding this chapter.) There was little dispute in the eighteenth century about what territory was Italian and what was German; the terms were then defined in cultural-linguistic terms and began to assume intense political importance only in the nineteenth century.

The princely county had been put together from bits and pieces of land gathered by the medieval Counts of Tyrol who took their name from the Castle Tirol, just outside Meran (Merano). These counts served the Prince-Bishops of Trent and Brixen as *Vogt,* the official who took care of the

13

CHAPTER ONE

ecclesiastics' temporal obligations and interests. From the vantage point of the *Vogtei*, the counts gradually extended their own authority, territorial holdings, and influence until Meinhard II (1258–95) welded the pieces into a single political entity, the (Princely) County or Land Tyrol, soon recognized as an independent state of the Holy Roman Empire. During the reign of Margarethe *Maultasch* (Pocket Mouth), the last of Meinhard's line, and her husband Ludwig of Bavaria, Tyrol received its *Magna Charta liberatum*, a 1342 document generally viewed as the first step in establishing the rights of Tyrol's peasantry. The charter guaranteed the Estates their freedoms, promised neither to change the laws nor levy new taxes without their consent, and pledged that Margarethe would not be taken from Tyrol nor foreign officials brought in. The document was directed to all four of Tyrol's Estates (prelates, nobles, burghers, and peasants) "as well as in general to all people in the County Tyrol, noble and nonnoble, rich and poor, whatever they are called or wherever they are situated in the County Tyrol."[2] In September 1363 Margarethe, by then bereft of two husbands and a son, transferred the princely county to Rudolf IV Habsburg, beginning three hundred years of Habsburg cadet-line rule, interrupted only briefly under Emperors Maximilian I and Ferdinand I.

Succeeding rulers made the peasantry's position increasingly more secure. Duke Leopold the Splendid (*Prächtige;* 1395–1411) issued a law code, or *Landesordnung,* that inter alia confirmed both the peasants' legal independence from the local nobles and their right to appeal directly to their prince. Within the next thirty years, the peasants' and burghers' positions were again strengthened as they came to the aid of the princely count in his struggles with some of Tyrol's richest and most powerful nobles, then seeking independence and recognition as free imperial knights of the Holy Roman Empire. With the help of his two lower Estates, Duke Friedrich with the Empty Purse (1406–39) broke the nobility's power and ended their aspirations for independence; from then on any influence the nobles had was derived primarily from whatever high offices they held. The two lower Estates, as their reward, received from Duke Friedrich a guarantee of their permanent role in the land's political life and in the various Estate assemblies, in some cases equal representation with the two upper Estates. The position of the peasants and burghers was further codified in the 1511 *Landeslibell,* agreed to by Maximilian I, Tyrol's Estates, and the Prince-Bishops of Trent and Brixen. The *Libell,* which came to be considered part of Tyrol's constitution, set the size of troop levies, guaranteed to all Estates the right to bear arms, and established other obligations and rights. When Tyrol's last cadet ruler died in 1665, Emperor Leopold I brought the county under the permanent and direct rule of Vienna; and in 1720 with their acceptance of the Pragmatic Sanction, the Tyrolean Estates renounced their right to have a ruler of their own, separate from the other Habsburg lands.[3]

Most of the Italian-speaking areas in eighteenth-century Tyrol had become part of the princely county in 1509 as a result of Maximilian I's wars with Venice. Originally fiefs of the Holy Roman Empire then subject to Venetian rule for a century, the areas that would become known as the Welsch Confines were not fully integrated into the Tyrolean economic or political system at the time of their incorporation. Except for the nobles who were gradually immatriculated and permitted to attend the Diet personally and the city of Rovereto that sent a deputy, the Confinants were politically disadvantaged because they had no representation in any of Tyrol's assemblies.[4] They did, of course, continue to enjoy their historical rights and role in their own cities, towns, and communes. Furthermore, the Confinants were economically restricted by a ban against their wine and brandy moving freely into the rest of Tyrol, a ban that had been in existence for two centuries before the Confines joined the princely county. As compensation, however, the Confinants were exempted from most of the taxes that other Tyroleans had to pay.

The Princely County of Tyrol, in which the Confinants sought full participation in the eighteenth century, was a land most unusual for its time. Tyrol's constitutional and social composition differed greatly not only from those of the five duchies[5] that formed the rest of the territory generally known as the Habsburgs' German hereditary lands, but also from much of Europe. In Tyrol the peasantry formed a separate Estate with voting deputies in all the land's assemblies. The largest of Tyrol's Estate assemblies was the general, or open, Diet where the nobles were entitled to attend personally and the other Estates sent representatives or deputies. Here, voting was not by curia or order; the prelates voted by religious foundation, the nobles by head, the burghers by city or town, and the peasants by jurisdiction. Nothing except economic considerations limited how many persons each town or jurisdiction might send to the Diet to cast its one vote. Therefore, when voice votes were taken, the shouting of the two lower Estates often exerted a decisive influence.

The open Diet that ratified the Pragmatic Sanction in 1720 was the last one convoked for seventy years; but other Estate institutions continued to function. The large *Ausschuss** (40 members) and the small *Ausschuss* (20 members)—kind of miniature Diets—met with greater or lesser regularity. At each meeting the four Estates were represented equally and had an equal number of notes. The members of each *Ausschuss* were technically chosen by the open Diet, but in fact certain areas had traditional seats, with none going to Italian Tyrol. The large *Ausschuss* with ten deputies from each Estate was supposed to meet when the Diet could not to deliberate on

---

*The modern meaning of *Ausschuss* is committee. In the earlier periods, however, at least in Tyrol, an *Ausschuss* often functioned as a small Diet. A deputation was then closer in function to the modern committee. I have therefore chosen to retain the German word throughout this manuscript.

important affairs of the land. It also had the right to elect the *Landeshauptmann*, the traditional leader and spokesman for the Estates and their interests. In the eighteenth century the small *Ausschuss* with five votes from each Estate met irregularly until 1728 when Charles VI began to convoke it annually, and his successors continued the practice.[6]

The small *Ausschuss* also took another form: with the same voting members but assembling at different times and with different names and functions, it became the *Steuercompromiss* or *Postulatcongress*. As such, this group met twice a year, usually for one month, to receive the ruler's tax postulates, allot taxes, and examine accounts. During the eighteenth century the Estate spokesmen at the *Steuercompromiss* began to use these meetings to present grievances, a practice that became more frequent as the other assemblies met less and less regularly.

Still another Estate institution appeared in 1721 when Charles VI introduced the *Aktivitäten,* one in Innsbruck and one in Bozen, each with one member from each Estate, chosen by the Estates themselves. These *Aktivitäten* met every fourteen days to take care of day-to-day Estate business when the small *Ausschuss* was not in session. The *Landeshauptmann* presided over the Innsbruck *Aktivität,* and his administrator (the *Landeshauptmannschafts–Verwalter*) presided over the Bozen group.[7] At none of the Tyrolean assemblies that functioned in the eighteenth century did the Italians have any deputies; the open Diet at which they did have a small voice did not meet during most of the century.

When Maria Theresa applied her tax legislation equally to all Tyrol, she in effect removed the Confinants' tax exemption together with any valid reason for limiting their rights. But the Confinants continued to be barred from political participation in the affairs of their land. By the time the open Diet was convoked again in 1790, the Italians—now paying taxes and enjoying virtually unrestricted commerce in their wines—were ready to seek political integration into the princely county *or* separation from German Tyrol and perhaps union with Mantua (then also under Habsburg rule). This was, as far as we know, the first time the request for separation was made, even in these either-or terms. And when the Italians sought equitable representation in 1790, the German wine-growing interests opposed them at every turn.

Because Tyrol had been patched together from lands that had been under different sovereigns at different times, no unified legal system existed for the entire land. By the eighteenth century, in addition to the numerous local statutes governing cities, market towns, and rural areas, three separate law codes were in effect. The Tyrolean *Landesordnung* applied to most of German-speaking Tyrol and the Principality of Brixen; the old Bavarian law, or *Buchsag,* of 1484 was observed in the former Bavarian domains of Rattenberg, Kufstein, and Kitzbühel; and a form of the 1527 Trentine Statute was in effect in the Italian areas.[8]

HEART AND SHIELD OF THE HABSBURG REALM

The organization of Tyrol's local administration was roughly the same in both Italian and German Tyrol. Each city and market town had its own historic ordinances and privileges, the towns in German Tyrol under a somewhat different general legal tradition from those in Italian Tyrol. The rural areas were divided into jurisdictions (*Gericht* in German areas and *pretura* in Italian areas), which formed the basis for peasant representation at the Diets. In Tyrol, "jurisdiction" was to "peasant" as "city" was to "burgher"; it was not uncommon, for example, to speak of the cities' bench or the jurisdictions' representatives at the various assemblies. A jurisdiction might include one commune or village; or it might include several, in which case the communes sent delegates to a jurisdiction meeting to choose deputies to the Diet. Although a city and jurisdiction might sometimes have the same name (for example, the city of Rovereto and the *pretura* of Rovereto; the city of Bozen and the *Landgericht* of Bozen), they were different political entities and might often have different interests.[9]

On the *Ausschüsse*, the smaller assemblies with equal representation for each Estate, the peasants were represented according to *Viertel* (Quarters), which were the traditional pre-Theresian divisions of Tyrol and were named after valleys, rivers, and even older *Gau* divisions. Taxes were alloted and troops levied according to *Viertel*; but not until Maria Theresa introduced, and superimposed, the *Kreis* system (retaining many of the older *Viertel* names and boundaries) was there a political authority for such areas.[10]

Population records were not kept according to nationality or language in the eighteenth century; nevertheless, most of Tyrol's Italian population lived in the Welsch Confines (see table 3-1). So, taking the total for that *Kreis* as an approximation of the Italian population, about 367,000, or eighty-four percent, of Tyrol's approximately 426,000 inhabitants were German in 1781, and about 59,000, or sixteen percent, were Italian.[11] The Italians therefore constituted a numerically significant and economically advanced proportion of the population, certainly enough to entitle them to equitable political participation in Tyrol's government. A breakdown of the population by Estate is more elusive, however. The available data were gathered at the end of the eighteenth century primarily for recruiting and taxation. Census categories therefore classified people, one way or another, as recruitable, taxable, or neither. The result was that females, minor children, and family dependents of any kind, regardless of Estate, fell into the "neither" category. Most nobles were counted as "nobles," but others were counted with burghers and even some peasants in the categories of "officials" and "burghers and professionists"—professionists being those who lived in rural areas and engaged in independent trades or professions. There is no way of knowing how many of the officials (*Beamte*) were noble and how many were burghers, or how many in the category of burghers and professionists were actually burghers. Although having a right to take part

CHAPTER ONE

in political affairs did not depend on owning land, the census category of "peasants" usually referred only to those who owned land; "cottagers" were counted separately, and the rest of the rural population were in some other category, if counted at all. Furthermore, since Tyrol was united with Brixen and Trent for purposes of defense and taxation, the population figures for the three areas were often combined. And because under Joseph II Tyrol and Vorarlberg were administratively united, their populations were often counted together. The available figures therefore offer a mix of information, none of it directly indicating the number or proportion for each of Tyrol's Estates. However, by combining figures from different sources (either totals or ratios) and making some assumptions, a rough picture of Tyrol's 1780 population emerges (including wives and children of the nobles, burghers, and peasants) (see table 1-1). Although Tyrol's Estate demography may be difficult to ascertain, the princely county's social texture is far more accessible.

TABLE 1-1

Estimate of Tyrol's Population by Estate, 1780

Clergy	3,000
Nobles	3,100
Burghers and Professionists	42,000
Peasants (in effect, all others)	375,000
Total	423,100

SOURCES: Otto Stolz, "Handel und Gewerbe, Märkte und Städte": *Tirol, Land und Natur, Volk und Geschichte, Geistiges Leben* (Munich: 1933), 1:326; Joseph Egger, *Geschichte Tirols* (Innsbruck: 1880), 3:119.

The German Tyrolean peasant, in addition to having representatives and a role in the land's assemblies, was free, generally literate, and sometimes university educated; at least a third of the student body of the university at Innsbruck (from its founding in the 1670s) tended to consist of peasants, many from Italian Tyrol. This Tyrolean peasant was usually economically secure, though not necessarily prosperous; he was politically experienced and had the right to bear arms and elect his own officers, except for his commander-in-chief who was appointed by the ruler. A peasant could become a burgher without great difficulty and occasionally even be ennobled. Tyrol's peasants (except for a very few) were the immediate subjects of their land's prince and not of the local nobility. But Tyrol was not, like Switzerland, a peasant democracy: the princely county's nobility, especially the old noble families, or *Dynasten*, still played an important role. Truly noteworthy, however, was that the Tyrolean peasants had attained as much as they had in the presence of a nobility and a prince, while the Swiss had not had to contend with either.

By the middle of the eighteenth century, Tyrol's peasants owned more than half the land of the county. Yet German Tyrolean peasants often had to seek seasonal work abroad, in part because the rural economy of the German areas could not support everyone (especially in the winter) and in part because the inheritance system encouraged such migration.[12] In Italian Tyrol when the peasants owned land, they usually owned dwarf holdings, which supported families only with difficulty and which were redivided with each generation unless heirs could be induced to give up or sell their claims and move off the holding. To supplement or replace income from the land, these Italians therefore tended to seek employment in the towns or vineyards where a continuing need existed for extra hands. Unlike German Tyrol, in fact, the Italian areas had to import labor, usually from nearby Venetian territory, to fill the needs of the growing silk and wine industries.

The *Freisassen* (freeholders) were another, small part of the German Tyrolean social structure. *Freisassen* families, although they were not noble, enjoyed nobles' privileges. For example, they were subject to the nobles' court at Bozen rather than to the court of the local jurisdiction; they paid taxes to the special fund for the nobility rather than to their communes; when called on, they had to render military service wearing armor and on horseback. The most prevalent theory explaining this anomalous group is that originally the *Freisassen* were peasants who purchased noble land and then claimed nobles' privileges for themselves by asserting that the privileges adhered to the land, and that later the land's prince had confirmed their claim to gain their support.[13]

The mythos surrounding the peasant was different in Italian and German cultures. In the German areas the peasant's way of life tended to be positively valued as he focused on cultivating the soil and on life among his fellow peasants. In Italian areas the peasant's life tended to be negatively valued as "a way of life without profit and honor, and one to which one is wedded by necessity, not by choice." The German peasant therefore looked to the village, the Italian peasant to the urban centers, as bearers of the good life and as a cultural focus. These views were beginning to emerge in the eighteenth century. They would become extremely important in the next century when the German Romantics would glorify the peasant, his folk art, music, and way of life, and the Italian Romantics, instead of creating a popular literature, would create "a literature to educate the populace."[14]

The contrast between Italian and German burghers in Tyrol was not quite so sharp. The population of each town consisted of burghers (*Bürger*, or *cittadini*) who were citizens, and other residents who were not counted as such. Usually, only those who were burghers had the right to conduct a

CHAPTER ONE

business or trade and to take part in the town's government and affairs. Each town had a council or councils of some sort, and town government was headed by either a ˙*Bürgermeister* or a *Podestà,* usually elected by the town's citizens from among their own number. Each town had its own official list of citizens and its own statutes defining how one acquired the rights of a burgher. In Bozen, for example, each male member of the family had to be accorded the right of a burgher and be entered into the book, usually on payment of a fee that could range from a few kreuzer to several hundred florins. Town citizenship could also be granted gratis, or a local noble or wealthy burgher might pay the fee for trusted and favored employees or servants to become burghers. Wealthier or more prominent burghers might also be ennobled. So the lines were blurred, and movement from one class or Estate to another was relatively uncomplicated.

In Italian Tyrol's cities and towns, the leading citizens usually constituted an informal patriciate, some of whom were ennobled, some not. Members of these leading families occupied the most prominent positions in the area's economic, political, intellectual, and cultural life. By the eighteenth century these families were enjoying the prosperity that the booming silk industry had brought and were seeking new markets for their wines and a more equitable political and economic role for themselves and their fellow Confinants. German Tyrol's towns were not as industrialized or as prosperous as those in Italian Tyrol, although by the end of the century that was beginning to change.

Since the days of Friedrich with the Empty Purse, Tyrol's nobility had tended to become a service nobility as their prominence and political power increasingly depended on the office they held, not on the land they owned. Through the end of the eighteenth century, only the nobles in southern Tyrol had managed to maintain any real economic or political independence; yet even these families served. A few aristocratic families (for example, Lodron, Firmian, Spaur) tended to monopolize the highest offices in Tyrol and some of the surrounding areas. Members of these families were often Prince-Bishop of Trent or Brixen, Prince-Archbishop of Salzburg, or Governor of Lombardy. Tyrol's nobles were taxed and did not usually have subject peasants to whom they might pass along the tax. However, the nobility did pay their taxes into a separate fund. While a nobleman might conduct the local court and even technically own the land that a peasant occupied and cultivated, not the nobleman but the sovereign was that peasant's lord. And if the noble did conduct court and collect fees, he did so by appointment of the ruler. The privileges of matriculated Tyrolean nobles, by comparison with those of nobles elsewhere, were not especially impressive. They included the use of predicates with their names, seat and vote in the open Diet, precedence before nonmatriculated nobles, a separate court of the first instance conducted by the *Landeshauptmann* at Bozen, small hunting rights, and the right to wear a red uniform with the insignia of an immatriculated noble, the Tyrolean eagle. By the end of the eighteenth century, after the changes made by Joseph II, Tyrol's nobles had even less: their separate court was abolished, they could not be granted judgeships without passing an examination, and they were subject to the same inheritance laws as everyone else unless their property was entailed in some way.[15]

The position of Tyrol's clergy was anomalous. All of Tyrol's parishes were part of dioceses presided over by "foreign" bishops—those with seats outside the princely county's borders, often outside immediate Habsburg territory. Depending on who did the counting and in which period, as many as twelve *Ausland* bishops had parishes in Tyrol. Most of Italian southern Tyrol was under the ecclesiastical jurisdiction of the bishop of Trent; the Etschland, that is, sub-Brenner German Tyrol, was divided primarily between the bishops of Brixen and Chur (Ciora, Coire); and northern Tyrol, above the pass, was primarily under the bishop of Brixen. But other dioceses also had a few parishes in the princely county.[16] Since these Tyrolean parishes were only a small part of the dioceses to which they belonged, they usually did not merit a great deal of their bishops' attention. These "foreign" bishops rarely responded to state temporal interference in their Tyrolean parishes unless ecclesiastical interests were negatively and significantly affected. So Tyrol not only had no primate or chief prelate; it had no resident bishop either, and its clergy therefore had no single person to look to for leadership.

Tyrol was overwhelmingly Catholic, having only a handful of Jewish families (eight in the 1780s) and about a hundred Protestants who belonged primarily to what was called the industrial population and who had probably come from outside of Tyrol. This religious homogeneity was graphically underscored by the response to Joseph II's 1781 Toleration Patent granting civil rights and limited rights of public worship to Acatholics (that is, Lutherans, Calvinists, and Greek Orthodox). Within four years after the patent was issued (by the end of 1785), throughout the Monarchy the number of Acatholics who had openly declared themselves as such had reached more than 100,000, a phenomenon dramatically compared to a cemetery coming to life. "Only in one corner of the cemetery did everything remain as before: in Tyrol!"[17]

Tyrolean piety was legendary in this land with no ecclesiastical leadership and a high degree of religious homogeneity. John Owen, an Englishman traveling through Tyrol in 1792, was struck by what he called "the vast objects of superstitious worship" along the road. He was referring to those wayside shrines found in many Catholic countries, but in notably great numbers in Tyrol. Astonished, Owen recorded that "every little village has, at its entrance, a complete groupe of the Crucifixion, into which enter all

whom the histories relate as present at the event. These [crowded Cal-
varies] being executed in immitation of nature, present a very ghastly spectacle." He also noted the many statues of the Madonna and the Savior
along the road, commenting that in Protestant countries the place of
such monuments was "wisely" taken by posts of direction and distance.[18]
Some forty years later, another Englishman recorded not only the piety
but also the other statuary a person was apt to encounter in extremely
kaisertreu Tyrol: "Neither in Innsbruck nor in any other part of Tyrol is the
traveller ever in danger of forgetting in whose dominions he is. The
Austrian arms are everywhere blazoned, and monuments and triumphal
arches, and columns are seen in twenty different places of Innsbruck, dedicated to the members of the imperial family . . .—and adorned with
statues of Leopolds, and Maximilians, and Francis's. They have a rival
however in the Virgin Mary."[19]

The relationship between the Principalities of Trent and Brixen and
the Princely County of Tyrol was not merely ecclesiastical; there were also
historically rooted political connections. The principalities, that is, the
territories subject to the prince-bishops' temporal rule, were part of the
Holy Roman Empire and immediate to the Holy Roman Emperor. Each
prince-bishop was therefore a prince of the empire with a seat in the Imperial Diet or *Reichstag;* appeals from his courts went to the highest court of
the empire, to which he had to contribute support. Yet, as the result
of numerous agreements and treaties over the centuries, the Principalities
of Trent and Brixen were also politically confederated with Tyrol for defense
and taxation and therefore sent deputies to the Tyrolean open Diet.[20]

The medieval Counts of Tyrol had used their office of prince-bishops'
Vogt to enhance their own status by gradually acquiring territory from the
ecclesiastical principalities. The territory so acquired was put together to
form the County of Tyrol—a land subject to the temporal authority of the
count and to the ecclesiastical authority of the prince-bishops. Along with
the land he acquired, the count also retained some of his *Vogtei* rights over
the ecclesiastical principalities. For example, he still had the rights of protection, military occupation, and control of foreign relations; and he had
the extremely important right to administer and use the temporalities, that
is, the taxes and other temporal rights, of the bishopric during a vacancy in
the bishop's office. When a new bishop was elected, a representative of
Tyrol's Princely Count—and not of the Holy Roman Emperor—invested
him with these temporalities. The Counts of Tyrol therefore had the opportunity and sufficient leverage to force concessions or attach conditions in
return for investiture.

When Rudolf IV became princely count and acquired Tyrol for the
Habsburgs in 1363, he persuaded the Bishop of Trent to enter an "eternal
confederation." According to the agreement, which is the oldest extant
treaty between Trent and Tyrol, the two territories were confederated for

defense and taxation; the bishopric's fortresses were opened to the Counts of Tyrol; and strict limits were placed on the bishop's hiring of foreigners as officials. Any disputes between the prince-bishop on the one hand and the Count of Tyrol or his subjects on the other were to be decided in the Tyrolean *Landeshauptmann's* court in Bozen (the court then reserved for Tyrol's nobles). Disputes within the principality were still appealed to the courts of the empire. Brixen had concluded a similar agreement in 1348, but it was not "eternal" and was therefore subject to periodic ratification; theoretically it could be canceled at any time.[21]

The Counts of Tyrol and the Prince-Bishops of Trent and Brixen concluded a number of treaties over the centuries, the most famous of which was the 1511 *Landeslibell*, agreed to by Maximilian I as Count of Tyrol (not as Holy Roman Emperor, an office he also occupied), the Estates of Tyrol, and the bishops. The *Libell*, like all these treaties, gave the Counts of Tyrol control over military and tax levies in the principalities, treating each principality as a *Viertel* of Tyrol for this purpose. And since Maximilian was also Holy Roman Emperor, he exempted Trent and Brixen from the empire's troop and tax levies as he subjected them to Tyrol's. Through these agreements, the two bishops and their cathedral chapters became part of the Estates of Tyrol, sitting on the nobles' bench rather than on the clergy's, attending the various assemblies (later limited to the open Diet), and collecting from their cities and jurisdictions any taxes voted by the Diet.[22]

Several changes in the Trent-Tyrol relationship occurred in the eighteenth century, especially after midcentury when Maria Theresa began her long reign. In 1748 she ended the two-century-old Ferdinandean Transaction, which had permitted Trent's wines to be the only Italian wines allowed into German Tyrol without a heavy tariff. And in 1761 and 1762 she intervened to end an unfortunate dispute between Tyrol's Welsch Confines and the Trentine bishop and curia.[23] Then in 1771 her new tax ordinance changed the basis of tax and troop levies as it had existed since the *Landeslibell* of 1511. Now, instead of taxes being assessed on the basis of how many "armed men" (*fanti bellici*) had to be provided, they were assessed on the basis of how many "taxable men" (*Fanti steorali*) there were in the principality. In other words, instead of providing and paying for a 5,000-soldier contingent, the principality had to provide 1,600,000 florins.[24]

A 1777 treaty between Maria Theresa and Prince-Bishop Pietro Vigilio Thun defined more precisely the relationship between Trent and Tyrol and limited the principality's sovereignty even further by expressly declaring it to be eternally "an integral part of the County Tyrol." The treaty also united Trent and Tyrol in a small customs and commercial union and specified that toll stations be built along the principality's external borders, that is, those not shared with Tyrol. Each year Trent was to receive 10,000 florins of the tolls collected at these new stations, a third of the export duty on cattle, and half of any confiscated contraband. The treaty also abolished tariffs between the two territories on all goods except Trentine wine, brandy, and tobacco, and these remaining tolls were placed at the same level as those on Italian Tyrol's products.[25]

Many contemporaries believed the complete secularization of Trent and its incorporation into Tyrol were only a matter of time. Apparently Prince-Bishop Thun shared that opinion. Early in Joseph II's reign (1780–90), Thun approached the Habsburg ruler and offered to sell him territorial sovereignty over the Trentine principality in return for a lifetime "rent" of 100,000 florins. Joseph was advised that secularization and incorporation would not be welcomed by most of the princes of the empire, especially the ecclesiastical princes and their chapters, and that Austria would lose more than it would gain. He therefore turned down Thun's offer.[26] Secularization did not come until twenty years later, and then under entirely changed conditions.

The economics of the princely county changed in the late seventeenth and eighteenth centuries. Historically, Tyrol's primary source of income was the transit trade, most of it on the Brenner Road, between Germany and Italy. This income was raised either directly from a transit tariff or indirectly through spending in local taverns and inns and elsewhere along the route. The transit tariff was assessed either on goods going through Tyrol or on wares headed for one of the four annual fairs held at Bozen in southern Tyrol, or at Hall in northern Tyrol.

Tyrol's transit trade, especially on the southern, or Italian, part of the Brenner route, began to suffer as the Habsburgs started to foster the development and growth of the port of Trieste. In 1719 Emperor Charles VI declared Trieste and Fiume (Rijeka) to be free ports; he and his successors developed these port facilities and promoted the flow of goods through them. The policy, aimed primarily at taking trade from the Republic of Venice, also affected the Habsburgs' own lands. The southern part of the Brenner route was forced to compete for transit trade with the Pustertal route to Trieste. The latter road, favored by lower tariffs, followed the Brenner route until just below Bozen, then branched off to the east; and it soon began to draw goods and income away from the Bozen market fairs and from Italian Tyrol's part of the Brenner Road. The entire Brenner Road also had to compete with a new toll road that bypassed Tyrol entirely and ran through the Swiss canton of Graubünden (Grigioni, Grisons).

Tyroleans repeatedly protested to Vienna about the favoring of the Trieste route and the resulting adverse affects on their own economy. But despite these repeated petitions, the first presented as early as 1729, not much was done to make the Brenner route more competitive. Then, in 1763, Vienna ordered a study to find out just what had happened to Tyrol's transit trade; the findings showed that Bozen and southern Tyrol had clearly suffered as Trieste-connected commerce through the Pustertal and northern

Tyrol had increased. There was, however, a peculiarity to this new Pustertal-Trieste route: it attracted more trade going north than south. By the end of the eighteenth century, this route had almost half the northbound trade, but only a sixth of the trade going south. The southbound trade, much of which was cotton and wool, still followed the all-land Brenner Road.[27]

The importance of the transit trade gave Tyrol's economy a north-south economic orientation, unlike most of the Habsburg Monarchy where the economic axis ran along the Danube. The princely county therefore had a tariff system separate from the other Habsburg lands, even after the 1775 tariff put a customs barrier around the rest of what would later be referred to as Cis-Leithania.[28] Tyrol and Anterior Austria were even excluded from a preparatory study for the customs union that Maria Theresa ordered in 1749 to determine whether the tariff barriers between the individual lands should be removed and a single customs territory created. In 1751 she gave Tyrol its own new customs regulation. In 1763 she decreed several related tariffs for the princely county: the *Consumo* on wares imported and used within Tyrol; the *Esito* on exported grains and other foodstuffs that Tyrol normally had to import; and the *Transito* on wares of foreign origin passing through Tyrol—a proportionately lower impost. An *Intrinseco* on goods produced and consumed in Tyrol was also imposed from time to time. Each of these Theresian tariff regulations had one thing in common: they favored the Pustertal route to Trieste with a much lower transit tariff than the southern Brenner route to Rome.[29]

The most dramatic and damaging change came with Maria Theresa's 1780 tariff. Despite her earlier resolve to treat Tyrolean tariffs separately, she now tried to integrate Tyrol into the Habsburg customs union. The result was a drop of more than two thirds in the princely county's transit trade income: from 10 million florins in 1756 to only 3 million florins after the tariff took effect. Clearly, something had to be done. In November 1783 Joseph II issued a new regulation that, in Solomon-like fashion, seemed to benefit everyone. The new tariff brought relief to Bozen and its market fairs and helped Rovereto even more, and by the end of the decade the Pustertal with its route to Trieste was in percentage terms the greatest beneficiary (see table 1–2).[30] The Etsch Viertel, however, despite the granted relief, incurred high expenses and was left with a negative balance on tariff collections.

The drop in Italian Tyrol's share of the transit trade that resulted from the shift to the Pustertal route provided the Confinants with a good reason to seek a guarantee against tariff barriers or other impediments to the free movement of their wines within the princely county. The attempt began in Maria Theresa's reign and continued through the early 1790s. Both Maria Theresa and Joseph II gradually did increase the amount of the Confinants' wines that could be brought into German Tyrol, which compensated in

CHAPTER ONE

part for the transit trade that was lost. But the more the Italians' wines moved freely, the unhappier the Etschlanders became, until the increased competition led them to seek restoration of their old wine monopoly. The Etschlanders began to argue that the freer movement of the Confinants' wines badly damaged their own economy because wine was the only product they produced in sufficient quantity to export. On the other hand, the argument continued, the Italian Tyroleans earned a great deal from exporting their silks and did not need added income from wine.

TABLE 1-2

Changes in Tyrol's Tariff Income
(in florins)

KREIS	1788	1790	% CHANGE
Tariff Income			
Welsch Confines	166,196	186,936	12.5
Etsch	53,855	56,674	5.0
Pustertal	45,670	59,192	29.6
All Tyrol	374,897	417,272	11.3
Expenses of Tariff Administration			
Welsch Confines	24,483	28,115	14.8
Etsch	9,227	13,527	46.6
Pustertal	10,617	11,600	9.3
All Tyrol	67,340	74,654	10.9
Net Income from Tariffs			
Welsch Confines	141,713	158,821	12.1
Etsch	44,628	43,047	–3.5
Pustertal	35,053	47,592	35.8
All Tyrol	307,557	342,618	11.4

SOURCE: Hans Kramer, "Die Zollreform an der Südgrenze Tirols 1777–1785": in *Festschrift Hans v. Voltelini zum siebzigsten Geburtstage, 31. July 1932* (Innsbruck: Wagner, 1932), 255–56.

Indeed, after the transit trade, the most important factors in Tyrol's economy were wine and silk, the largest exports of southern sub-Brenner Tyrol. In northern Tyrol above the Brenner, the chief occupation was cattle raising, which produced not only enough meat for domestic consumption and export, but also a considerable supply of cheese and leather goods. In the eighteenth century in northern Tyrol, attempts were made to revive old industries and create new ones so that capital could be kept within the land, or at least within the Monarchy as a whole. But the attempt to revive mining met with little success, and the impact of the new cotton textile industry was not very great until late in the century. The products of southern sub-Brenner Tyrol were therefore extremely significant for the economy of the entire princely county.

As far back as records go, wine was important to the entire sub-Brenner region. It was the most important product of southern German Tyrol and second only to silk in Italian Tyrol. And since areas suitable for vineyards are often just as suitable for the cultivation of silk, the presence of both in Italian Tyrol should come as no surprise. However, despite Habsburg efforts in earlier centuries to introduce mulberry tree plantations into the Etschland, the area proved unable to support a silk industry. Where both wine and silk were produced, the relationship could be symbiotic. Because the wood of the mulberry tree is strong, durable, and easily worked, throughout northern Italy it was turned into barrels and casks that lasted as long as a century and gave white wines a beautiful golden color. In the princely county's best vineyard land, below the Brenner Pass in and around the Welsch Confines and the Etschland, the vines seemed (and still seem) to fill every available open space along the roadside and on the mountainsides. The scenery was so striking that it found its way into many a traveler's commentary.

While passing through southern Tyrol in 1769, Englishman Thomas Nugent described the picturesque hillside vineyards planted "in the form of arbours, with the branches of the vines tied to the frames of wood . . . in long narrow terrasses, whose fronts are kept up with breast-walls of stone."[31] And a nineteenth-century American traveler, George Waring, observed that on these trellises the vines' thick foliage "formed a series of 'lean-to' roofs, facing toward the sun, and supported by substantial timber at a height which makes it possible to cultivate Indian-corn under them. Excepting a strip a few feet wide along the rows of vines which is kept well hoed, the intervening ground is occupied by grass or corn, or occasionally by other crops."[32] In a land that had to import much grain, the Tyroleans were using a well-known technique to maximize land use.

The vineyard owners were equally creative in meeting other challenges, both animal and human, in the vineyards. A seventeenth-century traveler, Maximilien Mission, wrote of small straw huts just large enough to conceal a man armed with a carbine to kill the bears coming down from the mountains to eat the grapes. American Waring described a kind of scarecrow to guard the vineyards, "an example of 'costume' in its maddest development—wearing the Tyrolese dress, resplendent with unusual colors, and a huge head-dress of feathers and fox tails and all manner of outlandish decoration." The original purpose of this attire, Waring was told, was "to strike terror into the hearts of grape-loving boys and girls," but by the

CHAPTER ONE

nineteenth century it was intended primarily for the amusement of tourists. As in earlier times, the serious business of protecting property was the task of an armed guard.[33]

The yield of the area's vines was abundant—enough, wrote French essayist Michel de Montaigne with some hyperbole, to supply all Germany with wine. These bountiful harvests were, to some tastes, matched by the quality of the wines. In the early seventeenth century, Tyrolean nobleman Marx Sittich von Wolkenstein observed that Tyrol's wine was of such excellence that "one is seduced to drink it and must restrain oneself greatly."[34] On the other hand, Englishman Nugent found the white wines "of a very agreeable poignancy," but he noted that the red wines, which Tyroleans valued highly, seemed to strangers "not quite so agreeable, being somewhat too luscious, and sweet." And, he cautioned, white or red, "all the wines of this country must be drunk the very year of their growth, or else they grow luscious, and then turn crabbed."[35]

For hundreds of years, until the changes in the eighteenth century, the wine-producing Etschland Germans had totally dominated the princely county's political life. They had used their power to keep Italian wines from coming into German Tyrol, applying a ban first enacted before the Confines became part of the princely county and then maintained after their incorporation. But from the middle of the eighteenth century on, the economic barriers and other inequities suffered by the Italians in Tyrol began to fall, one after another, to the efforts of reforming monarchs. In the course of the century, Italian Tyrol became increasingly prosperous, primarily a result of the dramatic growth of its silk industry. From the seventeenth century on, the Habsburgs took the economic advice of the cameralists and supported and encouraged mulberry tree plantations and the silk textile industry in many of their lands. They granted charters and privileges to individual entrepreneurs, often gave them subsidies, and provided for the training of needed hands. In 1764, for example, Maria Theresa not only increased the court's annual support for Tyrol's silk industry to 10,000 florins, she set up schools to train what were termed "capable Tyrolean children" to produce the raw material and to retail the finished product.[36] The beginnings of the industrial revolution, which appeared on the Italian peninsula at about the same time, also contributed mightily to the industry's growth.

Two new kinds of machinery, both developed in Italy specifically for silk production, made possible the mass production of silk: a silk-throwing machine invented in the seventeenth century[37] and the *vallichi* or *varghi*, silk-working machinery already in place and functioning in Rovereto in 1740 (something like two later developments in England, the spinning jenny, ca. 1765, and the water frame, ca. 1769). A midcentury diplomat traveling through the area was struck by what he called "the great Wonder of Rovereto," an enormous spinning mill on the banks of the river, "which turns a large Wheel, and that Wheel communicates Motion to a Machine within the House, that spins raw Silk without any body's Touching it, farther than to set it going." He was also extremely impressed by the amount of silk the machine produced. "This same Mill," he wrote, "throws or winds off at least six hundred Pounds of Silk at once, and thus makes a prodigious Quantity of it every Day."[38] This miraculous machine was one of the numerous *vallichi* or *varghi* increasingly used in Rovereto, each with "108 spools hung perpendicularly and 108 parallel to the plane, or 108 spools and 18 skein-winders."[39] In the short span of two decades, machinery of this kind brought dramatic changes to the silk industry in Rovereto (see table 1–3).

TABLE 1-3
Changes in Rovereto's Silk Industry, 1740–60

	1740	1760	% CHANGE
Vallichi or *varghi*	238	590	147.9
Spinning mills (*filatoria*)	23	36	56.5
Merchant houses	12	23	91.7

SOURCE: Based on information in Nicolò Cristani de Rallo, *Breve Descrizione [sic] della Pretura de Roveredo del 1766* (Rovereto: G. Grigoletti, 1893), 9.

By 1765 the Confines' silk production had more than doubled from what it had been at the beginning of the century, and the population had almost tripled. By the end of the century, Rovereto was considered to be among the most important silk-producing areas on the peninsula.

Together with silk and wine, two other industries contributed to the prosperity of southern Tyrol and especially of the Confines. Third in importance was tobacco, not a formal business in Rovereto but carried on by persons who also had other livelihoods. Enough was produced to take care of local consumption, with a bit left over for export to Germany and Italy. The surplus could not be shipped to the Habsburgs' other lands, however, because the Monarchy's tobacco monopoly excluded the princely county.[40] Finally, two forwarding (*spedizione*) companies operated at Sacco. Protected by a charter, they had a monopoly on transporting all goods on the Adige River through the *pretura* between Bronzolo and Verona. Water transit was brisk, the Adige was an important part of the water route to and from Italy, and the monopoly was profitable. By the end of the seventeenth century, the two privately owned companies—Fedrigotti, Baroni, and Company and its related Fedrigotti and Company—had control of all the rafts and forwarding on the river. These two families, the Fedrigottis and Baronis, were among the most prominent in the area, and when the 1790 Italian movement began to take shape, they would supply a number of its leaders and participants.[41]

The Welsch Confines, so close to the cultural boundary between Italian- and German-speaking Tyrol, were by midcentury feeling the full force of these economic changes. The intellectual currents of the Enlightenment and especially those from the Italian peninsula had by then arrived in the area to produce new cultural institutions and a rising sense of *italianità*. These new currents were fed by and intertwined with the area's growing prosperity to produce some remarkable results.

Priests, Poets, and Academicians: Enlightenment and *Italianità* in Italian Tyrol

The Enlightenment in central Europe had some elements that differentiated it from that in western Europe. By the middle of the eighteenth century there was a growing sensitivity to foreign cultural domination—be it French or that of a politically dominant culture, such as German in Tyrol's Italian areas. These sensitivities were part of a larger process that included debates on history; on what constituted one's "fatherland" or "*patria*"; on what one's "nation" was and what the "national" language and literature should be; and on what language(s) should be used in government, schools, and universities. Journals appeared and proliferated, most of them patterned on Addison and Steele's *Spectator* in England. Local academies or learned societies, most of them modeled on Italian Renaissance academies, enjoyed a resurgence in the seventeenth and eighteenth centuries and provided forums where *illuministi* and *Aufklärer* debated and discussed such "national" questions as well as those that occupied the *philosophes* to the West. With the new concern for and pride in one's "nation" (despite the lack of general agreement in this period on the precise meaning of such words as "nation" or "*patria*") came the beginning of more intense and sometimes negative feelings against other nations and cultures.

Italian Tyrol, with its political and commercial center at Rovereto, appeared at the beginning of the century to be an intellectual and cultural wasteland, a place "abundant only in silk, cocoons and silkworms."[1] And the Enlightenment, which appeared in the Welsch Confines about a third of the way into the century primarily in the work of the Roveretan scholar and poet, Abbot Girolamo Tartarotti, did not find a ready welcome all around. By midcentury, however, the picture was vastly improved. As the

31

area's intellectual and cultural life began to match its economic prosperity, the city became home to a new academy, the Agiati, and to a public library—both of which still exist.

The Roveretans shared the eighteenth century's renewed concern with history, that is, the turn away from mere glorification of rulers and brave deeds toward document-based accounts of the past of a nation or national land, with important documents often appended or included in the text. The new spirit and emphasis stimulated both German and Italian Tyroleans. The work of Lodovico Muratori (1672–1750),[2] a churchman and the court archivist-librarian to the Duke of Este at Modena for fifty years, was especially influential in the area and throughout the Italian peninsula. To Muratori, the true historical origins of the Italian nation were in the Middle Ages, and he worked diligently to unearth Italy's own heritage separate from the one he (and others) considered to be ancient Rome's universal heritage. He produced three great historical works: a 28-volume collection of medieval Italian sources, Rerum italicarum scriptores;[3] Annali d'Italia, originally intended as a history of Italy from 500 to 1500 and eventually continued to 1749; and Dissertazioni sopra la antichità italiane, seventy-five discourses in which he attempted to cover every phase of medieval Italian life—society, culture, law, dress, crafts, amusements, language, religious controversies, and so forth.

Tyrol, German and Italian, produced its own crop of historians, most of whom wrote local history with the new attention to archives and documents. Two German Tyroleans, members of Rovereto's Agiati and of an earlier Innsbruck academy, produced notable accounts: Anton Roschmann, whose works included a history of Tyrol; and Joseph Sperges, who wrote a history of Tyrol's mining industry. In Italian Tyrol, Girolamo Tartarotti published his Memorie antiche di Rovereto e dei luoghi circonvinci and De Origine Ecclesiae Tridentinae et primas eius Episcopis Dissertatio, and both would get him into serious difficulties with the Trentine Church. The members of the Academy of the Agiati included a number of historians: Clemente Baroni-Cavalcabò did extensive research on the history of his patria (Rovereto) and produced, among other works, Idea della storia della Valle Lagarina; Adamo Chiusole wrote and published Notizie antiche e moderne della Valle Lagarina e degli uomini illustri della medesima, as a supplement to Tartarotti's Memorie antiche; and Carlo Rosmini produced some half-dozen biographies, a work on Trentine and Roveretan writers, and a four-volume history of Milan (where he lived from 1803 until his death). Of all these histories, Tartarotti's careful work had the greatest immediate influence on his contemporaries.

The abbot Girolamo Tartarotti (1706–61), a native Roveretan, studied at Padua and then returned home, a bearer of Enlightenment ideas and determined to root out the scholasticism-based system of thought that he found entrenched in his patria. For Tartarotti, reason alone could break and had to break what he considered scholasticism's "enchantment." He there-

fore devoted himself not only to Rovereto's cultural and intellectual development, but also to social reform and a thorough revision of Trentine
history (the ecclesiastical and the temporal territory).[4] He wanted to purge
that history of what he considered its mythical elements, and it was therefore inevitable that he would run afoul of the Church, especially its Trentine representatives.

Tartarotti first aroused the anger of the Trentine Church (and much of
the society around him) by attacking its stand on witchcraft in his *Del
Congresso notturno delle Lamie*, "a long journey into a world of horror."[5]
Prosecutions for witchcraft had ended in much of Europe by the eighteenth
century. In the diocese of Trent, however, and in other parts of Italy and
southern Germany, women were still being tried and executed for witchcraft through the first half of the century. To shatter the centuries-old
rationalizations on witchcraft, Tartarotti used one of the *philosophes'* favorite
weapons: ridicule. He asked, for example, how witches could possibly fly so
fast and so far, or how witches could lie with the devil and never become
pregnant. He showed, without much difficulty, that the whole concept of
witchcraft was incompatible with his age's scientific knowledge and with its
concept of good and evil. But however deplorable the phenomenon called
witchcraft was, even more horrible was the persecution carried out "by
educated, civilised people on poor ignorant wretches."[6]

Tartarotti did not stop with trying to tear down traditional beliefs; he
also tried to determine just what the phenomenon was that was being
called witchcraft. And here he became an empirical scholar, gathering data
and showing his readers the newer empirical method in the process. He
found with what he called "a monotonous regularity in the frightful chroni-
cles of the Inquisition" that those accused of witchcraft were poor rural
women who lived in wretched conditions in isolated villages. Their diet, he
discovered, consisted almost entirely of "milk, herbs, chestnuts, pulse vege-
tables and other such foods which make thick, sluggish blood and produce
horrible frightening dreams." He could not, he said, explain how the witchcraft phenomenon occurred in these poor rural women since "we still do
not have a complete history of the power of the imagination."[7]

Tartarotti's *Congresso* evoked a stormy and often bitter debate on
witches, magicians, and the Catholic Church's official position toward
these phenomena.[8] The *Congresso* also marked the beginning of his trou-
bles with the Trentine Church, especially with the prince-bishop, Francesco Felice Alberti. His difficulties increased in 1754 with the publication
of his two histories, *Memorie antiche* and *De Origine Ecclesiae Tridentinae*, in
which he attempted to separate what he saw as myths from Trentine history.
The former work was the more provocative to the ecclesiastical hierarchy in
Trent because it denied the sanctity and martyrdom of Adalpreto, the patron saint and twelfth-century Bishop of Trent. In his *Memorie* Tartarotti
claimed that Adalpreto had not died as a martyr in the cause of the church,

but only as a temporal prince in a struggle with the feudal lords of the valley. His death, argued the Roveretan, should therefore be viewed as a mere battlefield event, a heroic act in defense of territorial rights, not as the act of a martyr for the church.

The Trentine Church and its prince-bishop reacted quickly to the attack on Adalpreto's sanctity, reasserting unequivocally the martyrdom of their patron saint. Tartarotti, undeterred, responded in his *Lettura secondi di un giornalista d'Italia . . . intorno al B. M. Adalpreto,* published in 1760, again denying that Adalpreto deserved sainthood. Prince-Bishop Alberti, seeing that the printed counterattacks alone would not achieve his purpose, decided to carry his campaign against Tartarotti into the public arena. Supported by the Trentine Curia, Alberti ordered the *Lettura* to be burned in an open square by the public executioner. The sentence was carried out on 7 May 1761 before a huge crowd. A contemporary vividly described the scene in the piazza: a platform was set up, which the executioner ascended; he then held the book in his hands and tore the pages from it one by one, consigning them to the flames by hurling them onto the pyre, symbolically burning the voice of Tartarotti himself. The mob applauded as the execution proceeded.[9] Tartarotti was seriously ill when his book was executed, and news of the burning was kept from him. His illness worsened, and nine days after the spectacle in the piazza Girolamo Tartarotti died.

The controversy, however, did not die with him. The Trentine Curia had intended that the public burning reinforce its own authority and humiliate the Roveretans. But the Roveretans, while ecclesiastical subjects of the prince-bishop, were also temporal subjects of the Habsburgs. When they decided to honor their fellow citizen Tartarotti with a public memorial service and a statue or bust of him in the church of San Marco, where he was entombed, the *Gubernium* in Innsbruck approved the plans. The prince-bishop and the Curia in Trent did not. The memorial service was held on 31 July 1761, and the monument was to be installed in the church early the following spring. The Trentine clerics viewed the service and the monument to Tartarotti as acts of defiance and used the installation of the memorial statue to show the Roveretans that they could not act with impunity.

The monument was placed in the church on 1 April 1762. The curia immediately ordered it removed, but the Roveretans left the bust of Tartarotti in place. Two weeks later Rovereto's church of San Marco was put under interdict, all sacred objects were removed and taken to another church, the church building itself was closed, and its bells were forbidden to ring. Only the baptisery remained open. Despite appeals from the Roveretans, the *Gubernium* at Innsbruck, and Maria Theresa herself, the interdict remained in force for nine months, until after Prince-Bishop Alberti died (31 December 1762) and a new prince-bishop, Cristoforo Sizzo, took his place. According to the compromise worked out, the monument of Tartarotti was transferred from the church to the municipal building; it was replaced with a stone bearing the Tartarotti coat of arms and an inscription selected and approved by Maria Theresa.[10]

During his lifetime Tartarotti also took an active and direct part in improving the intellectual climate of his native city, a climate he labeled at the outset, "Albergo d'intelletti sordi, e loschi" (abode of dull and short-sighted intellects).[11] Tartarotti donated his entire personal library to the city. (The collection forms the nucleus of the present-day Biblioteca Civica Girolamo Tartarotti in Rovereto, which has a bust of its benefactor in the second-floor reading room.) In 1726 when he opened the first printing house in Rovereto, Tartarotti also founded the city's first learned society, or academy, perhaps taking as partial models the then-existing Academy of the Accesi (Burning, or Kindled)[12] in nearby Trento and academies elsewhere.

Girolamo Tartarotti named his academy the Dodonei, a name chosen from the sacred oak grove (Dodana) of ancient Epirus and because Rovereto's coat of arms included an oak. This academy, forerunner of the later and more influential Agiati, chose as its task not only to remedy what was considered "the sad literary heritage of the seventeenth century" in Italy, but also—and more typically for the eighteenth century—"to fight the harmful influence the French language has made on the Italian."[13] The Academy of the Dodonei did not last long, primarily because of increasing personal hostility between Tartarotti and another leading member. But while it existed, it brought intellectual ferment to Rovereto and provided inspiration for those who came later.

New academies and learned societies were founded throughout the Habsburg lands and Europe in the seventeenth and eighteenth centuries, but nowhere were they as numerous as in Italy. These new societies had a propensity for assuming unusual names, a phenomenon that a poet named Casti captured in verse:

> A voi gloria, Umoristi, Oscuri, Ombrosi,
> Infernali, Lunatici, Insensati,
> Stupidi, Rozzi, Indomiti, Fumosi,
> Umidi, Muti, Torpidi, Intronati,
> E tant'altri, di cui per dire i nomi
> Vi vorrebbero almeno un par di tomi.

> To your glory, Humorists, Obscure, Suspicious,
> Infernal, Lunatics, Senseless,
> Stupid, Uncouth, Indomitable, Smoky,
> Humid, Mute, Torpid, Deafened
> And all others, of whom to speak the names
> Here would take at least several volumes.[14]

During the eighteenth century, several societies of this kind were established on Habsburg territory. Typical was an academy founded in Olmütz (Olomouc) in 1745 or 1746, which was recognized by the state and existed until 1752. Others were founded in Brussels in 1769, in Mantua in 1773, in Görz/Gorizia in 1780; they were usually started by a local group that later received official recognition. Another extremely influential eighteenth-century academy founded in a Habsburg-ruled area was Milan's Academy of the Pugni (Fists, or Fisticuffs). This academy's influence extended far beyond northern Italy and other Habsburg territories to the entire Italian peninsula and to the European Enlightenment as a whole. Founded more than a decade after Rovereto's Agiati and sharing some members with it, the Milan group included such *illuministi* as Pietro and Alessandro Verri and Cesare Beccaria, men who, even had they not organized the Pugni, produced works of sufficient import to ensure their place in eighteenth-century intellectual history.[15] In setting up the Academy of the Pugni, they created something where the whole may well have been greater than the sum of its parts.

The Pugni began meeting in 1761 and, using the English *Spectator* as a model, from June 1764 through May 1766 published *Il Caffè*, generally considered the most important periodical of the Italian Enlightenment. In addition to discussing the general ideas of the Enlightenment, however, *Il Caffè's* founders also had another purpose: to arouse Italians from their complacency and inspire them to reacquire civic pride and take an active part in the new movements then beginning throughout the Italian peninsula. The result was that while *Il Caffè* promoted a concept of world citizenry and connection with the general European Enlightenment, it also fostered a strong feeling of Italian, as opposed to local patriotism. The most famous of these "national" essays, Gian Rinaldo Carli's "Della patria degli Italiani," appeared in *Il Caffè* in 1766.[16] In this essay Carli poked fun at regional prejudices and, using a literary device common at the time, had a stranger tell the astonished habitués of a Milan coffeehouse that the people he saw were neither Milanese nor foreign. In response to their questions, he told them: "They are Italian . . . and an Italian in Italy is never a foreigner, just as a Frenchman is not a foreigner in France, an Englishman in England, a Hollander in Holland, and so forth."[17]

The first academy in Tyrol was founded as the Societas Silentiariorum, but it quickly became known as the Academia Taxiana because it met in the library of Count Leopold Thurn und Taxis' *palais* in Innsbruck. Founded in 1738 or 1740, the Societas Silentiariorum encouraged both literary and historical studies. Like many similar societies, it included both nobles and nonnobles, most of the latter being scholars. The new academy's members, a number of whom were shared with the later Agiati, included some of the most prominent men in or from the area: Baron Joseph Sperges, historian, mapmaker, and statesman; Count Christoph Anton Migazzi, later a cardinal and archbishop of Vienna; Count Leopold Thurn und Taxis, host of the society and hereditary-land postmaster; Count Joseph Philip Spaur, later Prince-Bishop of Brixen; three Counts Firmian,

PRIESTS, POETS, AND ACADEMICIANS

one of whom (Karl) became Governor of Lombardy; historian Anton Roschmann; and Count Paris Wolkenstein-Trostburg, then *Landeshauptmann* of Tyrol. The Academia Taxiana kept records and had more or less regular meetings, but it never sought public recognition or confirmation from the government. It preferred to remain a friendly private society and existed as such until 1758.[18]

Most important for Tyrol's Welsch Confines, for the 1790 Italian movement, and for the subsequent history of the area was the academy founded at Rovereto in 1750: the Academy of the Agiati (Leisured, Leisurely, Well-to-Do, or Unhurried), which is in existence today. The founding members and most of the eighteenth-century Roveretans who subsequently joined came from the same informal patriciate that provided the leadership in other areas of local society and government. Founded as a literary society, this academy quickly became a transmitter of the Enlightenment and then a focal point and leading force in the growth of the area's national and political awareness.

Two of the Agiati's founders, Bianca Laura Saibante-Vannetti and her brother Francesco Saibante, were raised under the watchful eye of Girolamo Tartarotti, who was their tutor and lived in their home. The academy was founded in the Saibante home on 27 December 1750, the feast of St. John the Evangelist, whom the founders chose as their patron saint. The other three founding members, all friends of the Saibantes, were Giuseppe Valeriano Vannetti, who was also Bianca Laura's husband; and Gotthardo Antonio Festi and Giuseppe Felice Givanni, both priests and professors at Rovereto's gymnasium. Bianca Laura Saibante-Vannetti was much more than one of the founders; until her death in 1796, she was one of the academy's leading and most productive members. Giuseppe Givanni became the new society's first secretary; Guiseppe Valeriano Vannetti was the first president, or *Agiatissimo*.

The new academicians, or Agiati, took as their emblem and as a symbol of their circumspection or prudence a pyramid with a snail creeping up one side. This symbol was intended "to express the toilsome slowness of the ascent toward the conquest of knowledge, the difficulty of its attainment and therefore the effort and toil necessary for its acquisition."[19] The Chancellor of Tyrol, Joseph Ignaz von Hormayr (a member of the Taxiana in Innsbruck), interceded with Maria Theresa on behalf of the Roveretans, and in 1753 she issued a diploma to the new academy assuring it of her protection and requesting regular reports on their literary efforts. Until 1756, when Taxiana ceased to exist, the two academies had some members in common.

About the only important Roveretan who did not join the Agiati was Girolamo Tartarotti, apparently because of a "disinclination" toward some of the members. He chose not to join, preferring instead to refer to the Agiati (many of whom he had taught) as the Academy of the Asinelli

CHAPTER TWO

(Young Asses). Nevertheless, the Agiati grew; many members came from outside Rovereto, including some Taxiana members from Innsbruck and both central and provincial government officials. By 1755, five years after the Agiati's founding, its membership had reached 165; and by 1760, after a decade of existence, it had 388 members.

At the beginning the academy's concerns were primarily literary and cultural, but dissertations or discourses were also presented on scientific, philosophic, economic, and social questions. The Agiati's aim was to have a share, or "citizenship," in what was referred to as the Italian Literary Republic, an idea proposed by Lodovico Muratori as a kind of pan-Italian superacademy to be composed of the most famous or accomplished literati in Italy. They were to devote themselves to the study and reform of the liberal arts and sciences and to raise the level of Italy's cultural life, all of which was to be accomplished by improving the Italian language and persuading other peoples to learn it.[20] In fact, a large part of the discussions in these eighteenth-century Italian academies centered around what linguistically constituted good Italian. The Pugni's *Il Caffè*, for example, spoke out against those who insisted that only the language of Dante could form the basis of a "purified" Italian. Instead, the journal argued that as long as an author did not bore his or her readers and wrote reasonably and in a way that was clear to all Italians, the origin of the words did not matter; that writer had a right to be considered a good Italian writer.[21]

Like Muratori and *Il Caffè*, the Agiati were concerned with the Italian language, although members used both Italian and Latin in their works. At the first meeting in December 1750, *Agiatissimo* Vannetti held out two linguistic goals for the members. First, he urged that they increase the reputation of the city's dialect by writing about its affinity with Tuscan; second, that members should promote the Italian language in general. Italian should be learned and spoken, said Vannetti, to eliminate errors in grammar or meaning and because Roveretans had a duty to speak Italian even though "we are now separated from beautiful Italy by an act of war."[22] That "act of war," however, did not mean ignoring achievements published by their northern neighbors. Founder Vannetti and two other early Agiati— Clemente Baroni-Cavalcabò (the historian) and Valeriano Malfatti (who had also been a member of Tartarotti's Dodonei)—thought it was especially important that members of the academy, and Italians in general, have access to the literary and scientific works produced in Austria and Germany. The three Roveretans hoped that they could serve as a conduit between the two cultures, presenting and publishing translations and reviews of German-language works either at the Academy's sessions or in Italian literary journals. But lest anyone misunderstand their purpose, they made it clear that they wanted only to make German-Austrian ideas accessible to Italians and that their work was in no way to be interpreted as a "renunciation . . . of the defense of their nationality, or of their *italianità*."[23]

PRIESTS, POETS, AND ACADEMICIANS

From the beginning, therefore, the Agiati were concerned with *italianità*, especially with their own *italianità*. As early as the July 1752 meeting of the Agiati, Francesco Frisinghelli, a professor of rhetoric in Rovereto's gymnasium and a member of the academy, presented a memoir entitled, "Che questo nostro paese di Rovereto è parte della vera Italia" ("That this our land of Rovereto is part of the true Italy"). Frisinghelli used geographic-historical arguments, citing sources beginning with Pliny, to argue that his city and its *pretura* were indeed part of the "true Italy." Rovereto's origin was Italian, he said, since Roveretans had descended from the Etruscans "who were certainly true Italians and inhabitants of the heart of Italy." Frisinghelli thought his historical review of ancient and Roman times provided sufficient evidence that Rovereto and its surroundings had always been part of the true Italy and had been recognized as such. But, he added, if it were necessary, he could easily show that the same was true of the Middle Ages. And, he continued, when Maximilian I incorporated the area into the County of Tyrol, the Roveretans had indeed changed their political master, but they had not at the same time changed their nation— not even when the Trentino became part of the "Germanic Empire."

> Nations are distinguished principally by Genius, Customs, and Language. Italian alone is the Genius of our Land, Italian the thought, the dress, the manners and every other custom, and finally Italian is the language, although German is also spoken by many. . . . I think, Valorous Academicians, to have proved here sufficiently with powerful, and firm reasons, that our Land is a true, and not presumed part of Italy, and we likewise are true and not illegitimate Italians.[24]

Along with the growing sense of *italianità* came an increasing awareness of political geography as new maps were made of the area. One of these maps was the work of Baron Joseph Sperges, a member of the Taxiana in Innsbruck and the Agiati in Rovereto and author of a history of Tyrol's mining industry. Culturally German, he felt at home with the Italians and added a second *e* to his name (the original was Spergs) so that the Italians could pronounce it more easily. For several years just after midcentury, Sperges served as secretary to a commission negotiating disputed borders between Tyrol and the Republic of Venice, and he drafted a border map to aid the commission. He subsequently filled in the interior and produced a map of the entire Italian Tyrol and the Principality of Trent.[25] This Sperges map, first published in 1751 and dedicated to the heir to the Habsburg throne, Archduke Joseph, was readily accepted.

But another map, which appeared in 1778, aroused enormous controversy. Drafted by Francesco Manfroni, the new map was dedicated to Prince-Bishop Pietro Vigilio Thun and appeared under his auspices. Thun was then negotiating with Joseph II on the possible secularization of the principality under Habsburg rule, and the map may have been drafted in connection with these negotiations. Manfroni showed the Principality of Trent as part of Tyrol. The resulting outcry came primarily from two sources: the Trentine cathedral chapter and Italian-minded Trentines and Roveretans. The canons of Trent's cathedral chapter raised essentially political objections. They protested that the map prejudiced the rights of the Trentine church and injured Trentine sovereignty both because it showed the principality as part of Tyrol and because it was dedicated to, and apparently approved by, the prince-bishop.[26]

The most eloquent national-cultural objections to Manfroni's map came from Clemente Baroni, the Roveretan historian and member of the Agiati. His protest appeared in a December 1779 article that has since become one of the "national" documents of the Trentino. Baroni's attack, which appeared as an open letter, assailed the Manfroni map and called it "offensive to history, to language and to the customs of the Land." How, he asked, can the Trentino be part of Tyrol? There were, Baroni admitted, a few political connections, but "in a geographical and natural way it has never been and cannot be a part of this province. . . . Is the language of the Trentines not Italian? Are their origins, their history not intimately connected with that of Italy? And did the Trentino by itself not appear a long time before the name of Tyrol was known?" He asked:

> What sane reason, then, persuades a geographer to incorporate an Italian nation into a German one, a nation most ancient to one, it can be said, modern? . . . If the Trentino by origin, by uninterrupted continuation of government, by uniformity of language and custom had always formed a part of Italy, why would it choose now, without necessity, even against all reason to make itself part of Tyrol? . . . Why would it graft a province totally Italian to one totally German, from which it is separated by geographical and natural reasons? For goodness sake! Counsel this new geographer to correct his error, even though he has it in common with many small *intelligenti;* and counsel the Trentine Lords not to permit this wrong to be done to their considerable Patria.[27]

Clementino Vannetti, son of two Agiati founders and by now himself secretary of the academy (and destined to become the "poet laureate" of the Trentino), not only supported Baroni's attack on the Manfroni-Thun map; he also sent copies of the article to many of his friends. Vannetti was extremely sensitive on this issue and responded with patriotic ferocity whenever anyone referred to Rovereto or Roveretans as Tyrolean. He did not spare even Girolamo Tiraboschi, successor to Muratori as court librarian at Modena and a giant of Italian literary history in his own right. Vannetti carried on a correspondence of many years' duration with the eminent Tiraboschi and never held back pointed criticism if he thought it was warranted. For example, in 1780 Tiraboschi was preparing a new edition of his well-known and highly respected *Storia della letteratura italiana,* and he used geographic terms in a way that Vannetti found highly objec-

tionable: "If it ever occurs to you another time to speak of Trentine writers," wrote the Roveretan poet on 21 April, "do not say that they are born
in Tyrol, which is not true. We separate the Trentine province [in which he
included the Confines with Rovereto] from that German one to which it is
annexed, for political reasons, but is quite divided from it by reasons of
geography, language, customs."[28]

A month later, his anti-German sentiments more in evidence, Vannetti again reprimanded the Modenese prelate. "Heaven protect me," he
invoked, "from flying into a rage with a Tiraboschi," who had not removed
from his Storia "that absurdity of ascribing Trentine men of letters to the
German nation." Then, in an often-quoted passage, Vannetti continued,
"No, we are in Italy, and the accidental political dependence on Tyrol is
not able to change either the nation or the place. On the other hand, we
have every reason not to love very much a race of people [gens] through
which have come to us those sorrowful destructive influences in commerce,
in the sciences and in happiness."[29] Perhaps Vannetti was referring to the
results of Maria Theresa's unfortunate 1780 tariff, then still in effect, but
soon to be changed. Otherwise, considering the prosperity and cultural
development of the area, the poet was clearly overstating the case. Yet he
did not moderate his views.

When Tiraboschi's revised Storia was ready to publish, he responded to
Vannetti's attacks by teasing and "assuring" him. "You are therefore secure,"
he wrote, that in "republishing my Storia I shall remove from it the name of
Tyrol and shall add a note in which I shall say that Trento and Rovereto
belong to Tyrol, but that cav[aliere] Vannetti does not want to admit it—
and that conquered by his importunities I have deleted the name." Vannetti, not to be put off, wrote back approving the changes Tiraboschi
mentioned; he got a prompt response from the Modenese prelate, again
chiding him: "Now that you have approved my idea, I shall say that as of
the 1st of April 1783," the date of Vannetti's letter, "Trento and Rovereto
were not in Tyrol."[30] There the matter rested, at least for the time being.

Vannetti's admonitions to friends and acquaintances to speak properly
about his patria's italianità were accompanied by his poking, prodding, and
insulting the Germans, especially the German Tyroleans. Wherever he
could—in prose, verse, newspapers, letters, assemblies of academies, public
meetings—he aimed his biting satire and ridicule at the Germans. An early
twentieth-century historian wrote that Vannetti had "a sense of horror . . .
the horrible vision of a bastard Tyrolean spirit united in two different and
colliding bodies."[31] He probably would have considered the phrase "Italian
Tyrol" a contradiction in terms. Vannetti, like the dramatist Alfieri, con-
stantly fought against what he saw as the cultural, if not political, "barba-
rism" that had overtaken Italy. (Vannetti's barbarians were primarily
German, Alfieri's French, and others' Spanish—but all were foreign.)

Vannetti's chief weapon was his poetry, and his most famous anti-
German Sonnet was written in 1790. But it was not his first. In 1789 he

sent one to Tiraboschi, claiming he had found the poem in the public library. It was a poem that just happened to be not very flattering to Germans.[32] (Vannetti often attributed his works to other, unknown authors.) Tiraboschi was not deceived by the ploy and scolded the poet in reply: "You want to enjoy yourself at the expense of the poor Germans. . . . It appears to me that your hatred is very general. Some ill must have been done you by the Saxons, the Bavarians, the Palatinate Germans, the Brandenburgers, the Hanoverians and all the Electorals because you wrap them all in one bundle and call them all guilty of that which is truly the guilt of only one or of a certain few."[33] Vannetti rejected the censure, replying that his sonnet (he now frankly admitted authorship) was not against all Germans. But, he wrote, "if you were a neighbor to them as I am, and if you felt all the new brutal orders" (perhaps referring to the new language regulations; see chapter 3), his Modenese correspondent would not reproach him so. The Tyroleans, wrote Vannetti, had the Roveretans "by the throat, not by the purse."[34]

Vannetti's most famous and lasting contribution to irredentist literature was his anti-Tyrolean sonnet written in the summer of 1790—a sonnet that in the next century would become the "national anthem" of Italian irredentism. The "Regola geografico-morale," as the sonnet was originally entitled, was addressed to a Florentine actor and dramatist, Antonio Morrocchesi, who was in Rovereto in the summer of 1790 with a theatrical touring company. The actor and the poet met, swore eternal friendship "as on a consecrated altar," and Morrocchesi had Vannetti (as well as his own mother) written into his speeches in one of his plays. Morrocchesi, who kept a diary during his stay in Rovereto, recorded how the famous anti-Tyrolean sonnet came into being. The actor had commented that "a fecund genius of such rare flowering" as Vannetti should not be in Rovereto, among the steep mountain valleys of Tyrol, but in "the beautiful Italic Athens, or some other celebrated City of this happy peninsula." Vannetti interrupted his new friend and, as might have been anticipated, pointed out that Rovereto was not in Tyrol but in Italy. Then, as the actor recorded it, Vannetti sat down and wrote almost without hesitation the sonnet that would become known not by its original title but by the last line of its first verse: "Italiani noi siam, non tirolesi."[35]

> To the Government of Tyrol, o Morochesi [sic],
>> These valleys only by accident
>> Became subject one day; for the rest
>> *We are Italians, not Tyroleans.*
> And lest in the judgment of the poets
>> You don't mistake it with that lowly people,
>> That confuses things and doesn't grasp the truth
>> I've set out a little rule for you here.

PRIESTS, POETS, AND ACADEMICIANS

When you arrive in those areas where the sermon
You find is transformed into shouts, the soil is horrid,
The sun is in Capricorn every season
The cattle and the wagoners an immense swarm
The houses pointed and the people round
Then you can say frankly: here's Tyrol![36]

What Morrocchesi saw was a draft, made on 14 August 1970 (while the Diet in Innsbruck was rejecting Italian Tyrol's pleas for equitable treatment). The sonnet was then polished in a spirited exchange of letters with the abbot Giuseppe Pederzani, a local priest and friend of Vannetti's.[37] (The above translation is from the revised final version.) As might have been expected, the "sonnet" was labeled "hate-filled" by a German and "playful" by an Italian. Angelo Rosmini, Rovereto's mayor and a deputy to the 1790 Diet, said he had laughed when he read it because the sonnet was "roguish and true, but full of genius."[38] At first the sonnet was published and handed out clandestinely; but it was destined to provide the motto for the coming irredentist struggles. In the nineteenth century leaflets would be handed out covered in red, white, and green and labeled: "Italiani noi siam, non tirolesi."

As a kind of footnote to his famous sonnet, Vannetti also wrote a parody, poking some not very gentle fun at his fellow Roveretans who called themselves Tyrolean:

"Tyrolean am I, not an Italian"!
Protested a Roveretan gentleman.
And another said to him: "That for certain is the truth,
Because, even if you had been born Spanish,
Hungarian, Russian, French, Arab, English,
You would not be anything but a Tyrolean!"[39]

Such pro-Italian and at times anti-German sentiments were not unusual by 1790 as the intellectual and cultural revival initiated by Tartarotti began to take a political turn. The jurist Carlantonio Pilati (1733–1802), closer in his ideas to Tartarotti than Vannetti, contributed much to the cultural and intellectual life of the area; and his life well illustrates the differing political climates in which Trentines and Tyroleans (Italian or German) had to work.

Although he was a Trentine by birth, Pilati's outlook was much broader than that of many of his local compatriots and contemporaries. He was probably the most cosmopolitan thinker in the area at that time since his chief concerns were in the mainstream of eighteenth-century thought and argument rather than in problems of the Trentino vs. Tyrol or Italian vs. German. He traveled so widely that his contemporaries often referred to him either as a "literary gypsy" or, more frequently, as an "honored adventurer." He became a teacher of civil law at the legal lyceum in Trent in 1760, a position created just for him. With Pilati, wrote an early twentieth-century historian, "the revolution of the conscience of the Land, initiated by Girolamo Tartarotti, was fulfilled, the old Trentino finished, and the modern Trentino begun."[40]

In 1767 Pilati's strongly anticlerical work appeared: *Di una riforma d'Italia ossia dei mezzi de diformare i più cattivi costumi e le più perniciose leggi d'Italia* (marked Villafranca, but actually published in Venice). In *Di una riforma* Pilati sought the reform of all Italy. He argued against "the temporal usurpations of the Church, the Inquisition, the ecclesiastical courts, the right of asylum," and he proposed as remedies the abolition of monastic orders, torture, the privileges of caste, and an end to what he termed "the barbaric confusion" in the civil laws. Pilati wanted Italians to have a mentality that was both religious and enlightened, an intellectual life inspired by the culture of the universities of central Europe where he had studied and taught, and a morality "animated by the ideas of countries more progressive and active" than eighteenth-century Italy. Voltaire said that Pilati's *Di una riforma* was stronger and bolder than most works and that by comparison French books were "all circumspect and honest." Pilati "makes the priests tremble and inspires courage in the laity," wrote Voltaire approvingly. "When the author speaks of monks, he always calls them rabble [*cannailles*]. At the end all eyes are clear, all tongues facile, all pens sharpened in favor of reason."[41]

The Catholic Church condemned Pilati's *Di una riforma* along with another work of his published the following year and usually considered a supplement to the first.[42] Both treatises ended up on the Index, and Pilati found it prudent to leave the Trentine principality. After a brief digression he went to Chur (Ciora, Coire) in Graubünden (Grigioni, Grisons), Switzerland, where he stayed for almost two years. While there, he founded a literary society, a printing establishment, and a *Giornale letterario*, "one of the lively periodicals of our Settecento, not unworthy of standing beside *Il Caffè*." In autumn 1769 he went to Padua, but the Venetian Republic's inquisition quickly expelled him as "a very celebrated author of godless and subversive books."[43] Still persona non grata in Trent, Pilati sought and received sanctuary in Habsburg territory under the protection of Emperor Joseph II, who had read and admired *Di una riforma*. At Sacco in the *pretura* of Rovereto, Pilati stayed with the Baroni family and met often with many of the Agiati; Rovereto, in effect, became his adopted *patria*. In 1778 while on a journey of several years that took him all over Europe, Pilati visited Florence and was honored by Grand Duke, later Emperor, Leopold (or Peter Leopold, as the Italians call him). It was perhaps the first time, but not the last, that the two would meet.

Still under the emperor's protection, Pilati returned to Trent in 1779— just in time to see Prince-Bishop Thun name a favorite, a man of bad reputation (G. B. Gervasi), as magistrate for the largest judicature of the principality. Pilati was soon defending the inhabitants against Gervasi's victimization; and Gervasi, assisted by the bishop, fought back, heaping accusations on Pilati. The bishop planned to rid the principality of Pilati by forging some documents, but he was thwarted by one of the cathedral canons. Later, when Gervasi attempted to deprive a local widow (and relative of Pilati's) of her inheritance, Pilati defended her in a biting memorandum that enraged Prince-Bishop Thun. On 24 January 1783 the prelate wrote Gervasi: "In Council this morning the blind[44] Pilati presented a most offensive *Memorandum* against you personally. . . . he burst into a rage against you, but by doing this he also attacked me. So if you have some trusted friend, who has the audacity to administer a good beating with a cudgel, the blind one will learn better to open his eyes."[45] A couple of weeks later, Pilati was assaulted on a Trent street, beaten by two men with clubs, and left for dead. He recovered, but with his vision permanently impaired. Despite the uproar that ensued and the outpouring of sympathy for Pilati, Bishop Thun pardoned the men who had administered the beating. The Council voided the pardon but could not stop Thun from granting the two men clemency and safe conduct out of Trentine territory.[46]

Pilati, once recovered, turned to Vienna in a "letter of supplication," which brought the intervention of Carlo Antonio Martini, Italian Tyrolean by birth and member of the *Staatsrat*. A settlement was worked out by which the large and important aristocratic Thun family agreed to pay Pilati 400 florins a year for the rest of his life; Pilati agreed to stay out of Trentine territory and to take no action against the Thun family. Only in 1796, under very changed circumstances in both Trentine and Austrian territory, could Pilati return to his birthplace. Until then he made his home on Habsburg territory in sub-Brenner Tyrol. In 1785 he was named legal representative of the Bozen Mercantile Magistrate, which had jurisdiction over the four annual fairs in that city. In this capacity he would appear officially in Vienna in 1790, after the Tyrolean Diet had ended. Historians have generally agreed that Leopold called Pilati to Vienna in that year, but have offered no explanation as to why or for what purpose.

These intellectual and cultural changes in the Welsch Confines—the beginnings under Tartarotti, the expansion represented by the founding of the Academy of the Agiati and the work of Pilati and Vannetti; the pro-Italian (or anti-German) sentiments expressed more and more frequently in essays, map disputes, poetry, and elsewhere—fed this growing sense of *italianità*. The Confinants' sharpened sense of being Italian and their exclusion from participation in Tyrol's Estate assemblies would combine with their new economic position and with encouragement from their ruler to produce the 1790 Italian movement in Tyrol. In that year, their well-drafted, firmly stated grievances would be almost totally ignored at the Diet but would receive a more positive response in Vienna. Each of the particular Italian grievances had a history and development that in some respects was unique, and in others was shared by other Habsburg lands.

The Grievances

$\mathbf{B}$y 1790, when the long-awaited Diet was finally convoked, the Italians of the Confines had accumulated many grievances, some of their own and some shared with the rest of Tyrol. The Etschland-dominated Estates[1] sought to undo most of five decades of innovations by Maria Theresa (1740–80) and Joseph II (1780–90).[2] Their dissatisfaction began soon after Maria Theresa ascended the throne and refused to hold a ceremony of hereditary homage where she would have had to confirm Tyrol's freedoms, privileges, and constitution. When in 1749 the Estates submitted a petition asking that their previous rights be restored, she replied that although she would seek their opinion in many questions, she would do so only out of grace and not because it was a right of the Estates.[3] She also refused to convoke the open Diet, despite repeated pleas from the Estates, for the entire forty years of her reign. (She promised an open Diet in 1762 but never issued the order of convocation.)

In Tyrol Maria Theresa was very much the absolutist, but rather than abolish Estate institutions, she chose to ignore or bypass most of them. She simply created her own institutions to stand alongside and gradually take over the functions of the traditional bodies, especially those that dealt with the administrative business of the princely county. In 1774, continuing the Habsburgs' attempts to build a *Gesammtmonarchie*, she extended the *Gubernium* system to Tyrol, creating the office of *Landes-Gouverneur*, an official named by and representing the interests of the ruler. At the same time, she combined this new office with that of Tyrol's *Landeshauptmann*, traditionally chosen by the Estates and representing their interests. This new official was to be an intermediary between the Estates and their ruler, but he was in fact primarily and essentially a representative of his sovereign. By uniting these two offices, then, Maria Theresa effectively deprived the Estates of their own spokesman.

Maria Theresa's reforms touched the church only lightly, but Joseph II altered both the power of the Catholic church and the performance of religious rituals, all of which greatly unsettled the very pious Tyroleans, though not their various bishops. Joseph's Toleration Patent, issued on 13 October 1781, granted full civil rights and the open but still limited practice of religion to Lutherans, Calvinists, and Greek Orthodox (referred to as Acatholics). Tyrol's bishops made little fuss about the patent; their Tyrolean parishes were but a small part of their dioceses. Of all these ecclesiastics only the Prince-Bishop of Brixen, Joseph Spaur, openly opposed the patent; the Bishop of Görz, whose seat was in another Habsburg province, was slow in confirming it, but an invitation and visit to Vienna persuaded him of his duty.

In Italian-speaking Tyrol the arrival of the Toleration Patent caused a minor flurry. The new law was ordered to be published in local newspapers in German, Italian, or Latin, or in all three languages. But the newspapers that most Italian Tyroleans read were published in Trent, a territory directly subject not to the Habsburgs but to the prince-bishop. Perhaps as a result of pressure from Prince-Bishop Thun or because the Trentine newspapers feared his displeasure, these papers denied the Rovereto *Kreis* office's request to publish the patent. The *Gubernium* at Innsbruck then stepped in and took the request directly to Thun, who ordered the patent published[4] (perhaps in exchange for some sort of quid pro quo). From the time toleration was decreed in 1781, Tyrol's Estates tried repeatedly, and unsuccessfully, to have the patent rescinded, at least for the princely county. They protested that it would lead to discord and unrest and affect Tyrol's prescribed oaths of homage and duty, which were based on the Catholic religion. And—not of least importance—the patent also violated their traditional constitution because Tyrol's laws could not be changed without the Estates' agreement.[5]

Further changes also disturbed the pious Tyroleans. In October 1784 Joseph II began dissolving monasteries throughout the princely county (and the rest of the Habsburg lands) until most, both male and female, were closed. The proceeds from the sale of the confiscated properties were placed in a state-administered Religion Fund, which was used to establish parishes and churches in remote or poorly served areas and to support retired or sick priests and schoolteachers.[6] He also closed churches where the population was not sufficient to fill the pews; decreased the number of religious (and hence work-free) holidays, pilgrimages, and processions; and altered the manner in which mass was celebrated and bodies buried. Although the Tyroleans protested these changes, their "foreign" bishops said little.

The bishops did react, however, to Joseph's innovations that challenged and greatly undermined their ecclesiastical power, particularly the establishment of general seminaries to train new priests. These new institutions were run by the state and replaced those run by the prelates themselves. Book censorship, long the domain of the clergy, was also taken over by the state, and new textbooks appeared that the state, not the church, had approved (in Tyrol's case multiple ecclesiastic imprimaturs would have been required). Joseph also extended his educational concern to the universities, where the clergy taught many of the classes. He thought one university (the one in Vienna) was enough in the Habsburgs' German hereditary lands and that too many university-educated persons would constitute a plague of sorts on the land. He therefore demoted the universities in Innsbruck and Graz to lyceums. The move pleased neither the Tyroleans nor the Styrians.

Then, in 1784, Joseph created a major grievance for Tyrol when he extended conscription to the princely county. The 1772 conscription law had omitted Hungary, Tyrol, the Austrian Netherlands, and newly acquired Galicia; Vienna feared that if the issue were forced in these four lands, the reaction might be violent. Tyrol's 1511 *Landeslibell* had set up the county's basic defense system and military obligations, and by the eighteenth century it was considered a contract between ruler and ruled, part of Tyrol's fundamental constitution. The *Libell* recognized all Tyroleans' right to bear arms and obligated them to provide troops only for use in and for the defense of Tyrol. Although the numbers had been altered slightly over the centuries, the principle had not. Therefore, in 1784 when Joseph decreed conscription for the princely county, the protest was emphatic. The Tyroleans were so opposed to wearing the white coat of the Habsburg army that many of them fled or maimed themselves to avoid the recruiting officers. An experienced administrator wrote that "the disinclination for the white uniform is so great that the Italian Tyrol, which constitutes half the population [Trent was included for defense], prefer life long prison to the soldier's Estate, and the Germans too would rather choose prison."[7] The war with the Turks, with its need for troops (and increased taxes), only exacerbated the situation by the end of Joseph's reign.

German Tyroleans were especially hard hit by Joseph's 1782 Emigration Patent, which banned free movement into neighboring lands without permission. German Tyrol had historically exported seasonal surplus labor into southern Germany (usually to Swabia and Bavaria), but now that safety valve was closed. Joseph's intent was to keep track of those eligible for conscription and to have workers available for the domestic industries he was fostering. But German Tyrol's own industries were not yet able to absorb all the idle hands, especially in winter. Labor-importing Italian Tyrol was not especially affected by the ban on emigration, its needed hands usually coming from neighboring Italian-speaking regions; and German Tyroleans rarely looked for work in Italian Tyrol.[8]

THE GRIEVANCES

Joseph's more radical changes that denied the Estates effective political power created the greatest opposition to his policies. His mother had merely ignored the traditional Estate bodies; Joseph abolished them altogether. Quickly gone were the open Diets at which all four Estates had seat and vote and the Diet *Ausschüsse* on which all estates had equal representation. In 1784 he merged the two *Aktivitäten* that his grandfather had created into one eight-member body, the perpetual congress, presided over by the Governor–*Landeshauptmann* and subordinated to the *Gubernium* and therefore to Vienna.[9] Now, instead of several autonomous institutions chosen by the Estates themselves, only one group existed, no longer autonomous and with its members named by the emperor. Only the *Steuercompromiss/Postulatcongress* remained, with powers restricted, to approve and allocate taxes. All other Estates' business was transferred to the new perpetual congress, to be convoked by the *Landeshauptmann* to take part in decisions on "more important matters."[10]

The coup de grâce to the Estates came in early 1789. Tyrol's Governor-*Landeshauptmann* Count Wenzel Sauer, who had the reputation of being more Josephian than Joseph, submitted a report on the effects of the earlier institutional reforms. He described the administration of Estates' business "as bad and costly beyond all proportions" and proposed that the perpetual congress be abolished and replaced by a single Estates Referent at the *Gubernium* in Innsbruck. For that office he suggested that his associate, Joseph von Aschauer, already Tyrol's Estate Syndicus, hold both offices. This syndic-referent was to represent all four Estates, speak for their interests, and be their legal adviser. He would take care of all the business previously handled by the perpetual congress (which had itself taken over the work of the Diet, the *Ausschüsse,* and the *Aktivitäten*) and "which required no special deliberation." Joseph accepted Sauer's suggestion and embodied it in a court resolution of 26 February 1789, thus ending at a stroke almost all Estate participation in governing the land.[11] Only the *Steuercompromiss* remained.

To make room for Aschauer's appointment, Sauer saw to it that the then-referent, Johann Christof von Unterrichter—whose power had not been so extensive, who did represent the Estates, and who had not allied himself with the governor—was dismissed and soon made the object of an investigation.[12] (Unterrichter, acquitted of any wrong doing, joined the camp of Sauer's most ardent foes in 1790.) But despite their apparent success in 1789, within eighteen months Sauer, his appointee Aschauer, and his Gubernial Secretary Eppstein would be forced from Tyrol.

Joseph II's changes in the administration of justice were also unsettling to the Tyroleans. He saw no need for a separate Upper Austrian appeals court in Innsbruck, so he transferred it to Klagenfurt and united it with the appeals court for Inner Austria (Styria, Carinthia, Carniola, Görz, and Gradiska). All appeals from Tyrol and Vorarlberg (which he had united with Tyrol) now had to go to Carinthia to be heard. Joseph also abolished the separate nobles' court at Bozen and put an end to the old communal constitutions of Rovereto, Bozen, and Innsbruck. In these three cities he set up new centrally appointed civic magistrates to take care of all judicial, political, and economic business and in the process he destroyed much of the municipalities' historical and traditional autonomy. Joseph did retain the *Kreis* system that his mother had instituted in Tyrol as an intermediate level of administration between the *Gubernium* and the villages or towns, but he reduced the number from six to five. Tyroleans themselves rarely used the label *Kreis*, however, continuing to identify these intermediate divisions by the traditional name of *Viertel*. At the 1790 Diet calls would be heard for dismantling the Josephian civic magistrates in the cities and for restoring the nobles' court at Bozen. But Tyroleans accepted the *Gubernium* and *Kreis* officials to look after their ruler's interests, as long as they could have their own institutions to see to their own interests.

Most of these grievances were shared by all Tyroleans, but the Confinants had four major complaints of their own to present at the 1790 Diet. They sought the right, in the restored Estate assemblies, to have an equitable number of seats and votes or be separated completely from Tyrol. They also asked for a guarantee of their relatively new right to bring their wines freely into the rest of Tyrol, recognition of their right to use their own language in their schools and courts, and relief from Joseph II's inheritance laws that allowed daughters to inherit property and then, when they married, lose control of it to foreign husbands.

Seat and Vote in the Assemblies

A few Italian nobles and jurisdictions appear in the oldest extant Tyrolean Matricle (the list of persons and places entitled to attend or send representatives to the open Diet), the one of 1474, along with the bishop, the cathedral chapter, and the city of Trent. After Maximilian I reconquered most of what became the Welsch Confines in his wars with the Republic of Venice, he joined the territories to Tyrol and made some limited provision for their representation. But during the sixteenth century Rovereto refused to be considered part of Tyrol and instead demanded recognition as an imperial free city of the Holy Roman Empire. To make their point, the Roveretans refused to pay taxes or render homage to the Count of Tyrol. This tax *Renitenz*, which would be repeated in 1790, did not end until 1564 when troops were finally sent in.[13]

In the seventeenth century more Italian noble families were enrolled in the Tyrolean Matricle; and in 1640 the city and jurisdiction of Rovereto (as a single entity) were immatriculated with seat and vote on the cities' bench at the open Diet. More Italian communes appeared, without vote, at the 1646 Diet. And by the 1720 open Diet, the Welsch Confines formed a separate *Viertel* with 20 jurisdictions, all of which were invited to this Diet called to ratify the Pragmatic Sanction—but they were still without vote. From 1720 to 1790 there was no general or open Diet and thus no opportunity for the Confinants to seek seat and vote in the Tyrolean assemblies.[14]

As that long-awaited Diet approached, Roveretan historian Clemente Baroni (author of the article attacking the Manfroni map that had included Trentine territory in Tyrol) again set down his thoughts. This time he argued the Confinants' case for seat and vote and countered objections already raised against their political participation, ably summarizing the positions of both sides. Baroni intermixed older ideas of local versus provincial rights with the newer ideas, then coming to the fore, of a nation's rights: his plea was not merely for justice for a territory, but also for a national group; and the blending of old and new occurred with the greatest of ease. His fellow Confinants, Baroni noted, had always been excluded from Tyrol's *Ausschüsse*, and only Rovereto had seat and vote at "those insignificant general Diets that are held scarcely once every half century." The German Tyroleans had claimed that because the Confines were conquered territories, the areas could not be admitted to full participation in the princely county. But, Baroni pointed out, other parts of Tyrol that had come under Austrian rule at the same time as the Confines had been allowed full participation in all the land's assemblies. Here he was referring to the so-called Bavarian domains (*Herrschaften*) of Rattenberg, Kufstein, and Kitzbühel, and to the Valsugana. The Confinants, Baroni asserted, had not been allowed to participate because the "old" German inhabitants "took umbrage at having to share their authority with so many strangers and particularly with those of the Italian Nation, toward whom they never did demonstrate much benevolence." Emperor Maximilian I may have conquered the land, wrote the Roveretan, but he had not conquered the people who had voluntarily subjected themselves to him. "The Prince-Conqueror could not divest them of that unalienable and imprescriptable right of equality that belonged to them at the moment that they came to form a Body of another Land."[15]

During the seventeenth and eighteenth centuries, Baroni recorded, the Italian Tyroleans had repeatedly sought remedy, and twice the Counts of Tyrol (1627 and 1630) had decreed that Italian Tyrol be admitted to the consultations and deliberations of the province. Yet, they were not admitted, at least not with the right to vote, because of "the intrigues and the power of the Most Serene German Provincials who had the public Treasury at their disposal," that is, the Etschlanders. Until Maria Theresa's reign these German "provincial lords" had had a ready weapon to fight the Confinants' admission: the fact that the Welsch Tyroleans did not bear as heavy a tax burden as the rest of the princely county. But with Maria Theresa's new and equal tax assessment, that weapon no longer existed. In 1790, said

Baroni, the people of Italian Tyrol were united to claim their rightful role; and now that "a most just and wise Prince" ruled them, they had great hopes of being successful.[16] The Italian Tyroleans had good reason to be optimistic about support from Leopold II: he supported them unofficially at first and then quite openly in their quest for representation and in the closely connected question of unrestricted commerce for their wines.

Wine

Wine, the most important product of southern German Tyrol, was second only to silk in Italian Tyrol. Wine cultivation, though not limited to the southern part of Tyrol, was primarily concentrated below the Brenner Pass in and around the Etschland and the Welsch Confines. The sub-Brenner Etschland Germans, with the economic prosperity their wine gave them and with their numerical superiority, had for centuries dominated Tyrol. They had been able to enforce both the exclusion of Welsch wines and the consumption of their own wines in northern Tyrol by limiting the availability of other beverages and not even permitting their northern brethren to build new breweries. Over the centuries at the Estate assemblies, the wine-consuming northern Tyroleans had repeatedly—and without success—sought a lower price on wine, usually urging that Welsch Tyrolean and foreign wines be imported as competition.[17]

To the Germans Welsch wines originally meant the wines crossing the main ridge of the Alps toward the north. Differentiations began to appear around 1300 as Welsch wines came to include wine from northern Italy or Friuli, and Bozener, or Etsch, wine indicated wines of present-day South Tyrol/Alto Adige. The Tyrolean ban against Welsch wines dated from the fourteenth century, when the areas that became the Welsch Confines were part of the Holy Roman Empire but not yet part of Tyrol. Concerned about competition from the South, the Etsch *Viertel* sought protection; and the Counts of Tyrol responded. In 1370 Duke Albrecht of Austria issued a ban against "Easter wine." More important and of greater effect was the ban imposed by Duke Leopold II in 1372 on the import of all Welsch wines into his lands, that is, wines from below the Nevis (Lavis*).[18] This 1372 ordinance specifically stated that Welsch wines were being banned so that they would not interfere with the markets for Etschland wines in northern Tyrol and Bavaria. Some thirty years later, in 1404, foreign wines were forbidden to everyone except "lords, knights or noble servitors," and then only for their own use.[19]

When the Welsch Confines were incorporated into Tyrol, the prohibition against their wines moving freely into the older, German areas of the county was not removed. Maximilian I confirmed his new subjects' privi-

---

*On the border between the Etsch *Kreis* and the Confines, just below Salurn.

leges and granted them the right "wherever they like, in our lands to sell their foodstuffs and goods, *except the wine*." The members of the Roveretan city council accepted Maximilian's limits on their wines but asked in return that he ban foreign (including German Tyrolean) wines from their city and its jurisdiction "under penalty of loss of the Wine, Cart, and implements, and the animals that brought the aforesaid foreign Wines."[20]

Some foreign wines could come into Tyrol legally if they were for the needs of the court, the military, or the treasury and if the importer had the required license or patent. The exception grew into a gaping hole, and the number of permits or licenses often reached heights unsettling to the Etschlanders. Courtiers and officials used this privilege so extensively that they were in fact carrying on a direct trade in foreign spirits.[21]

The Etschlanders' complaints about the import of wines, whatever their source, were continual. In response to one such complaint in 1594, the Innsbruck government told them to sell their wines more cheaply so that the imports would stop and admonished them to be sure that their fellow Tyroleans received a fairly priced product. The Bozen wine lords (*Weinherren*) were also taken to task for tending to press their wine too early, causing "podagra, contractures, colic and other illnesses" so that foreigners avoided Tyrolean wine. A few individuals, said the authorities, were spoiling the wine by an untimely harvest and causing everyone to suffer. The Etschlanders did not agree. Their wines, they said, still had a good reputation and were produced in a way that benefited the health of those who used them moderately as well as, if not better than, foreign wines did; and, they continued, their prices had remained essentially unchanged.[22] By the mideighteenth century, Etschland wine merchants found themselves facing new competition in their German markets: the Welsch Tyroleans, still unable to bring their wines into the rest of Tyrol, had set up their own warehouses in cities of the Holy Roman Empire. The new competition made the wine rivalry at home even more intense.

One of the most anomalous elements in the Tyrol-Welsch wine relationship was the special privilege accorded Trentine wines. Until the mideighteenth century, although the Confinants' wines were excluded from the rest of their own land, the wines of the Trentines (subjects of another temporal ruler) came into Tyrol under a special arrangement known as the Ferdinandean Transaction. The original agreement, concluded by Ferdinand I and the Prince-Bishop of Trent in 1529, allowed the principality to bring duty free into Tyrol 325 wagon-kegs of wine (approximately 400,000 liters) each year from St. George's Day (23 April) until the next harvest. Repeated appeals from the Etschland wine interests led Emperor Rudolph II to void the Transaction in 1598, again banning all foreign wines and ordering the confiscation of any wagons bearing them. In 1721 Charles VI renewed and extended the Ferdinandean Transaction, permitting the Trentines to send into Tyrol another approximately 372,000 liters during the remainder of the year (between St. Michael's and St. George's Day), but with a small duty.[23]

The Confinants, too, objected to the Transaction. They at least wanted parity with the Trentines. In 1743, not long after Maria Theresa ascended the throne, the city of Rovereto sent her a memorandum[24] that was a petition asking that the area's wines be given the same access to Tyrolean markets as the Trentine wines, that is, that the centuries-old ban on the Confinants' wines be lifted. The Trentines, with a copy of Rovereto's memorandum in hand, submitted point-by-point counter-arguments, providing an indication that, at least when it came to wine, they did not yet have a sense of common nationality with the Roveretans; the argument had a distinctly unpleasant coloration.

In their memorandum the Roveretans asked that between St. Michael's and St. George's Day (over the winter months) they be granted the same rights for their wines that the Trentines had. The Roveretans pointed out that they had suffered greatly from the quartering, passage, and encampment of troops that had twice passed through their area and retreated; furthermore, they now had a great deal of unsold old wines on hand but could not find sufficient customers in their own *pretura*, even though their wines were lower in price than the Trentines'. The Trentines replied, claiming that their own wartime sufferings had been even greater and that there was a lot of old wine throughout the lower Etsch or Adige valley because of an unusually abundant harvest and because enemy armies had blocked access to markets. Furthermore, said the Trentines, Rovereto's wines did not cost less. And to the Roveretans' reminder that they had advanced as much as 130,000 florins to help Maria Theresa fight Prussia, the Trentines countered colorfully: "One cannot without nausea hear the glory that the city of Rovereto openly gives itself for having advanced the considerable Sum of money." Individual Trentines, they continued, had together given the empress much more financial assistance.[25]

In their memorandum, the Roveretans also pointed an accusing finger at their neighbors, claiming that the Trentines purchased grapes and wines around Rovereto at the lowest available price, took them to Trent, then resold them in Germany at a high price, enriching themselves at the expense of the "poor supplicants." The Trentines retorted that they found very bizarre and false the assertion that they purchased grapes and wines around Rovereto at a paltry price and then "enriched themselves with the wares of the Supplicants." It all depends, said the Trentines, on the way one used the verb *purchase*. The city records, they asserted, showed that only one such case had ever been proved against Trent, that involving a certain Caldonazzi in 1694![26]

Finally, the Roveretans asked for permission to sell their wines throughout the Adige Valley both within and outside of Tyrol and without special licenses or patents from St. George's to St. Michael's Day. They argued that the increased sales would enrich the empress's treasury and benefit all her lands because their wines would be available at a price lower than the Trentines'. The Trentines termed this a "crafty proposal" that would mean not only their own ruin, but the ruin of all the inhabitants of the Adige Valley who were loyal subjects of the empress.[27]

Whether as a result of this 1743 petition or for other reasons, Maria Theresa did open all Tyrol to some Welsch Confines' wines. By 1748, five years after Rovereto's petition for equality with Trent, some Roveretan wines were entering German Tyrol without paying a tariff at the border; but they were assessed a higher excise at Innsbruck than were Trentine wines (see table 3-1). Then in 1753 Maria Theresa, along with increasing the Confinants' taxes by making their assessment equal to the rest of Tyrol's, admitted more of their wines, tariff free, over the Nevis Bridge.[28] Joseph II continued this policy, gradually increasing the amount of Welsch Tyrol's wines that could go over the Nevis without paying a tariff. In the ten years of his reign, the Confines brought into German Tyrol almost 18 million liters of wine and about 4 million liters of brandy, an amount significant enough that the Etschlanders were feeling the pain of competitive pressure by 1790.[29]

TABLE 3-1
Taxes on Sub-Brenner Wines Entering Innsbruck, 1748

Origin of the Wine	Tax in Florins per Orna (approximately 77.5 liters)
Meran	2.55
Bozen	2.24
Salurn/Salorno	3.5
St. Michael	3.13
Mezzotedesco	3.13
Trent	3.31
Rovereto	3.58

SOURCE: Giuseppe Dal Ri, *Notizie intorno all'Industria ed al Commercio del Principato di Trento dal sacro Concilio (1545) fino alla secolarizzazione (1803)* (Trento: 1888), 27.

The Roveretans not only paid a higher wine tax at Innsbruck, but they also had higher shipping costs. The slightly longer distance that their wines had to travel led to an unofficial increase in cost because tradition allowed carters to tap the wine kegs up to a certain amount (and the distance traveled tended to increase the dipping, often beyond the permissible vol-

CHAPTER THREE

ume). The practice was centuries' old, and the abuse of the practice was equally as old. An early seventeenth-century Trentine noted that the carters "expanded their traditional right to be allowed to drink the wine up to a thumb's depth of the barrel, with the help of a little tube, to the point of fraud. To make up the volume they often replaced what they had taken with water."[30] The Roveretans' shipping costs were high, but they would not have been so exorbitant "if the carters had not been permitted to open the casks more than once, and to bring the purchaser of wine not quite adequate [amounts] with the considerable regrets of the sender."[31]

The few remaining disparities between Trentine and Welsch Tyrolean wines were removed in 1777 when Maria Theresa and the Prince-Bishop of Trent concluded a treaty, part of which abolished tariffs on most wares going between Tyrol and the principality. The agreement also set the fees on Trentine wine, brandy, and tobacco, fees which were to be no higher than the tariffs "on the import of the same wares from the Austrian Welsch Confines."[32] In 1785 Joseph II, referring to this 1777 agreement and its clause on wine tariffs, noted that the provision had generally been ignored; he therefore removed the tariff on Trentine wines first imposed by his grandfather. Now all Trentine products were considered "Tyrolean," although those of Brixen continued to be viewed and treated as foreign.[33]

Another factor in the wine equation was the group of tax farmers known as the Wine Deputation, originally established to collect the import and excise (or Umgeld)* taxes on wine. Made up of Etschland Tyroleans and headquartered in Bozen, the Wine Deputation also took as its task "to thwart the importation of foreign wine and wine products from south of the Nevis bridge, and to establish each year the price of the grape vines (graspato)." The Wine Deputation's members were therefore more than tax farmers; they also served as guardians of, and lobbyists for, the wine-producing interests in the Etschland. As the tariffs on Welsch Tyrolean wines gradually decreased, the Wine Deputation found itself with less and less to collect, more and more to protect, and a lot to be unhappy about. Joseph II had abolished this Wine Deputation, at least as tax farmers, but it remained intact and continued to function as a lobbying group. By April 1789 the central government was well aware of the Wine Deputation's and Etschlanders' growing unhappiness with the continuing import of Welsch wines and with the loss of revenue and income that resulted.[34]

A final aspect of Tyrol's wine problem adversely affected both Italian and German wine interests, as well as the agriculture of all Tyrol: more and more Tyroleans were turning from growing grain to growing grapes because vineyards yielded the greatest profit per acre of all the princely county's agricultural products. But Tyrol did not produce enough grain to feed itself

---

*All Austrian documents and secondary sources use the spelling Umgeld, and that spelling has been retained here. Another accepted spelling is the north German, Ungeld.

and badly needed the grain that could be grown in those same fields and meadows. Land conversion of this kind was not a new problem. As early as 1404 the Habsburgs had begun issuing bans against the continuing, though illegal, expansion of arable land used for vineyards. As the eighteenth century progressed, the regulation of the Etsch river had made more land arable and tempted more Tyroleans to ignore the ban on land conversion. Therefore, in a 1730 patent for all the hereditary lands, Charles VI again forbade the conversion of arable land to vineyards without the ruler's permission, except in areas not suited to growing grain. The patent also prohibited unauthorized reconversion of any land that had once been used to grow grapes but had since been turned to other agricultural purposes. Under Maria Theresa intensive efforts to regulate the Etsch made even more land arable, so that in 1754 she found it necessary to renew her father's patent. But she added a provision meant to make the ban enforceable: if someone disobeyed or ignored the law, he would be fined 10 florins for each *"Viertel"* of illegal vineyard; half the fine would go to the informer, whose identity would be kept secret. Nevertheless, two years later she had to repeat the threat that those who planted new vineyards without permission were to be punished. And yet again in 1770 she found it necessary to forbid turning arable land into vineyards in an effort to ensure that the needed grain would be produced.[35] The repeated need to enact such a law was testimony in itself to the lack of compliance. And the more land devoted to growing grapes, the greater the competition for the established wine interests, Italian and German. By the last decade of the century, the question of land conversion became closely bound up with the whole issue of Italian Tyrol's economic and political situation.

Language

The Confinants' language grievances in 1790 were the result of new regulations, enacted both by Maria Theresa and Joseph II, requiring knowledge and in some circumstances the use of the German language in the courts, administration, and schools. Beginning with a school ordinance of 1752, Maria Theresa ordered that gymnasium teachers pass examinations proving a basic knowledge of Latin language and German orthography before they could be appointed.[36] Her most extensive educational reforms began in 1774 with a 24 January patent creating the Court Commission on Studies (*Studienhofcommission*), a kind of ministry of education, subordinated to the Chancellery. This commission was given responsibility for overseeing education and was to be assisted on the local level by bishops in the provincial capitals. Tyrol, however, had no such bishop, so a special school overseer was installed in Innsbruck to work with the governor in carrying out and watching over the Theresian school reforms.

As she established the Court Commission on Studies, Maria Theresa also stated her firm resolve to introduce the German language in all higher schools. At the end of the year she did exactly that, and much more. On 6 December she issued the extensive and encompassing General School Ordinance (*Allgemeine Schulordnung*). The new law required compulsory attendance in the lower schools (*Volksschule*) and an end to "a spirit of hierarchical separation of pupils according to Estates." Instruction in these primary schools was to be in the mother tongue, and education was to be general rather than vocational. But for attendance at a higher school (a gymnasium or one of the newly created normal schools), the ordinance required a knowledge of German.[37] The requirement was extremely important because the gymnasia trained those who would enter state service and the normal schools produced the teachers who would teach in the gymnasia. Under this 1774 General School Ordinance, two normal schools were established in Tyrol: one in Innsbruck to train teachers for the German-speaking areas and one in Rovereto for the Italian-speaking areas. The Rovereto normal school opened on 6 February 1775 and consisted of three classes plus a German class. The school director was an ecclesiastic named Giovanni Marchetti, who was also the overseer for all the schools in the Welsch Confines. For some reason he was never visited or inspected by his superior from Innsbruck, so by default he had more room for action, or inaction, than school overseers in Tyrol's other *Kreise*.[38] Rovereto quickly discovered that it could bend or interpret regulations as it saw fit, without fear of interference or reprimand from the authorities in Innsbruck or the Court Commission on Studies in Vienna.

The new gymnasium regulations that appeared in November 1775 were, for the first time, issued only in German and therefore had to be translated. The work of translation provided an opportunity for Rovereto's city school commissioners, one of whom was Clementino Vannetti, to accomplish "an assiduous work of interpretation and adaptation." They were determined to keep their hundred-year-old gymnasium Italian and, despite the new regulations, to save what they considered the traditional spirit of the school. Vannetti, as might be expected, both as a member of the city school commission (it existed only from 1774–76) and later, worked unceasingly against Germanization of the upper schools. Vannetti was intensely interested in the schools. He gave advice on how to improve teaching methods, negotiated with the authorities on scholastic affairs, and examined and criticized the government-approved gymnasium textbooks— especially a geography text that referred to Rovereto as an "Austrian" city. He, and others, also wrote textbooks to replace those ordered by the government.[39] His strong feelings about what should be taught and how led Vannetti in 1779 to accuse school director and overseer Marchetti of making cow manure (*guazzabuglio*) of the normal school by using the wrong teaching methods, teaching the wrong subjects, and—worst of all—replacing Italian with German.[40]

The law that required a knowledge of German for admission to the higher schools and its use as the language of instruction also set a deadline.

As the grace period approached its end, most of the students (and perhaps many teachers) in the area did not have the requisite linguistic skills. Therefore, in a petition to Vienna on 12 December 1779, the city of Rovereto asked among other things for relief from the German-language requirement in the higher schools. Vienna refused to void the requirement but on 29 June 1780 granted a three-year reprieve. The deadline was moved to January 1784, after which no one was to be admitted to the normal school or gymnasium who did not know German.[41]

Joseph II became sole ruler of the Habsburg lands on 29 November 1780. Soon thereafter, he received a request from Rovereto's gymnasium that the textbooks prescribed for teaching the Greek language be translated into Italian so that their students could understand them, but to no avail. Joseph repeated his mother's order that delayed the German-language requirement until 1784 and denied the request to translate the Greek language text on grounds that an Italian version would not be useful after that date. Furthermore, in what was certainly one arc of a circular argument, Vienna claimed that because the number of students involved was small, a translation would not be worth the expense involved. The result was that the number of Roveretan students who wanted to study Greek remained small, and the class remained closed because of low enrollment.[42]

Not only were Rovereto's students reluctant to study Greek, they did not rush to learn German either. The 1784 deadline therefore proved to be no deadline at all, so on 27 August of that year, Joseph decided to offer an inducement. To encourage the youth of the Confines to learn German more rapidly, they were to be told that only those who had expertise in that language would be appointed to positions in government service. This order also produced few results. By 1788 Vienna realized that the German-language requirement for the Confines' higher schools had to be brought into line with reality. On 16 July a new order was issued with two provisions. According to the first, members of the faculty still had to know German or be barred from appointment to a teaching post; but in the second provision, the German-language requirement for admission to the gymnasium was waived.[43] The Confinants and Vannetti had won at least one round.

Joseph II's concern for language extended beyond the classrooms to governmental institutions. At the beginning of his reign, he found four basic administrative languages in use: German, Italian, Latin, and French— the "four usual languages" in which decrees were often issued. He wanted to reduce that four to one and therefore issued his new language ordinance ordering for practical reasons rather than nationalistic ones that government business would be transacted in German. Those who customarily used one of the other three languages predictably opposed the decision. A March 1787 court decree on language evoked enormous protests in the Confines, as well as in Trieste, Görz, and Gradisca where it also applied. The decree required that at the end of three years, all the courts in these areas stop using Italian and instead conduct their judicial proceedings in German. This restriction applied to judges and advocates and to parties in a dispute. Furthermore, after the three-year grace period expired, no one was to be installed as a judge, allowed to enter a lower judicial office, or permitted to become an advocate who was not able to prove a sufficient knowledge of German by passing an examination. Joseph did permit an exception for the free port of Trieste: as long as one of the parties concerned was not a Habsburg subject or an inhabitant of Trieste, they could continue to use Italian in concluding contracts, keeping accounts, and the like. But if both parties were subjects of the Monarchy or were inhabitants of Trieste, they had to use German.[44] How this exception was to be enforced is unclear, and it may well have amounted to an intentional loophole for the port city, part of the same policy that put lower tariffs on the roads through Tyrol leading to the Adriatic port.

As he had for the Confines, Görz, and Gradisca, Joseph decreed similar language regulations for other parts of the Monarchy; almost everywhere the protests were so strong that before the year ended he had to make concessions. Noting that men were serving as chief magistrates and councillors "who were not learned in the language customary in the Land or in their judicial district," that is, the so-called *übliche Landessprache,* he instructed the appeals courts to issue their decrees in German and in the customary language of their land.[45] Judicial officials therefore had to know both German and the customary local language, a provision that tended to favor residents of the area over outsiders. By January 1790 (about a month before he died), Joseph recognized that a sufficient number of his subjects had not yet acquired the necessary language skills despite the grace period he had given them, so he prudently extended the deadline for another three years. (By that time the entire situation for the courts and administration would have changed, and the ruler would have changed twice as well.)

Joseph also bowed to necessity on other aspects of the language question. The Bozen Market Privileges and Statutes were revised and new ones published in January 1787. Section 18 provided that no one could be elected as a chancellor or actuary who had not proved his knowledge of both Italian and German by passing an examination. And since Joseph's subjects could not obey laws they could not understand, in February 1787 he decreed that all ordinances were to be published both in German and in the "National language."[46]

Daughters' Inheritance Rights

On 11 May 1786 Joseph II issued his Inheritance Patent "for all Estates without distinction," establishing legal disposition for "freely inherited property," that is, property not encumbered by some sort of entail or testamentary arrangement. According to the patent, all children, "be they of male or female sex, already born at the time of the death of the person leaving the inheritance or only after his death," were legal heirs and would inherit the entire estate (*Erbschaft*). If there were several living children, they would divide the estate equally "without distinction according to the number of persons." In a patent at the end of the following year, on 27 December 1787, Joseph ordered that all provincial inheritance laws conform to the provisions of the 11 May 1786 patent and make daughters equal heirs, that is, "participatory in all hereditary privileges which are ascribed to the sons." And by yet another law, Joseph decreed that women, who previously had had to transfer completely the administration of their property (*Vermögen*) to their husbands, now retained free disposition of that property.[47] The new arrangements also did away with a daughter's so-called voluntary renunciation of property when she married.

The result of all this legislation was in some places revolutionary. The daughters' new rights of inheritance and continued control after they married could create problems, especially when they married non-Habsburg subjects who were from areas where husbands still took control, if not outright ownership, of their wives' property. A family that owned a business or a landed holding might therefore suddenly find itself with a foreigner for a partner. This was the situation now facing the Confinants when their daughters married "foreign" Italians.

The law making daughters equal heirs with the sons apparently did not create that great a problem in German Tyrol, where all the children were somehow provided for with some kind of inheritance even though the landed holding itself traditionally passed to one son (or daughter, usually if there were no sons). The father could designate which of his children would inherit the property; but that child then had to postpone marriage and beginning a family until he actually took possession because the holding usually could not support two households. Elder sons often grew tired of waiting: they struck out on their own if the economic alternatives were favorable; or they might migrate or join the church. Therefore, younger sons usually inherited the land because they were still at home and available to run the holding. In general, the son who was reaching maturity just as the father retired or died had the best chance of becoming the heir. The holding could also be willed to a daughter, but tradition considered that "not right" if a son was present and willing to run the property, and especially if the daughter had already left—usually to marry. Once the land had passed to the heir, any remaining siblings either had to leave the property, perhaps with cash compensation as their legal share, or remain as subservient dependents of the sole heritor. The entire holding and everyone on it—including aged parents, since a father often passed the property on during his lifetime—were now subject to that single heir's decisions.[48]

In Romansch-speaking Ladin areas of Tyrol, all the children traditionally inherited equal shares. But to prevent the property from breaking up, the heirs sometimes agreed on joint management or, rarely, sold all their shares to one heir during the father's lifetime. The preference was to stay on the land, and the number that stayed tended to be the maximum number the holding could support. When daughters married, they therefore had to move off the homestead and give up their claim. But when any son married and tried to add to the household, it threatened the stability of the whole. The entire family therefore became involved in the courting process—to make sure that the prospective bride would fit in and to incorporate her gradually into the household. If serious friction developed, the courtship ceased—a development that might favor another son who also happened to be considering marriage. Another threat came from the children of newly-weds, since the new arrivals would eventually crowd out the other adults. If a second son married after the first marriage had taken place, he had to move off the holding because it simply could not support another family.[49] Presumably, the tradition of family control of property was strong enough here to convince a daughter of her duty to her kin when she married, despite Joseph's law that gave her ownership and control.

The Italian Tyroleans were most openly aggrieved by the new inheritance arrangements. In Italian villages all the offspring, male and female, traditionally had an equal share in the homestead; here, the concern was to make sure that each child had something with which to begin life. The result tended to be dwarf holdings or tenant farms. However small the holding, the Confinants did not want their land claimed by a foreigner when their sisters or daughters married. Rather, they wanted to keep the land in the family, maintain it together as a single productive unit and, above all, prevent further splintering. Before Joseph II's inheritance laws, when a woman married she gave up claim to support from her father's land, especially if she moved away. Or, at most, she got a cash settlement. If she did not marry, she frequently bequeathed her share to her brothers or nephews. Or during her lifetime her family might "encourage" her to draw up and sign what amounted to a fabricated family annuity contract, which encroached on her rights to such an extent that she often was left with nothing.[50]

Joseph II's inheritance laws made the daughters of the Welsch Confines the objects of matrimonial pursuit by neighboring foreigners, especially Trentine and Venetian Italians. Because of the transit trade and because Italian Tyrol was labor importing, many such foreigners were in the area; and after Joseph's laws were published, the inevitable began to happen with greater and greater frequency—or at least it seemed to. Italian Tyrol's businessmen faced a similar problem. They did much business with and were in constant commercial contact with Italians from other parts of the peninsula, so that their daughters frequently met and married men from outside the Habsburg lands. For both landowner and businessman, the new laws therefore meant—depending on the laws where their sons-in-law resided—that at least partial control of a family business or property might

THE GRIEVANCES

well fall into the hands of foreign Italians and create havoc in administering the enterprise. Or it might lead to years of lawsuits and countersuits.

Contributing in all likelihood to the Confinants' difficulties with the new inheritance laws was a demographic peculiarity: the number of males in the population was generally greater than the number of females. This anomaly meant either that more females were leaving the area or that more males (for example, foreign vineyard workers) were coming in, or both. The presence of more foreign men increased the likelihood that local women might marry them, especially since the Confinants and most of these for-eigners spoke the same language. The Etschland, which was also a wine-growing area, had a similar disproportional male-female ratio but not the problem of their daughters marrying foreigners, perhaps because of nation-ality differences (see table 3–2). Whatever the explanation, the Confinants did indeed have a problem as a result of Joseph II's inheritance legislation, and in 1790 they would bring this grievance to the Diet. In fact, of all Italian Tyrol's grievances, only this one was accepted by the Diet and in-cluded among the grievances of the land submitted to the emperor. And of all Welsch Tyrol's grievances, this one would be the most easily resolved.

TABLE 3-2
Tyrol's Male and Female Population by *Viertel,* 1777–81

	1777		1778		1780		1781	
Viertel	Male	Female	Male	Female	Male	Female	Male	Female
Lower Inn Valley and Wipp Valley	56,203	60,182	56,190	60,255	53,622	58,025	53,457	58,144
Upper Inn Valley	32,256	33,098	32,399	33,090	33,007	34,766	33,093	35,435
Burggrafenamt and Vintschgau	24,526	25,404	24,699	25,510	25,331	26,105	25,538	26,361
Etsch and Eisack	35,845	30,708*	36,096	30,879*	32,761	31,361*	33,223	31,612*
Puster Valley	32,559	36,591	32,625	36,527	32,564	36,616	33,098	36,927
Welsch Confines	28,046	27,713*	27,648	27,683	29,341	29,125*	29,748	29,336*

*More males than females

SOURCE: Based on information from Ferdinandeum, Dipauliana, Dip. 1194, census data for the years 1777, 1778, 1780, and 1781; as reproduced in Helmut Reinalter, *Aufklärung—Absolutismus—Reaktion. Geschichte Tirols in der 2. Hälfte des 18. Jahrhunderts* (Vienna: A. Schendl, 1974), 49.

Joseph II had begun to deal with the dissatisfactions of the Welsch Confines and all Tyrol and with rising discontent elsewhere, but he had not resolved very much before he died on 20 February 1790. All the problems therefore fell to his brother, Leopold II, who would convoke the Tyrolean Diet (and the Diets of his other lands) to channel the discontent and provide a legitimate forum for the expression of grievances and wishes.

A New Ruler and Renewed Hopes: Leopold II and the Convocation of the 1790 Diet in Tyrol

The Italians in Tyrol would prove helpful to Leopold II and he to them, but Tyrol was just one item on the list of domestic problems he had to deal with when he inherited the throne in Vienna. The mood throughout his new lands in 1790 was menacing, ranging from open grumbling to outright rebellion. The general European situation did not afford him much comfort either. In alliance with Russia, he had a Turkish war going on in the East; Prussian meddling was threatening his coronation in several of his own lands and in the Holy Roman Empire; and the French Revolution imperiled more than the well-being of his youngest sister, Marie Antoinette. The situation in the princely county, in many respects similar to that in the other Habsburg lands, was the result of a half century of generally unwelcome reforms, little opportunity to present grievances, the Estates bordering on revolt, and a national minority seeking equity. The way in which Leopold shaped his policies for the Italians and Germans in Tyrol reveals much about him and his domestic strategies in general, about his plans for Tyrol in particular, and about the Tyroleans themselves.

Even before Leopold's accession, during Joseph's last months, two main parties had begun to emerge in Tyrol. The smaller, reform party was led by the Governor-*Landeshauptmann*, Count Wenzel Sauer, who was fiercely pro-Josephian, supported the Italians, and earned the intense enmity of Tyrol's Etschland–dominated Estates. Governor Sauer, Joseph's man in Innsbruck, was a capable, industrious, and honorable man, but he was also peremptory and abrupt; and his enthusiasm in carrying out his monarch's policies at times bordered on the fanatic. The result was that Sauer became as great an irritation to the Tyroleans as the reforms he represented, and by 1790 he was the focus for anti-Josephian feeling. The Estates' dislike of Sauer was so intense that it extended to his two chief lieutenants: his secretary Wenzel Eppstein, a converted Jew originally from Prague; and Joseph von Aschauer, the syndic and Estate referent at the *Gubernium*, whose promotion Sauer had engineered.[1] It was in this small and extremely unpopular group that the Italians would find allies at the 1790 Diet.

Opposing Sauer and his supporters was the Bozen party, or Etschlanders. Initially, this by far larger party was led by Count Franz Wolkenstein (who wanted to be the next *Landeshauptmann*), Franz Gumer (a Bozen banker who had lost much influence under the Josephian regime), and Johann Christof von Unterrichter (who had been expelled from office when Sauer's friend Aschauer was made Estate referent at the *Gubernium*). The Etschlanders, who controlled and were therefore synonymous with the Estates, were staunchly anti-Josephian (and therefore anti-Sauer). They also opposed the Italians, whose claims threatened the Etschland's economic and political dominance.

Joseph's actions during the final two months of his reign tended to inflame the already overheated situation and brought Tyrol's Estates to the brink of rebellion. The atmosphere was so tense that when the *Steuercompromiss/Postulatcongress* met in December 1789 at Innsbruck, the delegates asked for and expected a thorough airing of grievances. They also asked for permission to send a deputation directly to the emperor to present their case rather than go through the *Gubernium* (that is, Sauer) as required by the new system. But Sauer, in control of the assembly and perhaps with his ruler's instruction, would not allow anyone to present grievances in Innsbruck or Vienna, even though many delegates had insisted on it as a condition of their attending.[2]

While the *Compromiss/Congress* was still meeting, Governor Sauer sent a report (6 January) to the Chancellery in Vienna, summarizing what the deputies were doing, or trying to do. He admitted that he supported some of their points and warned that the smoldering discontent might erupt with consequences "all too dubious for the general welfare;" as he put it, the current dissatisfaction might "gradually expand more generally."[3] The Chancellery submitted Sauer's report along with its own recommendations to the *Staatsrat* (State Council) and the emperor on 22 January 1790, suggesting remedies that amounted to a repeal of much that Joseph II had done in Tyrol. Joseph, now gravely ill, had begun to fear that the example of the rebellious Belgians and Hungarians might inspire the normally intensely loyal Tyroleans; so the *Staatsrat* moved swiftly, and the emperor's resolution was issued the next day.[4]

Responding especially to the Tyroleans' unhappiness with the new regulations on prayer and religion, Joseph resolved on 22 January that the *Gubernium* in Innsbruck would publicly announce "that it be my will from now on to allow to the people those old traditional exercises of devotion which they cherish according to their accustomed way of thinking" and that are "compatible with the genuine inspiration of our religion."[5] The decree on religion, issued two days later, also provided that some churches be reopened. As a further means of pacification, Joseph also decided on 24 January to abolish conscription for Tyrol, expressing the hope that in time of war the Tyroleans would voluntarily put the needed number of soldiers in the field.[6] But Joseph apparently did not have time to issue this decree before his death because his brother Leopold issued one on 29 March 1790 provisionally halting conscription in the princely county, and another almost a year later, on 4 March 1791, abolishing conscription altogether.

News of Joseph's decisions arrived in Innsbruck just as the delegates were preparing to go home. They asked Sauer to express to their monarch their "innermost feelings of thankfulness" for what he had done and their "most obedient respectful love as subjects";[7] and then they adjourned. But the Theresian and Josephian reforms had brought too many unwelcome changes, and the deputies were still extremely disturbed because Sauer had not permitted them to take their grievances directly to Vienna. They therefore met secretly and decided to work toward the convocation of the open Diet. There all the Estate officials and representatives would attend, and the Bozeners might well be able not only to have a decisive influence, but also to acquire important positions for themselves so that they would control the princely county in the future.[8]

The Tyroleans would have their open Diet, the first in seventy years, convoked not by Joseph, who died on 20 February, but by his brother and successor, Leopold II. On 11 February, nine days before Joseph died, Sir Robert Keith, the British ambassador in Vienna, wrote his sister of the dying emperor: "His intentions were always good; though he was often mistaken, both in plan and method. He has given the best proofs of his hearty wish to correct former errors, by restoring to many of his subjects their ancient privileges." And as a personal comment, Keith added: "He has been *kind, very kind* to me for twenty years."[9]

On 12 February Leopold, soon to be emperor, wrote his sister Maria Christine (governor of the Austrian Netherlands) from Florence, lamenting the condition of the Monarchy. Peace had not yet been made with the Turks, he wrote; the Habsburg lands had yet to be extricated from their difficulties with the King of Prussia; and their brother "needs to pacify completely Tyrol and Hungary, which are making a commotion." Affairs were, Leopold continued, being handled badly indeed and were getting worse: Things were being done "by halves and reluctantly," which gave to those one was attempting to assure "occasion to suspect that one is not [acting] in good faith."[10]

Because Joseph's illness left him increasingly weakened, he turned to his brother and heir, Leopold, and asked him to come to Vienna to help. Leopold may have preferred not to be saddled with his brother's policies when he himself ascended the throne, but he could not say no outright. In any event Leopold replied on 16 February that he planned to leave Florence soon, but "if by some accident or illness I would be prevented from leaving on the 22nd, I would let you know by courier." On 24 February (four days after Joseph's death, although the news had not yet reached Florence), Leopold wrote that he had indeed become quite ill: "I have been attacked by a very bad cold, sore throat and fever with headaches, insomnia, some repeated nerve attacks . . . [and] some nervous colic which absolutely prevents me from leaving."[11] That Leopold was prone to attacks of colic should also be noted.

News of Joseph's death soon arrived, and Leopold prepared to leave for Vienna. On 2 March 1790 he wrote Marie Christine that his cold, fever and colic, which had delayed his departure for eight days, had abated and that once in the capital he would need to face simultaneously "the war with the Turks in the southeast, Belgium in open revolution, Hungary ready for the fateful stroke, Galicia about to lose its reason, everyone dissatisfied, the treasury empty, Prussia in full readiness for war."[12] And there was Tyrol. His first concerns, he confided to his sister, would therefore be to make peace, to reassure foreign courts, and then turn his full attention to his own lands. He had already ordered that the Diets assemble in Hungary and the Austrian Netherlands.[13]

Leopold was sharply different from his brother in several ways. They had both been reared on ideas of enlightened kingship, and although they shared many goals, their styles and methods of government differed greatly. Where Joseph was more forceful, forthright, and perhaps headstrong, Leopold was more politically astute, cautious, and even suspicious. Leopold therefore brought to the chaotic situation now confronting him well-honed tactical and strategic abilities, a willingness to listen, negotiate, and compromise, and above all a desire that his lands and their Estates have a role in deciding their own affairs. Unlike Joseph, Leopold believed the Estates should advise and then preferably consent to policies he had decided on, even though they might need to be persuaded and prodded a bit on occasion to agree with him (as would be the case in granting seat and vote to Italian Tyrol).

Leopold admired the traditional constitution of Tyrol for the equality it gave to all the Estates, just as he admired the constitutions of Hungary, Bohemia, and the Austrian Netherlands because they included the participation of the Estates. His much-quoted "Confession of Faith," contained in a 24 January 1790 letter to Marie Christine, detailed his belief, expressed perhaps for public consumption, "that a sovereign, even a hereditary sovereign, is delegated and employed by the people," that every land ought to have "a fundamental law or contract between the people and the sovereign which limits the authority and power of the latter," that when the sovereign violates this fundamental law, the people are no longer obliged to obey him, and that the executive power "is in the sovereign, but the legislative is in the people and its representatives." Leopold added "that the sovereign ought to report and have approval for all the changes in the system, new laws, etc., . . . before publishing them."[14]

In reality, however, reporting to the Estates and seeking their approval was as far as Leopold was inclined to go. He was no more willing than his brother had been to cede legislative power to his subjects or their representatives. He probably came much closer to his own philosophy in an earlier, June 1789, letter to Marie Christine. Here he asserted that a land is fortunate if it has a constitution "which it has framed and to which the nation is attached, and since it then believes it is governing itself, it is indeed easier to direct, to govern, and to lead to its well-being and happiness, the only purpose for which any government is instituted." He added that where there were no Estates or constitution, they should be introduced "for tranquility and the good of the government itself."[15] He intended that these Estates be periodically consulted, but not that they enact laws.

Leopold's approach to government was among his most praiseworthy attributes. But he was also pedantic, suspicious, and sometimes petty, qualities he had displayed even as a child. His suspicion together with his interest in knowing what was going on in his realm and what the mood of the people was led to what he called his scientific method of government. Perhaps he called it that because it resembled the data-gathering methods of seventeenth-century astronomers and mathematicians which formed the basis for modern science. Leopold set up his own information-gathering system to provide him with large amounts of data from many sources so that he would not have to rely on single bits or single individuals.[16] He was neither covert nor subtle about his system. During Benjamin Franklin's tour of duty in France, the American envoy traveled in Italy, visited the Tuscan court, and saw firsthand how Leopold governed. Back in France, Franklin reported what he had seen to Phillip Mazzei, a Tuscan who had become a Virginian and then returned to Europe on behalf of his new homeland. Franklin described Leopold as "playing the cat" and "sniffing at all the holes," a ruler who had a famous informers' box into which people could drop bits of anonymous and even unsubstantiated gossip and accusations.[17] Yet, with all the suspicion and mistrust, all the agents and confidants at work (or perhaps in part because of them), Leopold was an enlightened, extremely capable—and extremely well informed—ruler; all these qualities he brought with him to Vienna.

Leopold laid the groundwork for dealing with Tyrol in the brief five-month period from 20 February 1790 when he took over from his brother to 22 July 1790 when the Tyrolean Diet assembled in Innsbruck. During these few months he developed his strategy, selected his lieutenants, and set in motion some of his policies. He included the princely county and other of his lands on his Florence-to-Vienna itinerary,[18] so that he could see things for himself, hear grievances, find out on whom he could depend, and what counterpressures were available, if necessary, to help calm the growing discontent. All along the route his new subjects greeted him with festivities designed to show their loyalty and devotion. In Tyrol these displays took place in defiance of Count Sauer's ban against public celebrations; Sauer, always with an eye on France, feared that public assemblies might provide the Tyroleans with the opportunity to turn their grumbling into emulation of the French. On his way through Tyrol, Leopold granted audiences to his new subjects and received grievances and petitions from Rovereto, Bozen, and Innsbruck.[19]

Rovereto shared many grievances with the rest of Tyrol and with the rest of the Monarchy. The city presented complaints about taxes, especially those levied for the war with the Turks, and protested against what they called "innovations in matters of religion." The Roveretans also objected to the new requirement that they pay to send their sons to school, especially a school where the courses were being taught in German. And they asked that all import tariffs between the Confines and the rest of Tyrol, including the tariffs on wine, be officially rescinded—a step, the Roveretans added that would carry the added benefit of stopping the smuggling generally going on in the area.[20]

Bozen's merchants and the foreigners who transacted business at the city's four annual fairs presented Leopold with grievances on the changes that had been made in the Mercantile Magistrate, the court with jurisdiction over the fairs. They found especially objectionable the new rules, fees, and procedures that required the services of advocates or lawyers at almost every step, even for consensual agreements. Everything, complained the merchants, had to be done according to the new protocols, and even trials did not finish matters because everything could be appealed. They wanted the Mercantile Magistrate restored to its pre-Josephian basis, which was, they said, "the most just and simple."[21]

Among those Leopold met with in private audiences at Bozen, the chief city of German southern Tyrol, was a Bozen banker and official of the Mercantile Magistrate, Franz Gumer (who would be the focus of many intrigues before, during, and after the Diet). He was accompanied by his brother Joseph and another man, Anton Menz, from a wealthy Bozen merchant family. The three men took almost an hour of Leopold's time discussing the status of the mercantile question and the damage that they felt had been done to commerce. They also tried to enlist his help for what they termed "the business already taking its course in Vienna," presumably the petition for convocation of the Diet.[22] In view of the difficulties that Franz Gumer would later have with Leopold, the banker apparently made a very bad impression on this March day.

At Bozen, Leopold also met with representatives of the city who asked that their municipal government be returned to what it had been before

CHAPTER FOUR

Joseph's reforms—that is, that the manufacturers, citizens, and peasants again elect the Civic Magistrate rather than have its members appointed by the central government and emperor in Vienna. The peasants of the jurisdiction (*Landgericht*) of Bozen asked only that the government be returned to what it had been at the time of Maria Theresa. The clergy complained about the deep feeling against the ecclesiastical innovations, claimed that the state was mishandling the Religion Fund, and asserted that "Acatholic principles" were being taught at the state-run General Seminary in Innsbruck.[23] Before leaving Bozen and in response to pleas from a deputation led by city official (and Diet diarist) Andreas diPauli, Leopold promised that he would soon convoke Tyrol's open Diet and reinstate the land's constitution.

Before leaving Tyrol, Leopold conferred with Governor Sauer and other officials and heard additional complaints both about conscription and about Joseph's reform of the judiciary, which limited the princely county to one court of the first instance and moved the Upper Austrian (Tyrol and Vorarlberg) appeals court to Klagenfurt.[24] Leopold promised his subjects that he would "view the Estates as the pillars of the Monarchy and therefore wished to return to them all their privileges and in union with them bring the good of the people into correspondence with its duty."[25]

From Tyrol, Leopold traveled through Styria and Carinthia, arriving in Vienna on 12 March 1790. That same day he issued a resolution permitting the Estates to present directly to him (rather than going through the *Gubernium*, as Joseph had required) any representations concerning changes in their constitutions or laws and to elect deputies for that purpose. And he repeated his promise to convoke the Diets of his lands soon. British envoy Robert Keith could write his sister by November of a whole new tone or image that Leopold had brought with him to the capital. "I have just now seen in my morning walk," he wrote, "what gave me real pleasure, but which if it had been exhibited in the reign of Charles the Sixth, or even that of Maria-Theresa, would have been thought to prognosticate the *downfall* of the House of Austria: the Archduke Francis, heir of the throne, walking in a great-coat, arm in arm with his new married *wife* in a warm gown, and without a single servant or living creature attending them. . . . in some respects the world alters for the better. Everybody blessed the couple as they passed."[26]

After three days in his new capital, Leopold wrote to Marie Christine confiding that his health was passable and that he was suffering now not so much from the effects of the journey as from "the sad state and situation of the monarchy and the confusion that reigns here and in all its lands. It is extreme; nevertheless, I flatter myself to be able to pacify them little by little, and that war with the King of Prussia will not take place."[27] Step-by-step pacification was exactly what he did, his relations with both the Italians and Germans in Tyrol providing an excellent case in point.

A NEW RULER AND RENEWED HOPES

As Leopold took over the reins in Vienna, the Tyroleans began to get ready for the promised Diet. And, as the different parties and individuals jockeyed for position, the new ruler's plans began to crystallize. He would retreat only as far as he had to in order to quell the disturbances; he would give the Estates a role, though not much power; he would encourage the Italians and grant them what they sought and were entitled to have and at the same time would make use of them as a counterforce to the about-to-rebel Etschlanders. Furthermore, if Leopold were to be truly effective, he could not allow the two parties then emerging in Tyrol to have a totally free rein in pursuing their separate goals. He therefore moved quickly to have his own men act as guides to events and hold important positions in each party. One of these emperor's men attended the pre-Diet assembly in Rovereto as the Italians drafted their grievances and elected their deputies. Another, Leopold's personally named court commissar to the Diet, took over leadership of the Bozen-Etschland party, thereby gaining a degree of control, but only that, over the budding Estates' revolt.

Initially, the Bozen party rallied around Count Franz Wolkenstein-Trostburg, the newly appointed administrator of the Land Marshal's office (*Landmarschallamtsverwalter*). Young and ambitious, Wolkenstein had hopes of becoming *Landeshauptmann* and immediately took a stand against the current *Landeshauptmann* and governor, Count Sauer. Wolkenstein was quickly joined by Franz Gumer, the Bozen banker-merchant and former *Bürgermeister* whose deceptive actions quickly earned him his new sovereign's disfavor, perhaps as early as Leopold's journey through Bozen on his way to Vienna. Gumer, by taking an active role now, hoped to regain at least some of the once great influence he had lost under Sauer's governorship. The third "musketeer" in the anti-Sauer camp was Johann Christof von Unterrichter, who more than once had found—and would again find—himself in difficulties with the authorities. Unterrichter, a former Estates' referent, had been dismissed in early 1789 so that Sauer's close associate, Joseph von Aschauer,[28] could be appointed to office. Unterrichter had then been subjected to an investigation for alleged misconduct in office.

Now cleared of charges brought by Sauer, Unterrichter quickly joined the Bozen party. At that time, he happened to be in Vienna and was therefore given the task of persuading the new ruler that someone favorable to the Bozeners should be named court commissar for the forthcoming Diet. The court commissar would preside over the assembly and in many cases control the flow of business. The Bozen party's candidate was Count Franz Enzenberg, then Vice-President of the Inner and Upper Austrian Appeals Court in Klagenfurt, son of an earlier governor of Tyrol, and godson of Maria Theresa and Franz Stephan. Enzenberg, who owned estates in Tyrol, had been a gubernial councillor (*Gubernialrat*) in Innsbruck for eleven years before going to Klagenfurt, and Unterrichter urged the count's appointment as the man "best entrusted with the local relationships."[29] The suggestion met with Leopold's approval; and it served his own purposes as well.

Leopold knew that while Enzenberg's personal sentiments were very much with the Etschlanders, he was also reliably *kaisertreu* and could be trusted to follow instructions. Once in Innsbruck, Enzenberg would rapidly place himself at the head of the Bozen party, which opposed most of what Leopold wanted for the Confinants and was in the vanguard of the Estates' revolt. In that position, Enzenberg could keep the Etschlanders from getting too far out of line, it was hoped; and, as commissar, he could attempt to obtain what Leopold wanted from the Diet. Enzenberg would carry out his mission with some success and at times with a bit too much zeal. But before Leopold could even appoint a court commissar for the Tyrolean Diet, other work needed to be done.

As spring took hold, the central bureaucracy began to deal with Estate complaints and requests, that is, their *Beschwerden und Begehren, Domande,* or *Desideria.* The grievances that Leopold brought with him from Tyrol and the other stops along his route and those complaints arriving from the other *Gubernia* followed the normal bureaucratic route: the *Vereinigte Hofstelle* (a single institution of government formed when Joseph II united several separate parts of the central government) organized and assembled them, then sent them on to the Bohemian-Austrian Court Chancellery, which in turn submitted its report to the *Staatsrat.* The *Staatsrat* considered the matter(s) and made recommendations to the emperor who, in the final step of the *Staatsrat* proceedings, issued his decision, or resolution. (Leopold's later abolition of the *Vereinigte Hofstelle* would eliminate one step in this process.) On 19 April, about two months after Leopold arrived in Vienna, the *Staatsrat* made its first report to him on Tyrolean grievances.

In these early days of Leopold's reign, one group of Tyroleans—the Bozen merchants—had as its Vienna lobbyist a familiar face. Carlantonio Pilati, now recovered from his beating and representing both the Mercantile Magistrate and the city, was there not only because Bozen had sent him, but also because Leopold had invited him (although why he was invited is not exactly clear). The jurist was graciously received and, as he himself reported, quickly succeeded in securing from Leopold the restoration, to the extent possible, of the Bozen Mercantile Magistrate's ancient statutes. Soon thereafter, Leopold commissioned Pilati to compile a mercantile code based on ancient rights and freedom of commerce and sanctioned this code at the beginning of 1791. The Bozen merchants had also asked Pilati to obtain certain "useful" changes in their taxes. Specifically, they sought the repeal of the customs tariff and road tax and of the *Umgeld* newly assessed on their wines. This *Umgeld* was intended to replace the income lost to the central treasury by the abolition of the former duties levied on the Confinants' wines at the Nevis Bridge. When these Bozen proposals came before the *Staatsrat,* Leopold decided only that the content of the protocol "serve as information." That is, the question was to be decided later. But either Leopold told the jurist something in confidence or Pilati was referring to the mercantile code when on 10 May 1790 Pilati reported back to Bozen that "the imperial response conformed to the desire of the city."[30]

While Leopold was taking charge in Vienna, all talk in Tyrol turned to the promised but not yet convoked Diet. Governor Sauer, with an eye still on France, was not yet reconciled to the idea of convocation and feared that the assembly would be only a first step to further trouble in the princely county. Therefore, he and his officials, and especially Referent Joseph von Aschauer, attempted to head off the convocation. In April, in a certainly unwitting emulation of France's Assembly of Notables, they organized a similar conference in Innsbruck to accept and approve a predrafted version of Tyrol's main grievances. That draft, according to their plan, would then be presented directly to the court at Vienna and would make a Diet superfluous. To this special conference they invited those officials and other individuals "who had formerly been subordinated to the so-called perpetual congress" and who happened to be in or near Innsbruck at the time.[31]

Sauer's handpicked assembly met secretly. To his chagrin the majority rejected the proposals worked out in advance (by Aschauer) and declared themselves in favor of an open Diet. When the Etschlanders learned about the secret conference, they defied Sauer's ban on public assemblies and held one of their own at Bozen where they drafted a protest against Sauer's private assembly—the first open, decided act of opposition to the government. And Sauer, instead of averting the rebellion he feared, now seemed to be precipitating it. Agitation for the Diet increased, and convocation could not be delayed much longer. The decree calling the Estates together was issued on 31 May; in Tyrol the Diet would assemble on 22 July.[32]

As the Etschlanders had requested, Count Franz Enzenberg was named court commissar at the open Diet; that is, he would be the emperor's plenipotentiary and the person who would preside over the sessions and hear grievances and requests in the emperor's name. On 25 April Kolowrat informed Enzenberg that he was the emperor's choice and would find special mandates annexed to his instructions. Enzenberg indicated that he would accept the appointment. But he seemed confused and asked which matters and postulates Leopold wanted him to present to the Diet. From time immemorial, said the new court commissar, Diets were called either to consider the prince's requests or to render the oath of hereditary homage. But, he continued, Kolowrat's message seemed to indicate that the emperor did not intend to offer any propositions and that the Diet was being called only so that the Tyroleans could openly submit their grievances and pleas to the monarch. That, despite Enzenberg's confusion and surprise, was

CHAPTER FOUR

precisely what Leopold did intend. Enzenberg received his actual commission and instructions on 31 May.[33] Meanwhile, on 26 April, the day after Enzenberg was notified of his appointment, Leopold restored the Estate constitutions not only in Tyrol, but also in Styria, Carinthia, and Carniola. He also decided that if the Tyroleans asked for the ceremony of hereditary homage, his sister Elisabeth (the head of a convent in Innsbruck) would accept the oath in his stead. Leopold's grandfather, Charles VI, had been the last to hold such a ceremony, at which the members of the assembled Estates swore fealty and obedience in their own name and in the name of every inhabitant of the land. The ruler, in return, renewed and confirmed the "rights and freedoms, graces and privileges" of the Estates.[34]

An anonymous Tyrolean historian of the midnineteenth century, writing on how close Tyrol's Estates came to revolt in 1790, praised Leopold for convoking the Diet that "raised the national spirit out of the swampiness of a half century," but he noted that the ruler had favored the "submissive" whom he could use "to rattle [anscharchen] and get rid of complainers." Leopold's instruction to Diet Commissar Enzenberg, claimed this historian, had been, "Let them in God's name vomit forth whatever they have in their stomach. Then we will have our way."[35] That in fact was—more or less, though perhaps not so picturesquely—one piece of Leopold's plan. Another piece, which he used in other parts of the Monarchy as well as in Tyrol, was to champion the rights of an "out" group within a land as a counterweight to an "in," or dominant, group causing trouble. In Tyrol, this meant taking the side of the Italians against the German Etschlanders, who were the primary source of the discontent there. Not that Leopold did not think the Italians' cause just; he did. But he also found it useful in helping him pacify the Etschland.

The emperor had set 22 July as the day of convocation for Tyrol's first open Diet in seventy years, and he had also invited the Italian towns and jurisdictions to send deputies and to express their grievances and desires. Therefore, throughout Tyrol representatives of localities met to discuss their problems and draft their grievances. At one such gathering on 9 May 1790 at Strigno, in and for the *pretura* or jurisdiction of Ivano, representatives of Ivano's eight communes drew up a 37-point list of grievances, including the reaction that had been growing against language reforms in the schools and courts of the Confines. Ivano asked that the local Italian population no longer be obliged to learn German and that the officials of their superior courts be completely fluent in Italian so that when someone was brought to court, he or she would be able to understand the complaint and its significance. Ivano also asked that the Confinants again be permitted to send their children to the lower schools of the colleges at Trent and Feltre, which would be much less expensive for the parents (and would provide an Italian education). Finally, along with other areas of the Confines, Ivano requested relief from the new inheritance laws so that a family would not lose control of any of its property when a daughter married a foreign, non-Habsburg subject.[36]

While the Ivano group was meeting at Strigno on 9 May, representatives from the city and *pretura* of Rovereto were also deliberating at their second pre-Diet session. There, in the home of Felice Baroni di Cavalcabò of Sacco (who would be one of the Confines' deputies both at the Innsbruck Diet and later in Vienna) appeared the first concrete evidence of Leopold's interest in the 1790 Italian movement—in the person of Baron Georg Adalbert von Beekhen, a *Hofrat* (Court Councillor). A contemporary chronicler and member of the Agiati, Baron Giambattista Todeschi, attended the 9 May meeting at Sacco and recorded the proceedings and the presence of this unusual visitor, "the most illustrious Signor [Georg] Adalberto Barone di Becken Court Councillor of H. M., who lodged in the above-mentioned house on the occasion of his passage from Milan to Vienna."[37] Since Rovereto was not on the most direct main route to Vienna (a route not likely to be blocked by snow in May), it is highly probable that Beekhen was there at Leopold's behest. And, if Leopold needed someone to take care of business for him in Rovereto or elsewhere along the way, he could not have found a more appropriate person than Beekhen.

Beekhen, a man with some financial expertise and a knowledge of several languages, began his climb up the bureaucratic ladder in the latter part of Maria Theresa's reign. He traveled widely both on state and personal business to many parts of the Monarchy. In 1773 he was sent to Galicia, the Habsburg share of the first partition of Poland, as a Gubernial councillor, where his duties included a confidential mission to Danzig (Gdansk) to investigate the sad state of Galician trade. Beekhen later claimed that there was no branch of public business in which he had not served while in the Habsburgs' new Polish territory. In 1782 he returned to Vienna's *Hofrechenkammer* (Court Accounting Chamber) as director of the department overseeing the property of abolished monasteries. And, as he himself said, he was involved "in more than one important matter, to which the documents attest,"[38] a formulation that Adam Wandruszka says is typical for a court agent. Two years later the future emperor, Leopold II, met Beekhen in Vienna; Leopold recorded the meeting in his diary, noting that he found the *Hofrat* to be "a man of animation and ability" who had 400 employees under his direction.[39]

A brief tour of duty to look into Lombardy's finances put Beekhen in Milan when Joseph II died; and Leopold, remembering at least his 1784 meeting with the *Hofrat*, summoned him to a new post in Vienna: director of two departments in the *Hofkammer*. Beekhen was en route to Vienna from Milan when he appeared in Rovereto on 9 May, clearly there for more than the silk and the wines. Even before he left Milan, questions had been raised about his new salary of 4,000 florins a year and especially the amount given him for travel expenses. The *Vereinigte Hofstelle* commented, in a note added to the protocol on such payments: "The advance of 1000 f[lorins] given to the aforesaid H. Hofrath on account (for future settlement) from the Cameral funds at Milan for the defrayal of his travel [expenses] appears to be excessive for the mere journey here."[40] This expense money, equivalent to a quarter of his yearly salary and far more than the annual wage of many others, was indeed excessive for mere travel expenses; it was probably given him to cover such extraordinary expenses as those he might incur on his stopover in Rovereto or other places he may have visited at Leopold's request.

Several local notables were also at the meeting that Beekhen attended on 9 May at Felice Baroni's. Among them were three men who represented the city of Rovereto: Luigi Carpentari, a local noble and silk merchant; Federigo Tartarotti, chancellor of the castle at Rovereto; and Carlo Betta, a local would-be noble who actually accepted unauthorized nobility with the predicate "dal Toldo" from the interregnum Vicar of the Holy Roman Empire, Elector Karl Theodor of Bavaria.[41] Rovereto's mayor, Angelo Rosmini, was also involved in preparations for the Diet and would later be the city's deputy at Innsbruck. The *pretura*'s eight communes also sent deputies to the 9 May meeting, one of whom was Clemente Baroni, the historian who had written against one of the maps of southern Tyrol and composed the arguments for giving the Confinants seat and vote (see chapter 3 and above).

Those assembled at Sacco decided to send two deputies to the Diet (one from the citizens of the city, the other from the communes), whose first task would be to ask "for Seat and deliberative Vote in the Diet," that is for immatriculation, which the Diet had the power to give. If the Diet granted them seat and vote, they would work with the representatives of the rest of Tyrol for the good of the entire province. But if the Diet refused them seat and vote, the Roveretan deputies were to leave immediately and go to Vienna "to seek from the Sovereign that justice which had been denied them at Innsbruck." Once in Vienna, they were also to propose to the emperor, as an alternative to seat and vote in the provincial assemblies, "a project of separation from German Tyrol and the formation of an autonomous Province composed of the 'Quartiere' of Rovereto, the Valsugana and the County of Arco."[42] This was the first time, but certainly not the last, that the idea of separation was advanced. It would be heard again and again with variants until 1918, when the irredentists achieved their goal—and took some of German Tyrol with them.

Although at their pre-Diet meeting the Roveretans proposed the alternative of a new crownland, they rejected the idea of union with the Principality of Trent. The Prince-Bishop of Trent may have been their ecclesiastical lord, but they did not seek to have him also as a temporal ruler, clearly preferring Habsburg rule to that of Prince-Bishop Thun. "The Count of Tyrol," they argued, "has provided enough to the ecclesiastical principality of Trent without need of resurrecting it into a new province in union with the Quartiere of Rovereto!" At this pre-Diet meeting, the Roveretans also agreed on four other requests they would make of their sovereign. They would ask for confirmation of their ancient privileges and statutes with modifications "as required by modern needs"; they would seek a guarantee of free commerce for their wines within Tyrol, commerce the Bozeners wanted exclusively for themselves; they would request exemption from the tax levied on most "necessary foods"; and, like Bozen and Innsbruck, they would petition for removal of Joseph II's civic magistrate and a return to the previous system along with administrative autonomy for the individual communes.[43] One can only speculate on what role Beekhen may have played at this meeting as the Roveretans drafted their plans, strategies, and tactics.

Tyrol's Italians held a final pre-Diet meeting at Sacco on 28 May. Here, all the communes of the Confines assembled, named their deputies to the Diet, and drafted a formal program of "grievances and wishes." This time the entire *Kreis*, not just the city and *pretura* of Rovereto, decided that if the Diet refused to give them a proportionate representation with seat and vote at the Diets, their deputies would go to Vienna to obtain justice from Leopold. (Whether Beekhen, or anyone like him, was at this 28 May meeting remains a question.) Among the deputies sent to the Innsbruck Diet were Federigo Tartarotti and Felice Baroni representing the *pretura* of Rovereto, and Rovereto's Mayor Angelo Rosmini representing the city. Carlo Betta had originally been selected as a *pretura* deputy; but with his new, though not quite legal, nobility in hand from Karl Theodor as a Vicar of the Empire, Betta adopted his new predicate "dal Toldo" and sought his own seat and vote as a noble at the Diet. He was therefore replaced as a *pretura* deputy by Felice Baroni.[44]

In Vienna, the central bureaucracy had begun to deal with the concerns of the princely county almost immediately upon Leopold's arrival in March 1790, the language laws in particular receiving early attention. On 29 March, about a month after he ascended the throne, Leopold issued a court resolution modifying the earlier language legislation: he ordered that for positions as appeals or land court president, if a "nationalist" with the qualities required for the office was available, he was to be given preference. Leopold also ordered that while *Landmannschaft* (in effect, citizenship in a land or province) was not necessary for an appeals court president, it was required for a president of a local court of the first instance, or *Landrecht*.[45]

Then, during the last week in April, the *Staatsrat* circularized and sent to the emperor a report of the *Oberste Justizstelle* on the use of the German language in the courts of the Welsch Confines, Görz-Gradisca, and Trieste. Leopold, accepting the *Justizstelle's* advice, issued a decree on 29 April ordering that the introduction of the German language in the courts of these areas not be further pressed. The decree also had a kind of grandfather clause, ordering that only for future installations of judges, judicial officials, and acceptance of advocates should "preference be given to those who, together with other abilities and merits, can be shown to have full knowledge of the German language." As a result, the people of the Italian-speaking areas would no longer need to know German to take a case to court; but those aspiring to judicial positions or to careers as lawyers in these areas would still be well advised to learn that language.[46] As for the schools, on 5 May the Court Commission on Studies sent its report to the *Staatsrat* and the emperor regarding the use of German in the schools of the Confines. Leopold accepted the advice of the commission and, judging by subsequent events because detailed documentation is lacking, permitted some class instruction in Italian.[47]

In the spring the central government also had to deal with southern Tyrol's reaction to Joseph II's new "systematization" of the wine *Umgeld*, or excise tax. The new regulations required the Estates of the Etschland to pay 16,000 florins into the central treasury in return for a contract that gave them the right to collect the excise tax on wine. The Etschlanders protested that the new tax raised the price of their wines and therefore might inhibit sales; they urged instead that they be permitted to raise the 16,000 florins by again collecting a tax on the Confinants' wines coming over the Nevis Bridge. The Etschlanders' opposition to the new *Umgeld* system grew intense and then menacing, and an urgent report from a local *Umgeld* official made it clear that something had to be done. But it was almost a year before any action was taken, probably because of the change in rulers. Then, on 24 June 1790 the *Hofkammer*, referring to Leopold's wish that "as far as it is possible" his subjects be pacified, made the following recommendation: that the assessment of a wine *Umgeld* in the Bozen *Kreis* be dropped for the term of the current *Umgeld* contract and that instead the Estates collect proportional head taxes (*Aversen*) in the amount of 16,000 florins and pay them to the central treasury. To collect wine fees again on Welsch wines crossing the Nevis Bridge, said the *Hofkammer*, would be "a true injustice to the so-called Confinants, who through the new Tax Regulation had been put into proper relation with the rest of the land" and were now retailing their product without restriction or additional duties. The *Hofkammer* also agreed with the *Gubernium* that the surplus in the Wine Deputation's Fund (that is, the tax farmers' fund) be distributed "according to the ratio of the tax base for the northern non-wine-growing *Viertel* and that each jurisdiction's share be added to its poor fund."[48]

As summer approached, attention shifted to the Tyrolean capital and to preparations for the Diet. On 9 June the court commissar to the Diet, Count Franz Enzenberg, left Vienna for Innsbruck; on the way he spent about three weeks in Passau to arrange, as he phrased it, "a few small whispered-about [*säussliche*] matters," and on 1 July arrived in the Tyrolean capital. He was greeted first by his court secretary for the term of the assembly, Karl von Seydel, who had arrived the previous evening, then more formally by two deputies from each Estate.[49] The opposition, or Bozen party, leaders were also in Innsbruck, having hurried to be there for Enzenberg's arrival. He was, after all, the man whom they had proposed as court commissar; now he would lead the Diet where they hoped to see their efforts rewarded and "their boldest wishes fulfilled."[50] From the beginning, Enzenberg joined with the triumvirate leading the Bozen party, three men who would control the Diet almost until the end: Land Marshal's Office Administrator Count Franz Wolkenstein, former Estates Referent Johann Christof von Unterrichter, and banker Franz Gumer.

Enzenberg took up residence at the *Landhaus*, living quarters that he had arranged in June through an exchange of letters with Governor-*Landeshauptmann* Sauer. The quarters, convenient to the assembly hall, the Chancellery, and the archives, afforded him the opportunity to take care of at least the most urgent business at all times of the day or night. Important to him and his mandate, noted Enzenberg, was his proximity to the quarters of "the two Baron envoys" and to Count Franz Wolkenstein and "several other important Voters," or *Vocalen*, at the Diet.[51] Enzenberg did not specify who the two barons were, which means that the reference was clear to Leopold and probably to his closest advisers, too. Most likely, one of these barons was Baron Marx Cazan, who represented the Etschland wine interests and later drafted the Diet's official reply to the Confinants.

Enzenberg carefully recorded all his activities from 1 July when he arrived in Innsbruck to 22 July when the Diet opened, providing an interesting picture of pre-Diet maneuvering, politicking, and activities in general. He took advantage of his proximity to the archives, he said, to gather and organize the documents that would tell him the rights, freedoms, privileges, and traditions that should guide the organization and running of the Diet. He also supplemented what he found in the documents with what he could glean from the oral histories recounted by members of local families on the constitution of Tyrol. In selecting the most useful documents for the Diet, he said, he also took the advice of experienced men who had long worked in the archives, had been displaced by salaried functionaries during Joseph's reign, and were now reinstated in their positions. He also relied on men who had knowledge of the law and those "who seek here the sole wish of the nation," that is, to have a Diet that is "the only dam against general upheaval." Enzenberg used the material he gathered both as a guide for the Diet and to write a history of Tyrol, which he appended to his report to the emperor.[52]

Enzenberg recorded several meetings with the Bozen triumvirate, that is, with Wolkenstein, Unterrichter, and the "everywhere-known" Gumer. The court commissar said he had accepted the last of the three because of Gumer's "clear-headedness and knowledge of matters," an opinion clearly in conflict with Leopold's. At these sessions the four men made plans for

CHAPTER FOUR

maintaining order and whatever else concerned the Diet to avoid "intrigues, ousters from office, husbanding of votes [against them], or other preliminaries disadvantageous to the common good." They also decided on how to handle all the documents that the Diet would generate and how to bring some order to the long-neglected nobles' section of the Matricle. Enzenberg also held preliminary meetings with Governor-*Landeshauptmann* Count Sauer and Count Franz Wolkenstein, especially to discuss preparations for the ceremony of hereditary homage, which the Tyroleans had requested, and for the Diet itself. Enzenberg recorded about his chief rival Sauer, "loyal to the truth, I must also indicate here that the L[ord] Governor in everything has shown himself outwardly very willing, indeed helpful and obliging," so that the two men no longer gave any outward appearance of misunderstanding.[53] But the apparent reconciliation went no deeper than the surface.

During these preparations, Enzenberg heard about a report from the *Kreishauptmann* in the Welsch Confines, Baron Sigmund Moll, which told of disturbances planned to be held during and after the oath of hereditary homage. The court commissar asked to see the report and learned that so far the uproar had been over a local dispute involving a bread baker. But he also found that Moll and Rovereto's mayor, Angelo Rosmini, had advised that further public security arrangements be made; this was done.[54] Enzenberg now wanted to know more about the mood of the Confines, since, as he recorded, he was already persuaded of the area's right to power and influence on the land's affairs. He therefore ordered, secretly, that Court Commission Secretary von Seydel go to the Confines, observe the local situation, and report back.[55] Seydel sent two reports from Rovereto, both of which Enzenberg forwarded to Vienna with his own report. The dossier's arrival was noted in a court resolution of 22 July (the day the Diet opened), but no action was noted on that day.

As the Diet's opening approached, the Confinants, helped by *Hofrat* Beekhen and supported by Governor Sauer and the emperor, were ready to face the assembly. The Etschlanders were ready too, with Count Enzenberg as their head, along with Wolkenstein, Gumer, and Unterrichter. Best positioned of all, of course, was Leopold, whose men headed both sides (though the Etschlanders at least were apparently unaware of their ruler's tactics or strategies). Everything was ready for the opening of the first Tyrolean Diet since 1720. More than 500 persons would attend; it would be in session for two months and would prove to be the last open Diet in Tyrol's history.

The Innsbruck Assembly:
German Tyrol versus the 1790 Italian Movement

Tyrol's open Diet was not, nor was it intended to be, a legislative body. It could petition for a redress of grievances and could accept, bargain over, or reject the ruler's postulates, but it had no legislative initiative and could not enact laws. The Innsbruck assembly could therefore not grant the Italians most of what they sought, but the Estates could decide (as could the emperor) on who was to be entered in Tyrol's Matricle and would therefore be entitled to seat and vote at the Diet. The assembly could also decide on the members of the *Ausschüsse* and *Steuercompromiss* and on which grievances would be presented to the emperor as grievances of the entire land. The Confinants, therefore, first turned to the Diet with their *domande*, and it was there that they first confronted the Etschlanders' opposition.

The Bozen party's initial attacks were aimed at the staunchly Josephian governor, Count Wenzel Sauer; his secretary, Wenzel Eppstein; and their ally, the Estates syndic and referent at the *Gubernium*, Joseph von Aschauer. As the Diet got under way, the anti-Sauer propaganda grew harsher, more intense, and more scurulous. The governor was now being attacked for more than being a forceful Josephian, opposing the convocation of the Diet, and supporting the Italians. An additional strike against him in the eyes of some at the Diet was that his secretary, Wenzel Eppstein, was a converted Jew. That fact led an anonymous writer at the Diet to compose an unpleasant bit of calumny against both Sauer and Eppstein:

To the Assembly
How long must you yet nourish the crafty vipers
Oppressed Land Tyrol! in your bosom?

They hiss destruction at you; poisoned sap and blood,
And seek to dishonor quite cruelly your honest heart.
They eat your bread, and still want to take your children,
Their selfishness devours more than a hyena;
To their tyranny must everyone submit,
Only let it not burn more intensely. To be banished, breadless.
O! would they go away from us soon, Count Sauer, Jew Eppstein
    and their band,
From the school of Mufti Defraine, Director Tartuf Sybul
Out of our Land,
How Innsbruck would hold a feast, how we would live in jubilation!
O King Leopold! hear the pleas of these children
O Brother Enzenberg! altogether we pray,
That this lawbreaker yet would leave our borders,
Quickly deliver us from this evil. Amen.
V. Plead for us, O Burg-countess Elisabeth
X. On that we become worthy of the promise of your brother.[1]

The Bohemian-Austrian Court Chancellery in Vienna was also discussing what to do about Sauer and Eppstein, whose actions in carrying out (perhaps a bit overzealously) their ruler's wishes had so enraged the Tyrolean Estates. According to Archduke Francis's careful records of the proceedings, the Estates claimed that Aschauer had become referent, that is, the single representative of all the Estates at the *Gubernium*, without ever having been elected or approved by them and that in any event they no longer needed any representative since they themselves were about to assemble. The emperor's court commissar Count Enzenberg, Francis recorded, had tried to reason with the hotheads but had been unable to calm them, and they threatened to break up the assembly if Aschauer was not sent away. As for Count Sauer, Enzenberg reported that he feared for the governor's life; and he also feared a repeat of events similar to those in the Austrian Netherlands, where the Estates were in open revolt and had to be subdued by military force. The Chancellery noted that Sauer, "who had done nothing other than to execute the commands of his ruler too hastily and without moderation," would be dishonored if he were now recalled. The councillors therefore proposed that for the moment the unpopular governor be left in Tyrol and supported until the Diet had been organized and was under way and that he be recalled as soon as this was completed. The matter, noted the Chancellery, required a prompt decision.[2]

In response to the Chancellery's urging, the *Staatsrat* moved quickly and on 24 July took up the matter. Leopold had learned firsthand of the high level of feeling against Sauer, Aschauer, and Eppstein during his Florence-to-Vienna journey and realized that to avoid inflaming the situation further, these men had to be removed. But they were loyal servants of the crown, and he did not want to injure their reputations. He therefore decided to inform the Tyroleans that Aschauer's office as Estate referent no longer existed because the Estates were now assembled and could speak for themselves. Sauer's position was a little more complicated, however. First, Leopold reminded the Tyroleans of their loyalty toward their ruler and his expectation that they would treat Sauer with the attention and respect due a governor. But Leopold also decided to avoid any suggestion of coercion that Sauer's presence at the Diet might have on an open and orderly presentation of grievances, by exempting the governor from having to attend the Diet sessions. Further, to avoid any dishonor, Sauer himself was to request the exemption. Therefore, although Leopold removed Sauer and Aschauer as the Estates had wanted, he tried to do it in a way that would preserve their reputations.[3] On 25 July Supreme Chancellor Kolowrat wrote to Sauer informing him of the emperor's decision. Sauer was present during the first sessions, which dealt primarily with formalities such as approving credentials. But by the time the hearing of grievances began on 28 July, he had ceased to attend, claiming indisposition;[4] on 1 August he submitted his formal request that he be exempted from attending Diet sessions.[5] It took him about two weeks to pack up and depart; but on Sunday, 15 August the Confinants' watched one of their staunchest supporters quietly leave Innsbruck for Vienna, accompanied by his wife and his secretary, Eppstein. Former Estate Referent Aschauer soon followed. The popular temper that drove these men from Innsbruck was vividly described three years later (and with a memory perhaps affected by time) by the then-governor Baron Maximilian Waidmannsdorf in a memorandum to Chancellor Kolowrat. A strong supporter of the Etschlanders, Waidmannsdorf wrote of discontent so general that severe outbreaks of what he called "public defamation" occurred and that rebellion was feared. The emperor, he added, had found it prudent to recall Sauer; Eppstein had found police protection necessary at his departure; and Aschauer had "considered it advisable to steal away quietly."[6] (Sauer subsequently became governor, or *Regierungspräsident*, in Lower Austria; Eppstein was ennobled and made a *Hofrat*; and Aschauer was appointed to state service elsewhere.)

An occasion as momentous as Tyrol's 1790 open Diet, the first in seventy years, brought out the diarist or memoirist in many of those who attended. Some of these diary keepers also collected documents dealing with matters put before the assembly and attached these documents to their journals. Several of these records have survived, the three most important manuscripts being those of the emperor's court commissar to the Diet Count Franz Enzenberg;[7] Bozen deputy and later celebrated Tyrolean citizen and benefactor Andreas diPauli;[8] and Italian nobleman and later police ministry employee Benedetto Sardagna.[9] The account that follows is based primarily on the records these three men gathered and preserved, supplemented by records kept by Archduke, later Emperor, Francis[10] and by the only published journal from the Diet, that of Franz Goldegg.[11]

There were few Tyroleans alive in 1790 who remembered the last open Diet of 1720. So, like the French Estates General in 1789, the ceremonies and proceedings had to be based on written records and oral tradition. The 1790 Diet would be longer than any other (two months), and more people would attend (more than 500). The backlog of grievances brought out all four Estates in record numbers: all the prelates entitled to seat and vote were there; towns and jurisdictions sent two to seven representatives each, although each area had but one vote; and most of the nobles either attended personally or assigned their proxies to someone else. An exact head count is difficult to determine, first of all, because none of the sources agrees on a number (it is never clear whether any particular total includes those who actually attended with or without proxies, those entitled to attend, or some mix of the two). The number in attendance also varied from day to day and week to week because some arrived late, left early, or had temporary business elsewhere. Nevertheless, by making some reasonable assumptions,[12] we can estimate the Diet's makeup, which at its peak had about 580 in attendance. The estimate would indicate that there were 17 prelates, 254 nobles, 45 deputies of cities and market towns, and 264 deputies of peasant jurisdictions. Although these figures are estimates, they clearly indicate that an anomalous situation arose every time a vote was taken. The approximately 260 peasant representatives from 88 jurisdictions were entitled to 88 votes, while the approximately 250 nobles could vote individually or through proxies. Yet in a voice vote, common at the 1790 Diet, each proxy holder could shout only as loud as one man, no matter how many proxies he held;[13] but each of the individual peasants and burghers, despite the number of votes to which their localities were de jure entitled, probably shouted as loudly as he could. The peasants' "votes" were therefore often the decisive ones as they "applauded or whistled or squawked according to the signals that came from their leader," that is, from Bozen party chiefs Gumer or Unterrichter.[14] And, by controlling the peasants, the Bozen party's Etschlanders controlled the Diet itself, or at least its first half.

The work of the Diet and the shifting alliances of the leading actors does suggest two separate segments to the assembly: the first from the opening on 22 July through 18 August when a new *Landeshauptmann* was elected and the Diet broke up into working committees or deputations; the second from 24 August when the Diet reassembled until 11 September when it adjourned. During the first phase delegates presented grievances and expressed opinions, attendance was heavy, and general sessions were held almost daily. During the second phase, many left proxies and went home to tend to their businesses or vineyards or take care of personal affairs; the sessions were less frequent, and work focused on preparing the grievances and wishes for presentation to the emperor and on organizing for the post-Diet period.

The Diet opened on 22 July with a solemn mass in Mariahilf Church; the members of all four Estates, "without order of rank," then formed a procession to the *Landhaus* where the Diet was to meet. Bozen deputy and diarist Andreas diPauli imparted a sense of rank and order to the scene in the assembly hall: "On both sides the seats are elevated like an amphitheater for the Prelates, Knights and Nobles Estates, but in a gallery built around the hall are the seats placed in the same way for the cities and jurisdictions."[15] DiPauli may have been describing the intent of the designers rather than what actually happened. Franz Goldegg, who also described the scene in the hall and gallery, added that during the sessions "one seated himself without consideration of rank, wherever one found an empty place."[16] If Goldegg's description is accurate, then counting votes had to be a chaotic procedure, easily subject to alteration or "interpretation."

By tradition the court commissar, the emperor's personal representative appointed to preside over the Diet and to hear grievances in his sovereign's name, did not appear in the assembly hall until after preliminaries were completed and credentials verified. The first couple of sessions were therefore conducted by the land marshal, Count Karl Auersberg. At the first working session, the day's business was solely concerned with the credentials of the first two Estates, and only the clergy and nobles attended. At the subsequent session when the hearing of grievances began, the assembly decided that two separate protocols of each session would be kept: one by Enzenberg's Court Secretary Karl von Seydel, the other by one of the Estates' secretaries. The two versions were to be reviewed, examined, and "harmonized" daily.

The overall presentation of grievances, as Enzenberg later reported, was orderly with "no abusive, offensive, disgraceful insults to honor." But, he admitted, people had come to complain, not to flatter one another. There had indeed been times, he said, when he wished he could have stopped "a few hasty invectives and expressions" or cut a speaker short so that the proceedings might have gone more smoothly or been more orderly. But he was not there to censor speakers, so everyone had the freedom to say whatever discretion allowed, and the decorum of the assembly, he concluded, had been noteworthy. "Socrates and Plato could not have been more easily heard," he commented, and he advised that such openness be retained in the future.[17]

Once Enzenberg got to Innsbruck, he saw that his instructions were not adequate to the situation; before the Diet even assembled, he therefore wrote to Vienna asking for guidance. During the second week of the Diet, he received his answer: he was instructed not to yield to the Estates' demands but to hear and accept their grievances in the emperor's name and

CHAPTER FIVE

to tell them he could decide nothing without hearing from the court.[18] By and large, Enzenberg would follow these instructions, although on occasion he would interpret them somewhat freely.

Seats and Votes for the Confinants

During the preliminary sessions that considered and voted on credentials and immatriculation, the Confinants won one small success. While the first and second Estates were being discussed, the assembly accepted the immatriculation of three Italian noble families "against payment": the brothers Barons Pizzini, the brothers Rosmini, and two Fedrigottis.[19] The Confinants, however, also claimed seat and vote on the prelates' bench when the Diet considered how to fill the vacancies created by Joseph II's dissolution of three particular religious foundations, urging that an Italian religious foundation be placed in one of the vacancies, but without success. The Diet awarded the seats to the Abbey at Innichen, the convent for aristocratic women at Innsbruck (of which the Archduchess Elisabeth was the abbess), and the Collegiate Abbey at Bozen. Not to be dissuaded, the Count of Arco then asked that a new seat and vote be created on the prelates' bench for the Collegiate Abbey at Arco. This request too was denied.[20] Later, in 1792, this Abbey would be immatriculated at Leopold's order, giving Italian Tyrol its first seat on the prelates' bench.

The Italians' claims for seat and vote for their third and fourth Estate deputies were treated no kindlier and opposition came not only from the Etschlanders, but also from the envoy of the Prince-Bishop of Trent. During the first credentials session for all four Estates, the city of Rovereto was called. Rovereto had been part of Tyrol for almost 300 years and was immatriculated with seat and vote at the open Diet. Nevertheless, the prince-bishop's envoy immediately protested, arguing that in their older Matricle, Rovereto was a Trentine fief and therefore should not have seat and vote in Tyrol's Diet; he demanded that this protest be entered in the protocol. Rovereto just as quickly took exception to the claim and asked to see the Trentine protest.[21] This was but the first instance of Trentine opposition to the Confinants at the Diet. In 1790 little commonality of interest existed between the two Italian-speaking areas, and throughout the Diet Trent sided with the Etschland against Italian Tyrol, at least in part because of the wine competition.

The first separatist sentiments were also uttered as part of the credentials discussion when the city and county of Arco (also part of the Confines) asked for clarification of their status. The Arcans noted that although they had been invited to attend, they were not being allowed to vote because they were not matriculated. The county of Arco therefore asked "either to be immatriculated or to be viewed as a county separate from Tyrol." Goldegg commented that as far as he knew, this request had not been entered in the protocol—if not, a curious omission.[22]

Several other Italian jurisdictions also asked for seat and vote in the assemblies. Among them was the *pretura* of Rovereto, whose eight communes requested their own vote separate from the city of Rovereto at the Diet and the other congresses of the land. They were entitled to this, claimed the communes, because the emperor had invited them unconditionally and separately from the city and because they now paid the same taxes as the rest of Tyrol. Governor-*Landeshauptmann* Sauer supported the Italians' petitions for the same reasons they had given but primarily, he said, because they had been invited at the emperor's command.[23] And by supporting the Italians, Sauer made himself even more unpopular.

The Etschlanders quickly voiced their opposition. Bozen party leader Count Franz Wolkenstein asserted once more that the Confinants could not have seats and votes because they were not entered in the Estates' Matricle. The Diet, of course, could vote that they be entered, but he did not suggest that course. Instead, he took the position that a formal invitation from the ruler did not automatically entitle them to seat and vote and that the emperor may have had nothing more in mind than for the Confinants to attend and be allowed to present their grievances. A stream of speeches against the Confinants followed, and the Diet finally offered what Wolkenstein had proposed: seat without vote for the Italian communes, but with the right to present grievances (which, at that moment, they had anyway).[24] The debate on the Confinants continued into the following day and threatened to block the discussion of any other business. A weekend recess intervened.

When the Diet resumed, the previous session's protocol was read aloud, a standard procedure so that corrections could be made. The Etschlanders apparently did not want the Italians' claims entered in the official record, at least not as they had been presented. So as soon as the reader began describing the deliberations over the Confinants' requests for immatriculation, a protracted dispute broke out over the wording, and the assembly spent several hours dwelling on trifles and trying to change the entry in one way or another. The haggling did not stop until the land marshal solemnly and finally ruled that the protocol would remain as it was. The record was again read aloud, from the beginning; and when the reader reached the section on the Confinants' immatriculation, the uproar began all over again. Count Sauer intervened and proposed that immatriculation and the constitutional questions involved be investigated by a special Matricle Deputation composed of an equal number of members from all four Estates. The suggestion was accepted and the deputation appointed, to report back near the end of the Diet.[25] That decision effectively barred most of the Italians from any seat with vote for the term of the current Diet.

The Confinants, of course, were not satisfied with the deferral. They again asked for a decision on whether they were entitled to their own seat and vote. And they now threatened that if this were not granted, they

CHAPTER FIVE

would retain the taxes they customarily paid into the Tyrolean treasury (though not those paid to the central treasury) and would contribute nothing more toward paying the princely county's debts. Although they did not mention the sixteenth-century tax revolt, they were indeed threatening another *Renitenz*.[26]

Finally, the assembly voted to turn to presenting grievances—the ostensible purpose for which the Diet had been convoked. Once the hearing of grievances had begun, Italian nobleman Pompeo Sardagna, a 70-year-old relative of the diarist Benedetto Sardagna, spoke in behalf of the Italians' rights. And he openly expressed indignation at the treatment being accorded the Confinants. It was valid, he said, to insist that they be placed in the Matricle before receiving seat and vote, but it was also wicked that more than 50,000 inhabitants of the land had to submit blindly to taxation. Then Sardagna formally claimed for the Italians of the province the right to vote in the Diet and pointedly announced that he and the Confinants expected no justice from the assembly in Innsbruck but only from the court in Vienna.[27]

The city and *pretura* of Rovereto had a chance to spell out their grievances in mid-August. The city's mayor, Angelo Rosmini, began by rejecting Trent's claim, made in the first days of the Diet, that Rovereto was a Trentine fief and therefore should not be granted seat and vote. The mayor pointed out that his city had submitted voluntarily to the Count of Tyrol in 1509, had been entered in the Tyrolean Matricle since 1640, and was therefore entitled to the seat and vote it had in the Diet; the Trentine claim was without merit, he asserted. Rosmini also said that the Estates should grant his city seat and vote on the *Ausschüsse* and *Steuercompromiss* because of the size of its population, because its prospering industry brought many benefits to the entire land, and because it now paid taxes equal to those paid by the other areas of Tyrol.[28] Felice Baroni spoke for the eight communes of the *pretura* and repeated their desire to have their own seat and vote at the open Diet, separate from the city of Rovereto. Then, to underscore the contention that they were not part of the city, the communes of the *pretura* entered a protest against any of the city's votes that they had not specifically endorsed. Four other Italian *preturas* also asked for their own representatives at the various congresses.[29] A few days later when the city and county of Arco came forward with similar claims for seat and vote, the city's spokesman, Dr. Carlo Marcobruni, proposed that the Confinants be granted not one but two votes on the prelates' bench at the open Diet: one to the Collegiate Abbey at Arco (proposed and denied earlier) and one to a representative of the Confines' parish clergy.[30] The Diet's negative response to these *domande* meant it was time for the Confinants to turn elsewhere.

Probably well aware that Leopold was championing the Confinants' cause, Felice Baroni left for Vienna to make a direct appeal to the emperor and presented his petition to his ruler on 19 August; the Chancellery took it up on the same day. The petition pointed out that the Diet had not agreed to equitable treatment for the Italians and therefore offered the alternative that if the requested seats and votes were not granted, the Confines should be separated from Tyrol, formed into their own crownland, and be immediate to their ruler. (At this point the further alternative of uniting them with Mantua was not raised.) Leopold had no thought of partitioning Tyrol unless he had no other alternative. The Chancellery also rejected the idea, emphasizing that the Confines now paid the same taxes as the rest of the princely county, were therefore equal, and recommended that Court Commissar Enzenberg persuade the Estates to treat the Confinants fairly and to settle everything "without compulsion." Leopold approved the Chancellery's suggestion and instructed Enzenberg to make sure the dispute was resolved amicably.[31] However, Enzenberg, whose sympathies were with the Etschland, did not rush to carry out his new mandate. The decision was made in Vienna on 19 August. It then took about five days to get from Vienna to Innsbruck, yet Enzenberg did not bring up the new imperial instruction to the Diet until 4 September, about a week before the Diet adjourned. Perhaps he deemed it prudent to let tempers cool or to let the numbers in attendance dwindle (as delegates went home to attend to their own affairs) before transmitting the emperor's message. Or perhaps he simply wanted to finish other business first. Whatever his reasons, the subject of the political rights of Italian Tyrol received no definitive answer from the Diet until just before the assembly adjourned. The Confinants, except for the City of Rovereto, were therefore effectively denied a meaningful role in the Innsbruck proceedings.

The Diet's first response to the Italians came in late August when it replied to the Prince-Bishop of Trent and his claim (made in the first days of the Diet) that Rovereto was not entitled to the seat and vote it already had because it was a Trentine fief. On 28 August the Estates denied the prince-bishop's claim, but they were also reluctant to violate anyone's traditional rights. They therefore asserted that while Rovereto's right to vote in the open Diet could not be taken away, the rights of the prince-bishop remained "unimpaired."[32] At this same session the Estates also rejected the *pretura* of Rovereto's attempt to have its own seat and vote, separate from the city, at both the open Diet and the *Ausschüsse*. Again arguing from tradition, the assembly based its decision on the fact that in 1640 the Archduchess Claudia had joined the city and *pretura* together and given them one vote in common. The Confinants had known that from the outset.

Then on 4 September, a week before the Diet ended, Gumer rose and spoke; he opposed giving the city of Rovereto, already in the Diet, a seat on any *Ausschuss*. He did admit that Rovereto's silk commerce made it deserving of some consideration, but other cities were equally deserving. And if the number of seats with votes was increased to accommodate all these cities, the votes of the other Estates would also need to be increased so that each Estate had an equal number of votes on each *Ausschuss*. That would make the small *Ausschuss* so large, Gumer argued, that it would cease to be small and therefore would cease to exist. The assembly supported Gumer and told the *pretura* of Rovereto that on this matter it "should not bother the Diet anymore."[33] On that same day, Court Commissar Enzenberg finally followed the instructions Vienna had sent him on 19 August and brought up, as he said in his report, the "ticklish matter" of the Confinants' petition to Vienna. He informed the assembly that Leopold had referred the request back to Innsbruck and had stated that if the Diet could settle the matter amicably, he, their sovereign, would gladly agree to the settlement. (The emperor had also requested a report containing the arguments of both sides in the dispute.) At the same session and knowing that *Ausschüsse* elections would soon be held, Rovereto's deputy urged that his city, as a fully qualified member of the Estates, be elected to both bodies. Enzenberg did not want to go that far and did not favor giving the Confinants seat and vote on either *Ausschuss*. He therefore asked the assembly to support a lesser step: immatriculation of the city of Arco and the larger Italian jurisdictions so that they would have seat and vote at the open Diet. At that large assembly, of course, they would be greatly outnumbered and could easily be outvoted.[34]

The Estates did not, therefore, reach the "amicable adjustment of the dispute" that the emperor had requested. In fact, their refusal was so sharp that Enzenberg felt obliged to respond. He reminded the assembly that the emperor wanted the Confinants to be treated fairly, asked the Estates to proceed less intolerantly, and again suggested they consider immatriculating the larger and more distinguished jurisdictions of the Welsch Confines. Then Gumer, perhaps afraid that Enzenberg might win on immatriculation, cut off discussion: he reminded the assembly that the Matricle Deputation, appointed early in the Diet to put an end to disputes and chaotic behavior, would soon report on the Confinants' requests. He therefore asked that the discussion be tabled until then. It was.[35]

All the members of the Matricle Deputation were German, and most had some sort of wine interest in the Etschland, which hardly made them an impartial group. The deputation's report, or *Elaboratum*, therefore favored the Etschland and denied the requests of the Confinants. It also contained some surprises. The report, which listed all the reasons for turning down the Italians' petitions,[36] was both a summary of all the arguments and a benchmark for all subsequent discussions. Baron Marx Cazan, a member of and later an envoy for the Wine Deputation, wrote the report. First, Cazan summarized the Italians' requests: The city of Rovereto, in addition to its seat and vote at the open Diet, sought seat and vote on the *Ausschüsse* and *Steuercompromiss*. The *pretura* of Rovereto wanted its own seat and vote, separate from the city, at all the land's assemblies, a goal other Italian jurisdictions also sought.

Cazan pointed out that the small *Ausschuss* already consisted of twenty votes and that granting all the desires of the Welsch Confines would add twelve more votes. Echoing Gumer, he claimed that by definition the small *Ausschuss* would cease to exist since it would be almost as numerous as the large *Ausschuss* (forty votes). The Confinants were claiming seat and vote both because they had been invited to the Diet and because of their new tax status. But, said Cazan, mere invitation was not enough since localities had often been invited without seat and vote; and many immatriculated jurisdictions, although they had seat and vote at the open Diet, did not have a right to send representatives to the *Ausschüsse* unless they joined themselves to another locality already represented. Cazan totally ignored the proposition that the Confinants' new tax status had given them new rights.[37]

Turning to the other points of argument, Cazan asserted that because the Confines had been conquered by Tyrol's ruler, they had a fair claim to his protection but no claim at all to those rights "which belong to German, and proper, Tyrol." Furthermore, granting the Confinants an equal share in the freedoms and constitution of Tyrol would diminish each individual's political rights (as if rights were a finite concrete substance) because of the greater number sharing them. However, said Cazan reassuringly, although the Italians could not have the seats and votes they were seeking, the German Tyroleans certainly bore them no ill will and stood ready "to render all brotherly assistance." And the Confinants had nothing to complain about, he added, since they had been able to appear at the Diet and express their grievances and wishes openly and freely.[38]

Then Cazan offered essentially the same concessions that Enzenberg had offered: to grant the city and county of Arco one combined vote at the open Diets with a seat on the cities' bench, such as that shared by the city and *pretura* of Rovereto; and to grant the other Welsch jurisdictions one combined vote at the open Diets with a seat on the peasants' bench. But he did not point out that these two new Italian votes would have had a negligible effect on an assembly as large as the Diet where voting was by head and often by voice. Cazan was totally unwilling to grant the Confinants any seat or vote on the two *Ausschüsse* or *Steuercompromiss*, since those seats would have given them a significant political role and, he argued, would violate the constitution and lead to extraordinary confusion. He conceded, however, that the cities of Rovereto and Arco could attend any of these smaller assemblies, depending on the needs of the situation, and could present their problems orally and in writing—but without a vote.[39]

Then came Cazan's coup de grâce: If the Confinants were not satisfied with what was being offered and if they believed they would prosper following a complete separation from Tyrol, Tyrol "would not want to begrudge them this prosperity. . . . They should leave our union, constitute a separate nation and be viewed equal to Lombardy"; and a wall should be drawn between German and Italian Tyrol. But, keeping the princely county's own prosperity firmly in view, he stipulated that the Confinants could not separate unless and until they had paid their share of their ruler's existing debts and abandoned their "unmindful" idea of tax retention by paying what they owed to the *Landschaft* (the province). Separating Welsch Tyrol from the rest of the princely county, Cazan concluded, would not cause anyone the slightest concern; the separated part could justly and suitably be incorporated into the Mantuan *Gubernium*.[40] It was the first and last time that German Tyrol was so willing to have its Italian areas detached. Leopold would neither welcome nor endorse such a solution.

When Cazan finished, Enzenberg, who had a better idea of Leopold's goals, tried again. Building on what the Matricle Deputation had offered, he tried to push them a little further. He suggested that together with the two new votes offered at the open Diet, the Confines have a permanent (not an incidental) representative without vote on the *Ausschüsse* and *Steuercompromiss*. The assembly quickly rejected this proposal; and the Italians probably would have, too. The Confinants' representatives then requested and were granted a copy of Cazan's report so that they could compose their rebuttal, or *risposta*.[41] This refutation, or *Risposta al Voto Cazan*, was quickly prepared and in the hands of the Vienna bureaucracy within two weeks; the Diet itself ended four days later.

The Italian areas' requests for seat and vote constituted one of the four grievances particular to the Welsch Confines in 1790. Equally as important to both the Confinants and the Etschlanders and closely connected with the political questions were the problems and grievances on both sides concerning the production, shipping, taxing, and selling of wine, especially the Confinants' wines.

Wine Production, Commerce, and Taxes

The status of Tyrol's wines, where and how they were moved, and the taxes assessed on them had begun to change in the early 1740s. After almost three decades of change, the whole matter came up at the 1790 Diet as grievances of both Confinants and Etschlanders. The Italians wanted a guarantee that the free transport of their wines into German Tyrol and their unrestricted retailing would continue. The Etschlanders wanted to restore their earlier, centuries-old monopoly on wine in German Tyrol. Closely connected with the competition between Italian and German wines was the question of taxes. Under the old monopoly, the Etschlanders (as tax farmers) had collected an assessment at the Nevis Bridge levied on any Confinant wine entering German Tyrol. Now that tax was gone, and the

Etschlanders were farmers for a new *Umgeld*, or excise, that was more difficult to collect. The German wine interests therefore sought a return to the monopoly with the assessment at the Nevis, or, failing that, a change in the *Umgeld* system. Additionally, both the Italians and the Etschlanders challenged the conversion of newly arable land (available as a result of the recent regulation of the Etsch/Adige River) into vineyards. The state too had an interest here, since that land had been drained and was needed to grow at least some of the grain that Tyrol had been forced to import.

During the second full week that the Diet met, on 2 August, diarist Andreas diPauli addressed the assembly for the city of Bozen. He spoke of the increasing competition that Etsch wines now faced from the Confinants, from foreign wines, and from new vineyard owners, and he asked that this competition be eliminated or be greatly reduced. He also specifically requested that the import of Welsch wines again be forbidden and that the Etschland's monopoly be restored. His theme was echoed a few days later when the peasant jurisdiction of Bozen (not the city, but the area in the countryside around the city) and two other Etschland jurisdictions protested against the legal import of Welsch wines and the far too common practice of smuggling Welsch wines and brandies from below the Nevis Bridge into German Tyrol.[42]

The Prince-Bishop of Trent was also interested in what happened to the Confinants' wines. During the first week of the Diet, his envoy had pleaded that foreign wines be kept out of Tyrol (Trentine wines, it should be recalled, were treated as Tyrolean); or if these wines were permitted to enter, that the tariff assessed on them be high. The envoy had also asked that foreign beer be completely forbidden and the production of domestic beer restricted to preserve at least the current levels of wine consumption. Then, on 4 August, the city of Trent added its voice to the chorus opposing the entry of Welsch wines into the rest of Tyrol, as well as the Confinants' freedom in retailing their wines. Once again, the Trentines and Etschlanders had found common cause.[43]

When Rovereto's mayor, Angelo Rosmini, presented his city's grievances, he accused the Etschlanders of being interested only in forcing the sale of wine at the highest price. The Etschland's monopoly, or wine privilege, had begun in 1440 when the Confinants were still foreigners and should not be reestablished, he said. The Italian Tyroleans were no longer foreign, and their wines were therefore not foreign either. Furthermore, with a population of 72,000, the Italian areas were paying higher per capita taxes than the Etschlanders, and they were benefiting the public treasury even more with their silk industry. Why then, he asked, should they be treated like stepchildren? Rosmini also requested, in an addendum to his wine grievances, that a permanent garrison be stationed in his city, not so much for defense as to consume the local wine and aid the area's economy.[44] Other Italian delegates also spoke against excluding Welsch Tyrolean

CHAPTER FIVE

wines from German Tyrol, especially the city and county of Arco and four other Italian *preturas*, most of which also wanted their own representatives at the various assemblies.[45]

Before Mayor Rosmini finished his economic grievances, he made an interesting and somewhat radical proposal concerning the four annual Bozen market fairs that he said gave the Etschland its great predominance. To equalize the burdens and benefits of the Etschlanders and Confinants, he suggested that goods or wares going from the south to the Bozen markets be sent instead to Rovereto! He argued that even if only part of the markets were shifted to his city, many more Italians would visit them because of proximity, language, and similarity of customs. And it would present no special difficulty to Germans coming from the north to travel down from Bozen by water and select the silk or whatever else they wanted to buy. Not of least importance, Rosmini emphasized, would be the greater sales generated by the higher attendance, which would mean increased tariff collections for the public treasury.[46] In short, the mayor was proposing that the traditional Bozen markets become Bozen-Rovereto markets, to the profit of Rovereto and the treasury. Bozen itself would lose in the change, but Rosmini's stated intent was to diminish the Etschland's domination of Tyrol's affairs. The proposal was interesting, but utopian, and the Bozen fairs stayed where they were.

Once Rosmini had finished, the Etschlanders rose with their grievances and pointed out that, in fact, they no longer had a wine monopoly—neglecting to mention that they were doing everything they could to have the ban against Welsch wines reinstated. They said that the Confinants' wine had begun entering the rest of Tyrol under Maria Theresa, the quantity had increased substantially during the ten-year reign of Joseph II, and now the Confinants were asking that their right to export to the rest of Tyrol be confirmed. The Etschlanders felt themselves injured by this claim and asked for a copy of the Confinants' petition so that they could "put pure truth into the true light" and show that Rovereto's requests were "exaggerated to the most ridiculous excess."[47] As the Italian jurisdictions sided with Rovereto, so the German jurisdictions called for restoration of the Etschland's monopoly and for restrictions on converting fields and new arable land to vineyards. The Etschlanders now went even further than the Trentines in their attempt to prevent other beverages from competing with their wines. An Etsch *Viertel* representative asked that coffee consumption be restricted since it "draws so much money out of the land and reduces the consumption of wine and brandy."[48]

Although many deputies sided with the Confinants and others with the Etschlanders, the lament of the jurisdiction of Steinach probably expressed what was the chief concern of most Tyroleans, who were not wine producers but wine consumers: "In the dispute of the Etschlanders and Confinants, it is to be seen then, that from this arises no increase in the price of wine."[49]

THE INNSBRUCK ASSEMBLY

No one liked the new *Umgeld* (*Buschen-Umgeld*), or excise tax, on wine, but the Etschland vintners felt especially injured. The Etschland Estates still had to pay 16,000 florins a year into the central treasury. That amount had previously been paid from the fees, or tariffs, collected on the Confinants' wine at the Nevis Bridge, but that tariff no longer existed. Now the 16,000 florins were to be paid from the new excise tax assessed on all wines, which would make the Etschland wines more expensive. The Wine Deputation, as tax farmers, had collected the fees once paid at the Nevis; now this deputation was only a locally appointed lobbying group charged with speaking for and protecting the area's wine interests in Tyrol and Vienna. But Vienna had imposed the new *Umgeld* on wine, and at the end of the Diet's first full week, the Wine Deputation was sharply criticized for permitting that to happen. Count Anton Firmian, presenting his personal grievances, proposed that the Estates follow Vienna's example and take away any remaining functions of the Wine Deputation since it had not faithfully represented the local situation to the court. Clearly, said Firmian, if the court had had a true picture of circumstances concerning Tyrol's wine, it would never have introduced the new wine *Umgeld*, a tax that seemed so devastating to the Etschland.[50] The deputation, however, was not dissolved.

As grievances were presented at the assembly, one town or jurisdiction after another spoke against the new *Umgeld*. On 2 August diPauli, speaking as a representative of the city of Bozen, expressed the city's grievances against this new arrangement and against Vienna's abolition of the Wine Deputation's tax farming privileges. The Roveretans too protested against the excise; their *Umgeld* assessment was higher than the one placed on Etsch wines, and they asked at least that their tariff be the same.[51]

The Vienna bureaucracy took up the Etsch *Kreis's* protests against the new *Umgeld* assessment during the third week in August, as the Diet was reaching its halfway mark. The Etschlanders had petitioned the emperor to restore the old duty levied at the Nevis Bridge so that they could impede the sale of the Confinants' wines. The Chancellery, in its report to the *Staatsrat*, labeled the earlier practice as "truly unfair" and recommended that there be no assessment of this kind again. The emperor agreed with the recommendation and refused to reimpose the Nevis tax.[52] But that did not solve the Etschlanders' problem with the new excise, nor the Italians' problems with the tax and with their northern neighbors.

The one wine-related grievance shared by both the Italian and the German wine producers was the increased competition coming from the continuing conversion of arable land to vineyards. On 2 August while presenting the city of Bozen's grievances, diarist Andreas diPauli complained about the increasing number of vineyards and asked that a general law be enacted to prevent any further land conversion. And during the third week in August, Roveretan Mayor Rosmini, speaking for his city, also asked that such land conversion be prohibited. Either the Tyroleans knew nothing about the existing legislation, or it seemed that no law existed because so many ignored it. The Bozeners also asked that the competition their wines faced from foreign wines, including the Confinants', be reduced. Mayor Rosmini subsequently suggested that instead of fighting each other, the Etschland and Confines work together against another common problem: the entry (legal or illegal) of truly foreign wines into the princely county; and he again reminded the assembly that the Confinants were no longer foreign.[53]

In late August as the Diet approached its end, the deputies of the German wine-growing areas met, discussed all aspects of the wine problem as they defined it, and decided to send their own Wine Deputation to Vienna. This group was to be separate and distinct from any sent by the Diet and was to carry their pleas and represent their cause to the emperor. Two men were entrusted with this mission: Baron Marx Cazan, a Brixen official and Tyrolean landowner who had drafted and delivered the Diet's formal reply to the Confinants; and Ignatz Atzwang, a colleague of Gumer's from Bozen.[54]

Language

The only time the language question came up at the Diet was just before the presentation of grievances. The representatives of the Italian jurisdictions asked that they be allowed to present their grievances in the Italian language or to have an interpreter. The Diet quickly denied the use of Italian, but it did decide to permit an interpreter on the condition that he be chosen from among those already at the Diet. The Confinants did not like the decision, though it can hardly have surprised them, and grumbled openly that they expected justice not from the Estates, but only from the emperor.[55]

Daughters' Inheritance Rights

The problem created for the Confinants by the new inheritance laws was adopted as a grievance of the entire land of Tyrol. Rovereto's Mayor Rosmini raised the issue as part of his city's grievances. The new laws, he said, granted daughters too large a share, especially because they could keep control of it after marrying someone not from the Confines. That arrangement, he pointed out, was even more disadvantageous to everyone than it appeared at first glance. Although the foreign men who married Tyrolean women usually gained control of their wives' property, and perhaps ownership, women from foreign areas who married men from the Confines brought no land with them because local laws in their homelands usually did not permit women to keep control of property after they married. The Roveretans therefore asked that a *Reciprolum* be introduced concerning the rights of Tyrolean daughters who married foreigners.[56]

The formal presentation of grievances ended on 16 August. The final item of business remaining for this first part of the Diet was the election of the *Landeshauptmann*, an office Leopold had returned to its pre-Theresian status by separating it from the office of governor. The *Landeshauptmann* would again be chosen by the Estates and represent their interests. As part of Leopold's decision granting the Tyroleans' request to have their own *Landeshauptmann* again, the emperor sent specific instructions to Enzenberg on how the election was to be conducted. The Estates were to vote by curia and were to submit to Leopold a *Terna* of three names, from which he would select one, preferably the one with the most votes. *Scrutatores* were to be freely elected to supervise the election, and Enzenberg was not to interfere in any way with the process. Until now Enzenberg had openly sided with the Bozen party, but the *Landeshauptmann's* election brought the alliance to an end. The Etschlanders supported Count Franz Wolkenstein for the office; Enzenberg (and presumably Leopold) supported Count Franz Lodron, who happened to be Enzenberg's brother-in-law. In addition, the court commissar ignored the last part of his instructions and interfered heavy-handedly; he made sure that his brother-in-law was elected by a very large margin over Wolkenstein (with a total vote that may have exceeded the number entitled to be cast). While Leopold was pleased with the result, he was unhappy with his court commissar's tactics, especially Enzenberg's role in the election of the *scrutatores* and his ballot-box stuffing.[57]

By assuring the election of his brother-in-law to the *Landeshauptmann's* office, Enzenberg won some new enemies for himself, including the unflagging enmity of Count Franz Wolkenstein and Franz Gumer. But Unterrichter, the third musketeer of the Bozen party leadership and early Wolkenstein adherent, joined Enzenberg after the election. The result was that the Bozen party, the focus of the 1790 Estates revolt and a party so strong that it nearly controlled the Diet, was in pieces. Leopold had snuffed out the threatening rebellion in Tyrol and, in doing so, had begun to pave the way for the Italians to achieve their goals.

Once the election of the *Landeshauptmann* was over, Enzenberg returned to the matters still before the Diet. About 2,000 grievances had been presented, and they needed to be sorted and consolidated so that they could be presented to their ruler in an orderly fashion. Enzenberg therefore proposed that a twelve-member deputation be named to handle the task. He also suggested that the grievances be divided according to subject, then according to those that could be granted only by the monarch and those that could be settled by the *Gubernium* or the *Hofstellen*. In any event, all the grievances would be submitted to Leopold so that he could "perceive the relation of the grievances from all aspects."[58] The Diet agreed to the deputation, and Enzenberg named the committees and subcommittees to sort and compile. Rovereto's Mayor Rosmini, along with diarist diPauli, was among those named to work on matters concerning the administration of justice, which included the inheritance rights of daughters. Rosmini was named spokesman for the committee, perhaps an indication that with the split in the Bozen party the animosity toward Italians was weakening and that Enzenberg felt he could name an Italian to the position without creating further difficulties. Gumer and Unterrichter were named to work on the organization of the Estates' government, that is, the *Landschaft*.[59] The committees were divided into subcommittees, each section to meet in the residence of its president. Enzenberg then declared a week's recess so that the groups would have time to do their work. Other special deputations— for example, the Matricle Deputation appointed at the beginning of the Diet—also used the time to finish their deliberations and prepare their reports.

This recess marked the end of the Diet's first phase, what might be called the active phase when grievances and wishes were presented, opinions expressed, and votes taken. The second part, which began when the assembly reconvened on 24 August, had three characteristics that distinguished it from the earlier period. First, the now-split Bozen party leadership could no longer effectively control the Diet. Second, the number of voting members (*Vocalen*) at the Diet steadily decreased as the deputies began to go home and the number of proxies rose; by the time the Diet formally adjourned on 11 September, only about 100 persons were still attending the sessions. Third, general sessions took place much less frequently and the deputations' sessions more frequently. And the assembly, which was pushed, prodded, cajoled, and nagged, finally agreed that the Italians should have a very small part of what they sought.

The grievance-organizing committees still had to complete their work, and the Diet itself needed to elect the large and small *Ausschüsse* and the deputation to take all the grievances to Vienna. When Enzenberg announced the election of the Vienna deputation on 26 August, he made it clear that there would be a departure from custom. Traditionally, four deputies had been selected, one from each Estate; the one noble nominated was the titular head of the group. That position would now fall to Count Franz Wolkenstein, an aristocrat, who had lost the *Landeshauptmann's* election to Enzenberg's brother-in-law. Enzenberg decided that he also ought to have his "own noble" in the Vienna deputation; so he announced that eight deputies would be chosen, two from each Estate. Enzenberg's "skillful chess move" made it possible to add Johann Christof von Unterrichter, who had left the Bozen party after the *Landeshauptmann's* election and allied himself with the court commissar, as the second noble and counterweight to Wolkenstein. It also meant that the disunity left over from the Diet would continue in Vienna.[60] The doubled Vienna deputation included not a single Italian; it did, however, have several Etschlanders. Formally chosen by the assembly, this Estates' Vienna deputation included[61]

THE INNSBRUCK ASSEMBLY

Prelates: Abbot of Wiltau, Markus Egle
Probst Gregor Tasser, Probstei of St. Michael

Nobles: Count Franz von Wolkenstein
Hr. Johann Christof von Unterrichter

Towns: Hr. Andreas diPauli, city of Bozen deputy
Hr. Peter Anton Aigner, city of Lienz

Jurisdictions: Hr. Joseph Praxmarer, Rattenberg Diet deputy
Hr. Johann Rottensteiner, Diet deputy for the jurisdictions of
Gries and Bozen

Accompanying them was the deputation secretary, Herr Josef Mayr, who had been a deputy for the jurisdictions of Gries and Bozen at the Diet. In Vienna these men would refer to themselves and be referred to as "the 7," excluding Wolkenstein, who henceforth would have only official contact with the other deputies. Secretary Mayr was not technically a deputy.

The large and small *Ausschüsse* had yet to be elected, and Enzenberg knew that it was also important economically to bring the proceedings to an end. "Wine cultivation," he recorded in his journal, "is the most productive source of livelihood; and the harvest time is a time equally important to the producer and the purchaser. This drew near with giant steps."[62] So that they could look after their own domestic affairs, many of the original Diet participants had already departed after reading their *Vota* to the assembly and had left their proxies behind. Now many others wanted to do the same. The remnants of the Bozen party saw that if they could collect enough proxies from those who left, they could control the rest of the Diet to their own advantage; they therefore began maneuvering to prolong the Diet and collect as many proxies as possible. But Enzenberg saw what they were plotting and moved to bring the Diet to an end by having the large and small *Ausschüsse* elected; on Monday of what would be the Diet's final week, he announced the elections. The larger body, he said, would finish whatever remained of the Diet's work and then would adjourn until the deputies sent to Vienna had returned. In the interim, he proposed that the small *Ausschuss* remain assembled in Innsbruck. The proposal was accepted, and the court commissar had successfully thwarted this last attempt by the Etschlanders to control the proceedings. Leopold had chosen his man well; the elections would be held on schedule, which was, as Enzenberg recorded, the preferable procedure and one more in accord with the constitution.[63]

When the assembly turned to these elections, however, the Italians objected. The smaller assemblies were in theory elected by the Diet, but, the Italians pointed out, the areas represented were in fact decided by tradition and were all German areas. Of Tyrol's five *Kreise*, the only one with no representation on either *Ausschuss* was the Welsch Confines.

CHAPTER FIVE

Dr. Carlo Marcobruni of Arco argued that the *Ausschüsse* should not be chosen until the emperor granted a place or places in these to the Italians. The protest had no effect, and the elections, such as they were, went ahead on 10 and 11 September. The closing ceremonies were also held on the eleventh, and Enzenberg made a final address to the assembly. "Farewell!" he told the Estates. "Go along under God's guidance, bring hope to your remote valleys . . . and with new courage, with new devotion for our Leopold." With some mutual expressions of thanks, the open Diet ended.[64]

The newly elected large *Ausschuss* met during the week following adjournment to complete some of the leftover business and to instruct the deputation going to Vienna; within a week after the Diet had ended, that *Ausschuss* also adjourned—but, as we shall see, without doing a very thorough job of getting things organized for Vienna.

Each person was now free to stay in Innsbruck and wait, at his own expense, for the return of the Vienna deputies, or return home. Fortunately, most of the participants went home; the deputies did not return until mid-March of the following year, six months later.[65]

Politicking and Maneuvering in Vienna: The Court, the Bureaucracy, and the Deputies

Vienna, the emperor, and his bureaucracy now became the focus of attention as the deputies, officials, and other interested individuals converged on the capital. The week after Tyrol's Diet adjourned, the princely county appeared on the imperial agenda with the arrival of two reports from Enzenberg. In the first, written shortly before the final session, Enzenberg said it was his impression that the Estates preferred that the Confinants be separated from Tyrol rather than entered in the Matricle. But he also noted a ray of hope because the Matricle Deputation had recommended giving the Italians two new seats and votes at the open Diet in addition to Rovereto's existing seat. One new seat was to be on the cities' bench for the city and county of Arco, the other on the peasants' bench for the other Welsch jurisdictions. That recommendation, by definition, meant immatriculation, as limited a step as it was. Enzenberg's second report stated that the assembly had agreed to grant the Confinants the new seats at the Diet but would not approve any for them on the *Ausschüsse*. These two additional Diet seats and votes in fact gave the Italians very little real influence or power since they could still be overwhelmingly outvoted by the Etschlanders and their adherents at the Diets. Nevertheless, Leopold and the Italians had won a point, and the emperor ordered that Enzenberg be advised that his news "has been very gladly heard."[1] The Confinants soon won another point on the free movement of their wines within Tyrol when on 23 September Leopold decided that the Nevis duty on their wines would not again be assessed. He also upheld his brother's wine regulations that required, among other things, the Etschland to be assessed 16,000 florins in *Umgeld*, an amount no longer payable from the collection of Nevis duties.[2]

CHAPTER SIX

By the third week of September, the Confinants' response to the Matricle Deputation, their *Risposta al Voto Cazan*, had reached the Chancellery in Vienna. The Chancellery sent it to Enzenberg, who was by then back in Klagenfurt, for comment. The content of the *Risposta*, itself apparently no longer extant, can be more or less reconstructed from two other existing and related documents: Enzenberg's paragraph-by-paragraph commentary and a summary of the *Risposta* that diPauli included in his Vienna diary.[3]

First of all, the Confinants objected to the makeup of the Matricle Deputation, which had offered them so little. It had, they argued, consisted either of Etschlanders or others who owned estates in the Etschland, a *Viertel* that had always opposed them because of the wine trade. And Tyrol's other wine-consuming *Viertel*, which might normally have sided with the Confinants to increase competition and therefore lower the price of wine, had been seduced by the Etschland into acting against their own best interests. This Matricle Deputation, the Confinants charged, was therefore no proper *Landesdeputation* at all, but rather a conspiracy hatched by Welsch Tyrol's adversaries accompanied by special interests.[4]

In their *Risposta*, as diPauli summarized it, the Confinants also pointed out that only they, of Tyrol's five *Kreise*, had no representation on either of the *Ausschüsse*. They argued that every jurisdiction that paid taxes to the land should be represented at the Diet, that every *Viertel* should have seat and vote on the large *Ausschuss*, and that every larger *Viertel* (that is, *Kreis*) should be on the smaller *Ausschuss*, with no act of immatriculation being necessary. Furthermore, the Matricle Deputation was advancing "a baseless chimera" when it claimed that including the Confinants would enlarge the small *Ausschuss* into nonexistence. Giving them seat and vote, the Confinants countered, would only increase the small *Ausschuss* by four, assuming the addition would be one city, one *Viertel*, one noble, and the prelate of the Collegiate Abbey at Arco. They rejected the idea that for purposes of representation they be joined to another *Viertel* because representation was too important in itself for them to be joined to another part of the land. This was especially true when the part of the land being suggested was the Etsch or the Eisack *Viertel*, with which they had long been in conflict because of the wine trade, and more recently in commercial matters. Cazan's report, they said, showed "the entirely unbrotherly tone of the city of Bozen and the *Viertel* on the Etsch, by whom the Confinants are perceived as an unbrotherly and hated Esau, who indeed would scarcely deserve the blessing of our Most Illustrious Jacob."[5]

Enzenberg's point-by-point refutation of the Italians' *Risposta* began with the caveat that he would be writing from memory and would be unable to verify his statements with appended documents and appropriate citations since these papers had already been attached to earlier reports and sent to Vienna. Nevertheless, he thought he could remember enough to refute the Confinants' arguments, which he found "brilliant indeed, high-sounding and fascinating, but upon closer examination . . . groundless." No longer Leopold's personal representative, Enzenberg now could, and did, speak for himself. He described the Confinants as trying to cast doubt on the mental abilities or intentions of those who opposed them: "Not to concur with their opinion is either great ignorance or calculated unfairness." He could not possibly take their side, he said, and by responding point by point to their *Risposta* (in addition to his formal and extensive memorandum on this subject already sent to the court with documents attached), he hoped to show the exaggerations in their demands.[6]

German southern Tyrol, said Enzenberg, was not opposing the Italians' requests simply because of the wine trade. The Etschland no longer had a wine monopoly, and a look at the tariff registers would tell the story: In the past ten years, the Welsch Tyroleans had brought over the Nevis Bridge a total of 254,736 eimer (almost 18 million liters) of wine and 56,873 eimer (about 4 million liters) of brandy. If one added smuggling to this, he said, "then a quite handsome round little sum of 300,000 eimer [about 21 million liters] results from the most moderate calculation." Enzenberg did not add that the Etschland was trying to have at least part, if not all, of the ban against Welsch wines reinstated. Then he admitted that as taxable, deserving, and loyal subjects, the Confinants must be allowed to share in the advantages of being Tyroleans; he questioned only how it might best be done. Giving them seat and vote on the *Ausschüsse*, he said erroneously, would destroy the old constitution by destroying equality of Estate representation in these bodies. Nevertheless, some sort of political participation should be granted to them so that they would have all the privileges bestowed by the constitution—which, he reminded his sovereign, had been solemnly confirmed by the act of hereditary homage.[7]

Enzenberg suggested several alternatives. The first was the proposal made by the Matricle Deputation and accepted by the Diet: to immatriculate the city and county of Arco as one unit and the other jurisdictions as another, giving them two more seats and votes at the Diet. However, the solution Enzenberg preferred was that the Confines' representatives attend Estate assemblies without vote. They could attend deliberations, examine documents and accounts, and present petitions; if they felt a decision was unfavorable, they would always have recourse to the throne. Enzenberg termed this alternative the "least harmful middle road" and commented that if the Confinants were not satisfied with it, their motivation was "not patriotism but mere private ends, not praiseworthy ambition, but *Puntiglio* [spite]."[8] Enzenberg's official report, already in Vienna, would go into far greater detail than this reply to the *Risposta*. The Chancellery received his comments, deliberated on what he had to say about the *Risposta*, then on 17 October sent its report to the emperor. There it rested for the moment.

Two weeks later, on 2 November, the Confinants were again on the Chancellery's agenda as Enzenberg's formal report came up for consideration along with a supplementary petition from the Confinants themselves for seat and vote at the assemblies. The Chancellery decided that it was now appropriate for the former governor, Count Sauer, to have his say; so they sent the entire dossier to him for comment. Sauer, now in Vienna, received the materials quickly and requested that all the remaining documents concerning the Diet also be sent to him for comment. By mid-November, after asking the opinions of the chancellery on the wishes of the Confinants,[9] Leopold decided that Sauer should have all the documents he had requested—with full confidence that the count would make his comments "without any personal offensiveness" and "only with regard to the true welfare of the State."[10]

After the Diet ended, Enzenberg sent a journal he had kept along with his formal reports to Vienna. For reasons that are not entirely clear, he included in his journal a couple of unusual sections. One was a handwritten history of Tyrol (section 3 of the journal) based on his research in the Innsbruck archives; he called it "a mere little thing that had been shoved in (*Einschiebsel*)" and that contained "merely the history of Tyrol in a compressed summary in regard to the origin, and consolidation of the National Constitution."[11] Another curious document was his essay, or discourse, on the differences between the German and Italian national characters (section 4); it was a discussion he ostensibly prepared for the benefit of the new, and at that point still-to-be-named, governor of Tyrol so that he would not make the same mistakes as his predecessor, Count Sauer. Having seen in a previous chapter what some of the Italians were thinking and saying about the Germans, it is worth pausing for a moment to see what this German (Enzenberg) was saying about the Italians, and about his fellow Germans.

> The *German* Tyrolean is religious in the highest degree, he depends totally on the words of his parish priest, and long habit has sanctified to him what mere pious innocence or self-seeking hypocrisy would have introduced: he desires that his son think about religion as he thinks; the school innovations are therefore extremely odious to him.
> The *Welsch* Tyrolean is already more enlightened on this point, and the hope of profit is inducement to him, unhesitatingly to work on an abolished holiday. . . .
> The *German* Tyrolean has courage and manly vigor; with his shooting iron [*Scheibte Rohre*] he is frightful to the enemy: on the other hand, he is almost useless in a white coat [of the Habsburg army] because he is discontented and seeks to end a position so contrary to his natural inclination toward liberty. If he enlists, he performs like any other.
> The *Welsch* Tyrolean is still unmilitary, and in general avoids all military service.
> The *German* Tyrolean has good common sense, is straightforward in his way of thinking, direct in his dealings. Rough in his manners, his word is his bond, and he requires the same [of others]; a handshake and

a glass of wine are to him what witnesses, notes and written documents are to his neighbors.

The *Welsch* Tyrolean has wit, spirit of inventiveness, craftiness, and is more polished in world events.

The *German* is restless, thrifty, loves order and cleanliness. The *Welsch* works only when the need presses him, has a good day at the expense of many others, is by far not so neat in dress or household furnishings, and hopes to acquire easily for himself by his wits what others gain only by unstinting labor.

The *German* Tyrolean lets himself be swayed, the *Welsch* has to be persuaded; to the *German* the rugged fatherland is everything; to the *Italian* wherever things go well for him, he feels at home. The *German* studies the history of his fatherland, he acquaints himself with the constitution, he gladly talks about politics; the *Welsch* does not concern himself with any of this. Finally, the *German* wants to be respected, the *Welsch* to be feared.[12]

While all these preliminaries were going on in Vienna, the numerous deputies, official and unofficial, were making their own preparations for the activities that would keep them busy from mid-November until mid-March of the following year. The emperor and his bureaucracy also mustered their forces, prepared their arguments, and plotted their strategies. All the documents, protocols, and pleas would make their way through bureaucratic channels to the emperor's desk.[13] Leopold would listen, then continue his attempt to persuade Tyrol's Estates to grant the Italians what he thought they ought to have.

Leopold, with his "scientific method" of government, had many sources of information about what had transpired at the Tyrolean Diet. On 18 August as the second part of the assembly was getting under way, one of those sources, court agent Giambattista Baroni, was in Vienna reporting to Leopold. Baroni informed his ruler that the proceedings were directed by the Bozeners who in turn were directed by the two Gumers (Franz and his brother Joseph), that Joseph was quite wealthy, and that Franz was "very boorish, a dangerous crackpot." These words may have been uttered in confidence to the emperor, but they were not long in getting back to Franz Gumer, who decided he simply had to go to Vienna to justify himself. However, he needed an excuse for a trip to the capital and decided to use the pretext of handling some business for the city of Bozen.[14] That information soon made its way back to Vienna.

Another source of information for Leopold may well have been the Trentine-Roveretan jurist, Carlantonio Pilati. An early arrival in the capital, Pilati had subsequently departed and now returned to a welcome by his ruler. At his audience with Leopold on 4 November, Pilati presented a draft of proposed new statutes for the Mercantile Magistrate (the autonomous court for the Bozen market fairs, which was abolished by Joseph II) and suggested that his proposals might be submitted to the legislative commission, then working on a new civil code. Leopold informed the jurist that he intended to restore the Mercantile Magistrate and promised that the draft statutes would have a careful examination. Pilati then delivered the news that Franz Gumer, sent by the Bozen merchants, was on his way to Vienna but had not yet arrived because of illness. Leopold retorted that Gumer was an intriguer, that his commission from the merchants was a pretext, and that the real reason for his journey was "an understanding with Unterrichter, *another intriguer and rogue,* to come to Vienna looking for an 'open door.' " As Pilati listened, he realized that the emperor had little use for either Gumer or Unterrichter. The jurist offered to tell Gumer not to present himself to the sovereign, but Leopold replied only that Pilati should do as he wished and promised again that the draft statutes would be closely examined, as requested.[15]

Leopold kept his word on the statutes. The next day when Pilati visited Baron Carlo Antonio Martini, the member of the *Staatsrat* who had earlier interceded in his behalf with the Thun family after Pilati's severe beating, the jurist found that the draft statutes were already in the baron's hands. As their conversation progressed, it became increasingly obvious that Martini disliked Gumer even more than the emperor did; the mere mention of Gumer was so upsetting to the baron that Pilati had to spend much time and effort trying to calm him. Martini too was convinced that Gumer was in Vienna both to support his own party against that of the former governor, Count Sauer, and to act for the Wine Deputation in an attempt to have all the assessments on the Confinants' wines reimposed at the Nevis Bridge. But Pilati felt it was important that Martini see Bozen banker Gumer, and after some urging, the baron agreed.[16]

The morning after Gumer arrived in Vienna, he was granted a 7:00 A.M. audience with the emperor. Leopold, Gumer later told Pilati, received him roughly, asked if he had truly come for mercantile affairs, and fell silent after the banker replied in the affirmative. Gumer claimed that he had explained himself to advantage but had then been dismissed. Pilati later learned that Gumer's audience had lasted about one minute. (Gumer wrote his brother, who was financing the stay in Vienna, that he had had a five-hour audience during which the ruler had been very well disposed toward the grievances and deputies sent by the Diet and had promised everything they had requested!)[17]

The behavior of Tyrol's Estate deputies while they were in Vienna was differently portrayed by several observers, none of them flattering. Baron Giovanni Battista Todeschi, who had also kept the records on the pre-Diet meetings at Sacco and Rovereto, described the group as "a numerous Commission that greatly irritated the Court with its improper manners and deceitful pretensions."[18] Another observer noted that the court considered

Unterrichter, the deputation's second noble, "a bigoted fanatic, an intriguing, dangerous man," and Supreme Chancellor Kolowrat reproached the group "for lack of uprightness, insincere intentions and for tailoring the Diet (*Diätenschneiderei*),"[19] that is, running the Diet to suit its own purposes. Finally, the deputies would make such nuisances of themselves that they would be asked to leave Vienna even before a full resolution of their grievances had been worked out.

The pleading, dealing, and politicking about to begin over Tyrol's grievances also attracted others to Vienna. The Welsch Confines had two deputies of their own in the capital, Felice Baroni and Angelo Rosmini. The wine interests of the Etschland sent two delegates from the Wine Deputation, Baron Marx Cazan (whose report at the Diet had evoked the Confinants' *Risposta*) and Ignatz von Atzwang. Counts Sauer and Enzenberg were also in Vienna and would be the chief spokesmen at court for the two opposing sides: Sauer for Italian Tyrol and Enzenberg for German Tyrol.

In the late spring after convoking all the Diets, Leopold had established a special commission to deal with Estate grievances. Two of his sons, Francis and Ferdinand, presided either jointly or separately over the proceedings. Although the commission had no official name, its membership was stellar, chosen from the uppermost echelons of the Bohemian–Austrian Court Chancellery and the *Oberste Justizstelle* (a combination supreme court of appeal and ministry of justice). Its permanent members were [20]

Leopold Kolowrat-Krakowsky *(1727–1809)*, Count, of an ancient Bohemian aristocratic family; Supreme Chancellor of the Bohemian-Austrian Court Chancellery

Johann Wenzel von Ugarte *(1748–96)*, Count, a Bohemian noble and Vice-Chancellor of the Bohemian-Austrian Court Chancellery

Franz Johann von Bieschin *(1742–1802)*, Baron, a Bohemian noble from the *Oberste Justizstelle*; also on Leopold's codification commission

Mathias Wilhelm Virgilius von Haan *(1737–1816)*, a Lower Austrian noble from the *Oberste Justizstelle*; also on Leopold's codification commission

Joseph von Koller *(1731–1800)*, a noble from Austria above the Enns and member of the Bohemian-Austrian Court Chancellery

Franz Karl von Kressel *(1720-1801)*, Baron, a Bohemian noble, member of the *Staatsrat* and President of the *Geistliche Hofcommission* overseeing Joseph II's church reforms. Under Leopold he became Bohemian Chancellor within the Bohemian-Austrian Court Chancellery, second only to Kolowrat.

Baron Joseph Thaddäus Sumerau *(d. 1817)*, the Tyrolean referent at the Chancellery, was present at all the commission sessions dealing with Tyrol. Others sat with the commission from time to time as outside experts on certain provinces or topics. Grievances and recommendations went from this group to the Chancellery or *Oberste Justizstelle*, depending on the sub-ject, then to the *Staatsrat* and the emperor for decision. Along with their official duties, the members of the commission were subject to frequent visits from Estate deputies (at least those from Tyrol) pleading their cause and attempting to influence the outcome.

The deputies used their first days in Vienna to make contacts that they hoped would be useful, especially among other Tyroleans and old friends now living in Vienna. By the time Leopold II returned from his coronation as King of Hungary in late November,[21] the Tyroleans were eager to get started. But when they called on Baron Sumerau, their referent at the Chancellery, they were criticized for the form and to some extent the content of their written grievances, which the Diet had not quite had time to prepare properly. Sumerau also told them the Diet had acted precipi-tously and without authorization in several matters, and he informed them that Tyrol would probably be discussed by the grievance commission before long. He therefore advised them to put their grievances in proper order and deliver them to the Court. He also mentioned that the entire deputation might soon be presented to the emperor. The deputies, anxious to meet their ruler, decided to turn to Count Wolkenstein, the official head of their delegation and its highest-ranking member, to arrange the audience as soon as possible. If Wolkenstein would not do so, they decided that they would seek the audience on their own.[22]

When the deputies called on Wolkenstein the next day, he hesitated about approaching the court in their behalf. He was afraid, he said, that if he sought the audience, the court would misinterpret their visit to him and think he was making the request because of "a knife wielded by Hr. v. Unterrichter." Unterrichter became furious and insisted that the others exonerate him; they hastened to comply, reassuring him that he had done no such thing. Wolkenstein then agreed to ask about their audience when he met with the emperor the following day. That evening, three deputies— Unterrichter and the two prelates of the deputation—continued their poli-ticking at dinner with Cardinal Migazzi (Archbishop of Vienna and a Tyrolean noble), joined by Baron Martini and Baron or *Hofrat* Beekhen,[23] three men who might well be expected to champion the Italian Tyroleans' cause.

The next day the seven deputies and deputation secretary Mayr went to see Baron Sumerau again and found Count Wolkenstein already there. First they discussed the Confinants' political goals: seats and votes in all the assemblies or separation from Tyrol. Inter alia, Sumerau said, echoing Leopold's words, he wished a way could be found for some sort of agreement and amicable reconciliation with the Confinants. Articulating another of Leopold's views, Sumerau noted that "the Tyrolean constitution and the equality of the 4 Estates founded on the same is beautiful, and would also be desirable for other lands." As long as that principle of equality of Estates was upheld, he added, it did not seem essential to maintain the current number of votes on each *Ausschuss*. One deputy replied, erring as Enzenberg had, that the number of deputies had always been the same and that the land would be "very displeased" if the Confinants were granted votes on the *Ausschüsse*. The best solution, said the deputy, would be to give the Italians their alternative request: separation from German Tyrol and union with Mantua. Once that was done, Tyrol should be united with Vorarlberg. Sumerau quickly made it clear that separation would be useful to no one, that is, that Leopold would not consider the idea. He regretted that he had no ready solution, asked the deputation to try to work one out, then offered an idea of his own—one quite in accord with an age that stressed reason, but for Tyrol it was radical indeed. Sumerau proposed that the population become the basis of representation, and that the total be divided by the number of seats on each *Ausschuss*. Then in each of the election districts thus created, everyone—Italian or German—would by definition have a representative on each *Ausschuss*. The deputation, with some justice, pointed out the extraordinary confusion that would result from such an entirely new division of their land and added the further objection, soon to be refuted, that the idea could never be used for the cities.[24] The group then turned to the economic problem: wine. The Estate deputies wanted some way to prevent the smuggling of Venetian wine into Tyrol and the unauthorized establishment of new vineyards: both of these illegal practices plus the wines the Confinants were now bringing in legally meant even more competition for the Etschland's product. Before the deputies left, Sumerau reminded them to put their grievances into some suitable form and deliver them to him for transmittal to the court.

In the meantime, Count Sauer had been working on the Diet documents sent to him. In late November his comments and the full dossier on Tyrol came before the special grievance commission, which the deputies did not yet know; but they did learn that their audience with the emperor was set for 28 November. The deputation secretary, however, could not go with them because no more than eight persons at a time were permitted at a private audience, and the deputation itself totaled eight. Beforehand, Count Enzenberg told them that because private audiences with their monarch were not granted very frequently, they were "to profit by a proper candidness." He also added that at his own audience the next morning, he would try to smooth the way for the deputation. But the day before the audience with Leopold, the deputation almost fell apart as Wolkenstein's anger erupted toward Enzenberg for cheating him out of the *Landeshauptmann's* office and toward the deputies for behaving badly. He raged at everyone; and the deputies, upset by his tirade, threatened to go to their audience without him (unthinkable, since he was the head of the deputation). The threat had its effect, and the count quickly calmed down and assured them of his good intentions. When the dust had settled, diPauli asked Wolkenstein please to keep the deputation informed of whatever Count Sauer might be doing and saying about their concerns, especially since all their petitions had been sent to him for comment.[25]

At their audience the next morning, Wolkenstein presented Tyrol's written grievances, which the emperor promised would be closely examined. Then, as head of the deputation, the Count presented each deputy by name. Leopold told them that work was about to begin on their affairs and that when it was completed, the deputies and the grievance commission would meet in conference, or "concertation." Wolkenstein requested a separate audience for deputation secretary Mayr, which was granted, and the deputation's audience ended. Two peasant deputies remained behind, however, and presented their own petition for Count Enzenberg to be named Governor of Tyrol, a post his father had held. Leopold replied that he had already named their new governor, Baron Maximilian Christoph Waidmannsdorf, and again assured them that Count Sauer would not return. Then Leopold advised them not to be taken in by the gossip they had heard about the Diet not being convoked again. "Don't let yourself be talked into anything," he said, "entrust yourselves to me; I want only to make you happy." Leopold did not hesitate to name names and point out the troublemakers: "Unterrichter and Gumer are not useful people either; Gumer would monopolize the treasury fund for himself in order to make use of it as a banker, and Unterrichter has another aim." Leopold said he was telling this only to them—confidentially. The two peasant deputies assured him of their complete loyalty to his "paternal heart," and said they knew nothing of all this plotting. They then went straight to diPauli and reported all the emperor had said (as Leopold probably assumed they would; there were many ways to communicate). DiPauli warned the two deputies not to say anything to Unterrichter "in order not to depress him."[26]

In early December, about a week after their audience, Tyrol's seven Estate deputies paid an official visit to Chancellor Kolowrat and learned that the emperor had not yet returned their written grievances to the Chancellery. Suddenly, in the middle of the conversation, Unterrichter asked Kolowrat to remove Baron Sumerau as Tyrolean referent at the Chancellery and replace him with someone well disposed toward himself (Unterrichter) and who knew Tyrol firsthand. (Perhaps Unterrichter had his own future in mind.) Kolowrat deflected the request with the explanation that this was not the proper time to consider such a question. Unterrichter was not deterred and on a visit to Vice-Chancellor Kressel (also a member of the grievance commission) asked if Kressel could arrange a new referent to replace Sumerau. When Kressel too said he knew of no one, Unterrichter decided he would leave the matter to the mercies of the emperor and the Chancellery.[27]

In the meantime, diPauli met with the Wine Deputation representatives, Marx Cazan and Ignatz Atzwang, who were now in Vienna. The two men informed diPauli that they would have nothing to do with the Estate deputies but would take care of their own affairs independently. They probably had heard of the deputation's unfortunate reputation and decided their best chance for success was to strike out on their own. After a few days in town, however, the wine deputies altered their position slightly and invited three Estates' deputies (the prelate of Welschmichael, peasant deputy Rottensteiner, and diPauli) to a meeting at Gumer's. They decided that they would all work together to let the emperor know that the Confinants' complaints about an Etschland wine monopoly were untrue. They would also ask that Venetian wine imports (including smuggling) be suppressed and that the Wine Deputation, as tax farmers, again be empowered to collect a tariff at the Nevis Bridge on the Confinants' wines.[28]

But the Confinants had one more surprise in store for the Etschlanders, one that hurt them economically over and above the wine imports. On 5 December the Estate deputies in Vienna received unofficial word from Innsbruck that the Welsch Tyroleans had refused to pay either taxes or *Umgeld* to the *Landschaft* until their grievances were settled. In an attempt to come up with a solution that would satisfy the Confinants' political demands, Lienz deputy Peter Aigner proposed that the city of Rovereto with its *pretura* have one seat and vote on the large *Ausschuss* and that the remainder of the Confines' jurisdictions be given a combined vote with the Eisack *Viertel*. Giving the Roveretans (city and *pretura*) one combined vote on the large *Ausschuss*, presumably on the cities' bench, would indeed have been a step forward. But attaching the rest of the jurisdictions in the Confines to the Eisack *Viertel*, geographically part of the Etschland, was not much better than giving them no vote at all, since the Confinants would be asked to share their vote with their already established economic-political enemies. The deputies, however, thought Aigner's idea was excellent and accepted it with applause. But they also decided to keep it in reserve and use it only if it became necessary.[29]

Having made this self-satisfying decision, the seven deputies went to see *Hofrat* Beekhen, apparently unaware of his role in helping the Italians before the Diet. They often called on him even though he was not part of the grievance commission and was not as high in the bureaucracy as the others they visited. Perhaps Beekhen was again acting for his emperor, this time befriending the German Tyroleans. In any event, during the deputies' conversations with Beekhen, Unterrichter commented that the Estates' deputies, and German Tyrol as a whole, would rather the Confines be separated from Tyrol and attached to the Duchy of Mantua, which was also Habsburg territory. Beekhen offered the thought that the Vorarlbergers might be inclined toward union with Tyrol, and the deputies leaped at the idea: "We would accept them quite gladly as Germans, but the now-fawning character of the Confinants is already repugnant to us." The Estates' deputies also brought up the wine trade and the fact that the

Confinants had two deputies of their own in Vienna. Beekhen did not respond directly but, digressing and probably speaking for Leopold, discoursed on the Tyrolean and English constitutions, noting that the two systems had much in common. In England, he said, representation was not based on population, but on having the right to send a representative to Parliament "at the beginning of their present constitution." The result, said Beekhen, referring to the rotten boroughs, was that villages with but a few houses had a Member of Parliament, but large cities like Manchester had none. Similarly, districts such as Kufstein, Rattenberg, and the Gorizian Pustertal, which had become part of Tyrol "late," were not permitted their own representation but had to be joined to other, older parts of the land in order to be represented. The Confines and their almost total lack of representation were not specifically mentioned (at least not according to diPauli's notes), but they were there implicitly and may indeed have been expressed.[30]

The next day (7 December) the seven Tyrolean Estate deputies received, through unmentioned channels, a copy of the Confinants' grievances with attached supporting documents, all of which had been presented to the court by the Italian deputies, Angelo Rosmini and Felice Baroni. Included was the complaint that Tyrol's constitution differentiated disadvantageously between the Welsch Tyrol and the German Tyrol, as well as a statement condemning the treatment the Italians had received at the open Diet and the refusal of the Estates to include most of the Confinants' problems among the land's grievances. Therefore, the Italians stated, they were sending their own grievances directly to the court with the assurance that the emperor, "a most reasonable and just monarch," would have the complaints investigated and would remedy them.[31]

As the seven Tyrolean deputies considered what to do about the Confinants' petition, they received documentary proof of the Welsch Tyroleans' tax revolt: reports sent to Unterrichter by the new *Landeshauptmann*, Count Lodron. A tax collector had reported that the cities and jurisdictions of the Confines refused to pay taxes to any Estate official until the settlement of their grievances and that their innkeepers and tavern keepers were refusing to pay the *Umgeld* on wine. Because the continued tax revolt represented a substantial financial loss to the Tyrolean *Landschaft*, Unterrichter asked Baron Sumerau (whom, it should be recalled, he was trying to have removed from office) what could be done about it. Sumerau wisely recommended that the Tyroleans take no action themselves, but that they present the problem to the emperor for decision. In the meantime, he suggested that they urge the Confinants to continue paying. Sumerau also said he had a plan for reaching agreement with the Italians, but he was not yet ready to reveal it.[32]

The deputies took Sumerau's advice to let the emperor decide about the tax revolt, but the feeling was that something should be done quickly lest the revolt spread to other jurisdictions. Using the documents that had been sent from Innsbruck, deputation secretary Mayr drafted a report that diPauli asked all the deputies to approve and sign. But Count Wolkenstein hesitated and asked where the information had been obtained. When he learned that the documents had come through Unterrichter, he announced that the *Renitenz* was a matter for the provincial authorities, that is, the *Landeshauptmann* and the *Activität*, and that the deputation should not meddle. He adamantly refused to sign the report. Unterrichter then stepped in and became the counterweight to Wolkenstein that Enzenberg had intended when he doubled the deputation. This second noble deputy now took the lead, readily signed the report, and urged the other deputies to follow. Before noon the next day, all seven had signed. They also learned that their first conference, or concertation, with the grievance commission would probably be held at the end of the week.[33]

By 9 December Sumerau and diPauli were again discussing the wine question, and they developed some interesting suggestions. Sumerau noted that the princely county had three separate wine interests: those of the northern Tyroleans, who were primarily wine consumers; and those of the Etschlanders and the Confinants, who were both wine producers. Was there not, he asked, some way to reconcile the interests of all of Tyrol's wine producers, Italian and German? DiPauli thought this might indeed be done and a fair manner found in which to settle their differences. Sumerau, curious, asked what diPauli had in mind, but indicated that as part of any settlement the Etschlanders would have to accept an equitable political and economic role for the Confinants. It was unfair, said the count, to keep subjects who paid equal taxes in an unequal position, even if they had become part of Tyrol somewhat later. Bozener diPauli agreed it would be absurd to demand that the Confinants not sell freely within Tyrol the wines they produced on their own land, but he added that in any event they always managed to sell all their wines. On the other hand, he continued, the Etschlanders could quite fairly ask that foreign, that is, Venetian, wines be kept out of Tyrol. Sumerau agreed, and diPauli commented that because the Etschlanders were economically dependent on the wine trade, their wine necessarily required favoring so that they could pay all their taxes, including some more recently assessed. They were now paying a new tax because of the new water system in addition to the levy resulting from the emperor's 23 September ruling on wine *Umgeld*. That ruling had denied a proposal that the Tyrolean treasury pay 6,000 florins to the Etschlanders to replace the discontinued duties previously imposed on Welsch wine at the Nevis.[34]

While the Estate deputies were occupied with tax problems, the Vienna bureaucracy took up the Welsch Tyroleans' petition for seat and vote or for separation from Tyrol. By now the Chancellery also had in hand the Confinants' *Risposta* to Cazan's Matricle Deputation report, Enzenberg's formal report and his informal comments on the *Risposta,* and Sauer's thoughts on Enzenberg's views and on the other documents. The Chancellery assembled all these documents, drafted its own report, and sent the whole dossier on to the grievance commission. A 25-point debate on paper, with Enzenberg's arguments and Sauer's counterarguments, survives as part of this commission's records.[35] Some of the assertions were not especially new; some of the answers were.

Enzenberg began by asserting that the Confines were conquered territory. Therefore, even though the Confinants were taxable, hereditary, and loyal subjects, it would amount to setting aside the constitution if they were made equal participants in all the benefits *"which, according to the unequal old constitution . . . are bestowed upon the rest of the Motherland, alone!"* Sauer replied that Enzenberg was confused and that his talk of constitution and motherland made no sense in a monarchical state. Furthermore, said Sauer, the Tyrolean Estates were exhibiting the same lack of sense by arguing that because the Confines were conquered, they were perpetually excluded from the privileges of the Estates even though they now shared all taxes and debt payments. That kind of argument, said the former governor, was rare in a monarchical province and had been heard in Tyrol only since the Confines had begun to pay equal taxes.[36]

Enzenberg, turning to the question of seat and vote, stated that because the Diet had accepted the Matricle Deputation's report (which denied meaningful new seats and votes to the Italians), its decisions should be regarded as the expression of the entire assembly and be adhered to as such. Sauer replied that what the Etschland begrudged the Confines was free retail trade in their wines and that the Italians had not had a fair hearing because the deputation's decision was inevitable. Eleven of its fifteen voting members owned substantial property and vineyards on the Etsch, including the report's author, Cazan. Further, the Diet's response could not be considered the voice of the entire nation since it was impossible at an assembly as large as the Diet had been to count the vote in the usual, or accurate, manner.[37]

Enzenberg then claimed that it was the Etschlanders who were being treated unfairly. The Etsch *Viertel,* he said, had only one vote on the large and small *Ausschüsse* and constituted only a small part of the Diet; by itself, therefore, it could not be accused of opposing the Confinants. Sauer countered first that the Italians competed with this *Viertel* in producing wine, again asserting that this competition was at the heart of the entire problem. The Etschlanders, he said accurately, feared that if the Confinants were admitted to the Estate assemblies with equitable arrangements for seat and vote, they would be in a better position to protect their own economic interests. Sauer also rejected the idea that the Etschland, with only one vote on each *Ausschuss,* was being treated unfairly. True, he said, on the peasants' bench the Etsch *Viertel* had only one vote, but on the cities' bench it had two, namely, Bozen and Meran. Further, most of the nobles on the *Ausschüsse* had vineyards in the Etschland, and a similar situation prevailed on the prelates' bench. The result, therefore, was that the whole political system in Tyrol was unfair not to the Etschlanders, whom it favored, but to the Italians. And the Confinants were not the only ones disadvantaged by the Etschland's political domination; the much more numerous population of northern Tyrol, who were wine consumers, were continually outvoted by the representatives of the less numerous wine producers.[38]

Enzenberg then addressed three questions that Arco deputy Marcobruni had raised at the Diet: What is the Matricle? What is the *Landschaft*? Do the jurisdictions of the Welsch Confines constitute part of the *Landschaft* Tyrol? Of these questions, the third is the most pertinent here. Enzenberg claimed that the Confines were indeed a part of the land or county of Tyrol, but not of the *Landschaft* or Estates. In other words, they were part of Tyrol politically and geographically by action of the land's prince, but they could not become part of the *Landschaft* because—that argument again—they had been "partly conquered by arms and partly by forced capitulation." Furthermore, Enzenberg said, Tyrol was a land with its own laws and statutes, constitution, and traditions; but the Italians had kept their own local statutes and were therefore barred from becoming part of the *Landschaft*. The Confines, he said, were only "attached" (*angeklammert*), not "incorporated." Sauer, perhaps with raised eyebrows, replied by pointing out that many localities in the princely county had their own statutes and also had seat and vote in the open Diet and on the *Ausschüsse*, and no one maintained that they were not really incorporated. Furthermore, the Italians were now paying equal taxes, and it was therefore truly unjust to deny them seat and vote any longer.[39]

Enzenberg insisted that the constitution required a specific number of votes on each *Ausschuss*, according to certain "recent" (1573) provisions. Sauer pointed out that Enzenberg was completely incorrect, that the number of votes had changed frequently over the centuries, and that the principle of equality had to be maintained, not the number of votes. Sauer also emphasized that the Italians were being treated unfairly by showing that the Confines paid more taxes (16,000 florins) than the Eisack *Viertel* (10,000 florins), which did have seat and vote on the small *Ausschuss*.[40]

Enzenberg, continuing his constitutional line of attack, argued that the Estates assembled at the Diet elected the members of the *Ausschüsse* and that the Confinants had no seat or vote because they had not been elected to these bodies. The answer begged the entire question. As Sauer pointed out, the former commissar was in theory correct, but the elections were merely pro forma. The very same jurisdictions had been on the peasants' bench at the *Ausschüsse* since 1573 so that in fact there were perpetual seats for the jurisdictions and towns. The Welsch jurisdictions, he said, were now claiming such a perpetual seat and vote for themselves, as were the towns of Rovereto and Arco. The nobles and clergy, the former governor admitted, were another matter; since they did indeed choose their *Ausschuss* delegates at the Diet, they could not have representatives mandated from any particular area. But at least the Collegiate Abbey at Arco and the parish priest at Rovereto could be immatriculated so that they would be eligible for election. Then Sauer suggested a change to be considered for the future: that as long as Tyrol was divided into *Viertel*, the prelates and noblemen should also be elected to the *Ausschüsse* from each *Viertel*. For now, he said, the total on both the prelates' and nobles' benches should be increased by one vote each; then, with a vote granted to the Welsch Tyrol on the peasants' and towns' benches, all four benches would still have the same number of votes. The Confines' population (a seventh of the total, or 61,280 out of 428,684), said Sauer, entitled them to two perpetual votes on the small *Ausschuss*: one on the towns' bench and one on the peasants' bench.[41]

After a brief exchange about the Matricle Deputation's report, Sauer proposed the solution that would, with a small change, be accepted by the emperor: that on the large *Ausschuss* the eleventh vote on the peasants' bench go to the Confines and the eleventh vote on the cities' bench either alternately or jointly go to the cities of Rovereto and Arco; that the prelates' and nobles' benches each be increased by one vote, resulting in 44 seats on the large *Ausschuss*. On the small *Ausschuss* Sauer suggested that the sixth vote on the peasants' bench go to Welsch Tyrol and that the cities of Arco and Rovereto be the sixth vote on the cities' bench, alternately or jointly. The other two benches should also have one more vote each so that the small *Ausschuss* would have a total of twenty-four. To be eligible for election to the *Ausschuss*, Sauer proposed that the Collegiate Abbey at Arco and the parish priest at Rovereto be immatriculated.[42]

After digesting all the argumentation, the grievance commission presented its opinion and recommendation to the emperor. Right and fairness were on the side of the Italians, the commission said, since they now bore entirely equal and proportionate taxes and other burdens with the rest of Tyrol. The claim that the Confines were conquered or acquired territory was beside the point because other such territories had long ago been immatriculated and given a role in the various congresses. The commission agreed with Sauer that the Collegiate Abbey at Arco should be immatriculated, but not the parish priest at Rovereto because then all the other parish priests could also claim immatriculation. The commission briefly considered the suggestion that Sumerau had made: that if it was important to give everyone equal representation and still keep the number on each *Ausschuss* the same, Tyrol should first be divided into five equal districts with each having one representative on the small *Ausschuss*; and then into ten equal districts with each having one representative on the large

Ausschuss. Bowing to tradition, the commission suggested that if this pro-posal were accepted, the new *Viertel* for the most part would retain their old names. The commission, however, went beyond Sumerau's proposal and extended the idea to the cities, overcoming earlier objections to this idea that the Estates' deputies had raised: each city was to be represented accord-ing to its population in such a way that there would be either ten or five votes total at the large or small *Ausschuss* on the cities' bench.[43] That either Sumerau or the commission seriously believed such a plan was possible in Tyrol of 1790 is difficult to imagine.

In any event, the commission, stepping away from its new plan (and back to the realm of the possible), said that if its task was to limit its advice solely to Enzenberg's and Sauer's suggestions, it would have to support Sauer because the spirit of the Tyrolean constitution required not a certain number of votes but only equality of votes for each Estate. The Chancellery received the commission's recommendation and suggested that the emperor issue a declaration informing Tyrol's Estates that since they had not acted as requested on the Confinants, their sovereign had reached his own decision. His declaration should say that justice and fairness required seat and vote at the Estates' assemblies for Italian Tyrol, especially a vote on the cities' and jurisdictions' benches at each *Ausschuss.* That was the Chancellery's recom-mendation on 11 December 1790.[44]

The deputies from Tyrol apparently learned nothing of the commis-sion's or the Chancellery's decisions. If diPauli's diary is an accurate reflec-tion of what was known either on that day or the following days, the bureaucracy simply did not leak information on this occasion. Tyrol's seven deputies heard nothing about the commission or Chancellery sessions de-spite visits to grievance commission members Haan, Koller, and Referent Sumerau (the latter two also members of the Chancellery). By 16 December the emperor had reached his own decision on the Confinants; he would take the Chancellery's advice but would first give the Estates one more chance. However, it was to be "clearly and decidedly given to the Estates to understand that in case they do not comply willingly in an amicable agree-ment for the traditional smaller *Ausschuss,* I will take into direct protection so fair a wish as that of the Welsch Tyroleans," and that he would satisfy that wish by making use of his prerogatives and rights as land's prince.[45]

Leopold greeted less warmly the Chancellery's proposal on how to respond to a report on the Confinants' tax revolt, that is, their refusal to pay *Landschaft* taxes and wine *Umgeld.* In its report to the *Staatsrat,* the Chancellery proposed that the Upper Austrian *Gubernium* at Innsbruck be instructed to attach everything it could that belonged to the Confines and hold it until the emperor had resolved the matter and that "in adverse circumstances" certain steps might need to be taken to execute the deci-sion.[46] No evidence exists that these Draconian measures were ever carried out, or even that Leopold ever seriously considered them.

CHAPTER SIX

In mid-December the Chancellery reported to the *Staatsrat* and the emperor on Tyrol's Diet protocols and Enzenberg's journal. Its report was especially critical of the way the Court Commissar had controlled the *Landeshauptmann*'s election, far overstepping his instructions. Both Enzenberg and the Diet were criticized for granting 100 ducats to Franz Michael Senn (whom the Diet had sent to Vienna in August to plead its case against Sauer and to whom the court commissar, without the Diet's knowledge, had entrusted his own secret report to the emperor) because the Estates did not have the power "arbitrarily to ladle out [*schöpfen*] remuneration from their treasury. . . . [which] is to be viewed merely as a branch of the general state treasury." The Chancellery urged that bounds be set on such activity and criticized the Diet for voting itself expense money beyond the traditional defrayal of expenses for burgher and peasant deputies. Leopold could not allow the Estates to continue "ladling out" money, but he also did not wish to injure Senn, who had carried out a trust and performed a service. His decision answered both those concerns. He expressed his displeasure with the Estates for high-handedly and without his permission voting the payment to Senn, and he allowed Senn to keep the payment. Then, acting out of grace and with confidence that the Estates would not again presume such high-handedness, he required that they repay the 100 ducats to the *Landschaft* treasury. Otherwise, he accepted the Chancellery's advice.[47]

Still, all of Tyrol's grievances had not been resolved. The deputies waited; Christmas came and went, and then they learned the reason for the delay. On the day after Christmas, Kolowrat sent them a lengthy reprimand informing them that the emperor, in his own handwritten note to the chancellor, had said he found it most incomprehensible that the Tyrolean representatives had left Tyrol without completing the compilation of their grievances. Their negligence had created difficulties and delayed the completion of their affairs. Leopold also accused the deputies of prolonging their business in Vienna either to have time and opportunity for intrigues or to extend the enjoyment of their expense allowances granted by the Estates. He demanded from them a written declaration stating when they promised to deliver their completed grievances. And, to save the Estates of Tyrol much expense, Leopold ordered that four of the deputies, one of whom had to be Unterrichter, were to return home "without further ado." Enzenberg, as mentioned earlier, had doubled the number of envoys to Vienna just to get Unterrichter on the deputation!) Further, if the four remaining deputies delayed delivering their grievances beyond the time that they themselves set, they would have to remain in Vienna at their own expense until the work was completed. Kolowrat said that the sovereign expected their written declaration at the earliest opportunity.[48]

The deputies sprang into action, got to work on their grievances, and within two days had their response to the emperor in the hands of his son Archduke Francis. In their covering note they told Francis that his father's message had been unexpected, shocking, and "piercing." They denied that they were prolonging their stay in the capital just for intrigue or for their own enjoyment at the Estates' expense, and they said that the attached note addressed to his father contained their vindication and that they had no further general grievances to add. They also asked the emperor for a formal investigation of their conduct so that each man could preserve his honor, adding that if any of them should be found culpable, they would submit to the deserved punishment; but if a rigorous probe should prove any innocent, these individuals should again have "the all-highest grace and favor." To underscore their honorable intentions, they voluntarily re-nounced any payments from the *Landschaft* until the investigation had been completed. They were, they said, asking for nothing more than justice and hoped that Francis would put in a good word for them with his father. Seven of the eight deputies signed the appeal; only Wolkenstein's signature was missing.[49] As if the deputies had not had enough bad news, a few days later they received more from Count Enzenberg. Their *Landeshauptmann*, Count Franz Lodron, elected with so much effort at the Diet, probably would not live long; he was very ill and extremely melancholy. Lodron's death, they lamented, would be yet another blow and "all that was lacking to make our confusion complete."[50]

Early in the new year, the Chancellery took up, inter alia, the inheri-tance rights of the Confinants' daughters and the request for a *Reciprolum*. Referent Sumerau supported the recommendation of the *Oberste Justizstelle* "that a daughter who married-out into a Trent or Brixen district, or into a foreign territory enjoy her hereditary rights only insofar as she might be able to prove that in the district where she is married, the daughters are also accorded equal hereditary rights with the sons." Otherwise, she might lawfully claim "only that inheritance right which is provably accorded to the daughters of the district" into which she had married. Most of the Chancellery agreed, suggesting only that the separate mention of Trent and Brixen be deleted. A mild dissent came from Count Ugarte and Baron Bieschin, who disagreed only about the timing; they felt the laws should be left as they were until the second part of the new civil law code was com-plete.[51] (The first part had been issued in 1786; the final version of the entire code would appear in 1811.)

The new year brought the deputies a break in their routine and per-haps a lift for their depressed spirits. On 4 January Count Enzenberg took them to visit Vice-Chancellor Kressel; diPauli devoted his diary entry to describing the vice-chancellor's inventions. "This man showed us his lan-guage machine, a detailed description of which would last until Easter. With his machine he produced the sound of a 4-year-old child; though monotonous, it was quite passably understandable as French. He said . . . he had already experimented on this machine for 20 years and that he would have brought it to still greater perfection if his official business had allowed him time." Kressel also showed them a machine for spinning cotton and a kind of silk but regretted that he could not display his chess machine because it was then dismantled.[52] Surely it was one of the deputies' more lighthearted days in Vienna; another difficult one was not long in coming.

The Estate deputies had a second audience with the emperor scheduled for the morning of 7 January, but he kept them waiting in the antechamber until after the noon hour. At the audience the prelate of Wiltau spoke for the group and for what he termed their most upright sentiments, but he said that their stay in Vienna had been extraordinarily painful and provoked because at every turn they found only the emperor's disfavor. Leopold did not respond directly; he asked only if they had finished with everything and then dismissed them. But Unterrichter, whom Leopold had ordered to leave town, approached the throne and said Enzenberg had portrayed him badly. Leopold admitted that some dirty tricks (*Schurkereyen*) had been attributed to Unterrichter and indicated that he should stay after the others left. The emperor questioned Unterrichter's handling of some Estate funds and his behavior at the Diet. "I already know, the emperor said, "that the peasants especially spoke only through you," and what they did at the Diet "also occurred only through your wink . . . in brief, you are known to me as a dangerous man; and you must answer to me for every disturbance which resulted at the open Diet." The Tyrolean protested his innocence and asked for a commission of investigation. Leopold merely repeated that Unterrichter was a dangerous man and dismissed him.[53]

A week after the new year began and in preparation for the concertation with the grievance commission on 18 January, the Chancellery took up the tangled matter of the wine *Umgeld*. The Etschland had refused to agree to the payment of 16,000 florins in return for the contract to farm the *Umgeld* but instead wanted to reintroduce the old tariffs on the Confinants' wines at the Nevis Bridge, to be collected by the Wine Deputation reinstated as tax farmers. The Chancellery now repeated the position it had taken on 4 August 1790 (while the Diet was still in session): that the situation had been truly unfair when Nevis Bridge tariffs impeded the Confinants in the retail sale of their wines and that it would be equally unfair to reestablish the Etschlanders' former wine monopoly by resuscitating the Wine Deputation as tax farmers at the Nevis. Leopold had upheld the Chancellery in a decision of 23 September and had abolished the Nevis tariff and replaced it with the *Umgeld*; that decision, said the Chancellery in January, "could not be departed from." But the Chancellery also deemed it unfitting to force the Estates to pay 16,000 florins for farming the *Umgeld* and therefore offered two alternatives: either to reintroduce the 1789 ordinance concerning the wine Umgeld on the Etsch or allot the 16,000 florins directly to the wine-growing localities.[54]

At the concertation, or open session, of the grievance commission, the Tyrolean Estates' deputies heard the decisions reached on their many grievances and had an opportunity to respond. The two Archdukes Francis and Ferdinand both presided, seated at a long table. To their right sat the entire commission and Tyrol's new governor, Baron Maximilian Waidmannsdorf. To the Archdukes' left sat the eight Estates' deputies, including Wolkenstein. As each grievance was brought up and its resolution announced, the deputies were given an opportunity to respond to the emperor's decisions.[55] The Confinants' request for seats and votes and for alterations of the language laws were not part of the grievances of the land and therefore were not mentioned at the concertation. But the daughters' inheritance rights and aspects of the wine problem were very much part of the proceedings.

On the inheritance rights of daughters, the emperor had adopted the recommendation that a *Reciprolum* be introduced. The laws decreeing equal inheritance and permitting married daughters to retain control over inherited property would be applicable only if the married daughters could prove that the same rights existed for women in the district or region into which they had married. The deputies said they found the decision fair and added nothing. It was, in fact, exactly what they and the Confinants had asked for. On the wine *Umgeld* the deputies heard the Chancellery's most recent recommendation: if the Estates did not want to be tax farmers for this *Umgeld* (which would cost them 16,000 florins), either the 1789 ordinance of Joseph II be renewed or the 16,000 florins be allotted directly to the wine-growing localities. This time the deputies did respond; they objected with some right that neither the *Landschaft* nor the Estates could agree to this because they had no treasury under their control. The deputies made their point, and the grievance commission recommended a delay in deciding on *Umgeld* assessment until after the *Gubernium* had an opportunity to investigate how such a sum might be raised.[56]

Leopold, like most monarchs, usually rewarded in some appropriate way those who served him. Among others, he now considered two men deserving of reward: Tyrol's former governor, Count Sauer, who had so staunchly supported and defended his rulers' policies and the rights of the Italians; and the former court commissar, Count Enzenberg, who had sided with the Etschlanders while for the most part carrying out his ruler's directives. Sauer was rewarded early in 1791 when he was named president of the Lower Austrian Government in Vienna. It was, in effect, a full vindication and expression of support since the position was equal in rank to that of governor of the Upper Austrian *Gubernium* in Innsbruck and perhaps even more important because of geographic proximity to the emperor. Sauer and his replacement in Innsbruck, Baron Maximilian Waidmannsdorf, both received the real privy councillor's dignity tax-free.[57]

Count Enzenberg was offered the presidency of the restored Upper Austrian Appeals Court in Innsbruck, but at his own request he was granted the same office for Inner Austria in Klagenfurt.[58] He was also informed officially that Leopold was "completely [and] most graciously satisfied with his performance at the open Diet, with his management of the course of business, and with the wise direction wherewith the Hr. Court Commissar had always maintained the peace at such a numerous assembly." Enzenberg, however, was not satisfied and petitioned for further assurance that his work had pleased his ruler. Leopold thought that he had given the Count enough recognition, that his promotion to Appeals Court president was "adequate confirmation of My goodwill . . . and my satisfaction with his performance." Enzenberg was informed of this, too, in writing.[59]

The Confinants' request for seats and votes at the assemblies was not part of Tyrol's official *Gravitorialschrift*. The emperor had made a preliminary decision in December that the Italians' requests were fair and were to be satisfied, but he preferred that the Estates endorse the decision. The Confinants' petition came up at the *Staatsrat* again early in February, and Leopold decided that the small *Ausschuss* should be convoked in Innsbruck so that the Estates could reconsider their position. Tyrol's seven deputies did not agree. They preferred that the large *Ausschuss*, which they believed they could control more easily, deal with the problem. Or they asked for assurances that their sovereign would summon the small *Ausschuss* "only according to past resolutions," that is, with no Italian members, to deliberate on the Confinants' requests.[60]

The Confinants too were concerned about the small *Ausschuss* being summoned precisely because it had no Italian members. On 10 March their deputies again asked for seat and vote on both *Ausschüsse* and the *Steuercompromiss*. This time the request had a sense of urgency. These bodies were to meet in a few months, and the Italians wanted to take part, with seat and vote, so that they would have some influence on the decisions made, including the free export of their wines (exactly what the Etschlanders did not want). The Confinants therefore asked specifically that the deputies of the cities of Rovereto and Arco, and of the rest of the Confines, be summoned to the summer *Ausschuss*.[61] But Leopold had already decided that the old rules would prevail for that meeting. He wanted the Italians to have the seats and votes, but rather than grant them by fiat, he preferred that Tyrol's Estates consent to the changes. Referring the matter to the *Ausschuss* would give the Estates another opportunity to sanction what their ruler wanted and, for the moment, effectively table the seat-and-vote question.

The wine issue was still unresolved, and the envoys of the Etschlanders' Wine Deputation were still to be heard from. In early February these two envoys, Cazan and Atzwang, submitted a lengthy petition that raised two primary points against the free traverse of the Confinants' wines over the Nevis Bridge: it was against the clear right of the Etschland Estates, and it was not to the advantage of the ruler's treasury. On the first point, they said that the Etschland's right to keep out all wine imports was not because of its liability to pay taxes to Tyrol, but because the Etschland had essentially a one-product economy. That product was wine, and it had to be sold at a certain price for the area to survive. Free trade in wine would therefore bring disastrous consequences, they said, because the Etschland's industrious population and productive land would inevitably decline and disappear; that, in turn, would mean the ultimate ruin of the adjoining non-wine-producing jurisdictions. But, they continued, free movement of wine in Tyrol would be clearly advantageous to the Confines and to the Venetians who could export their wines "on all sides *per Controbando*"; the petition also said that the Confinants needed and used Venetian-Vicentine wines to improve their own product. In their second point, Cazan and Atzwang argued that free commerce in wine would also be disadvantageous to the ruler because his income and Tyrol's income would both drop precipitously as a result of the depopulation and economic ruin that free wine commerce would bring.[62]

Their grievances expressed, the wine deputies then stated their wishes. The three wine *Viertel*—Etsch, Eisack, and Burggrafenamt—asked that the treaty with Maria Theresa, concluded "for eternity" in 1758 and again in 1774, be restored. It had permitted them to farm the wine *Umgeld* in return for 16,000 florins and to defray this payment by collecting duties from the Confinants at the Nevis Bridge (18 kreuzers for their wine and 1 florin 30 kreuzers for their brandy, which amounted to about 6,000 florins a year). But now that the Nevis tariff was abolished, the wine *Viertel* could not pay the entire 16,000 florins. Nor could the *Landschaft* treasury replace the 6,000 florins. So, unless the Nevis duty was restored, the central treasury would have to make up the shortfall. If Vienna chose to pay these 6,000 florins, said the Etschlanders, it would show preference for the Confinants and would thereby dig the Etschlanders' grave. The wine envoys recommended—echoing recommendations heard throughout the Monarchy in 1790—a return in this instance to the *status quo ante* Joseph II by restoring the freedoms confirmed in the eternal treaty with Maria Theresa. Then their treasury would be able to pay the 16,000 florins to the *Gubernium* in Innsbruck, everything would be put back in proper order, and the Etschland would be saved from ruin. On 14 February 1791 the Chancellery recommended postponing any action on this petition until after the emperor had reached a final decision on Tyrol's grievances and the deputies had met in final concertation with the commission. Then, suggested the Chancellery, the wine deputies' petition should be sent to the *Gubernium* where a new opinion on the matter should be drafted.[63] The *Staatsrat* and the emperor concurred. (*Gubernium* personnel were, of course, all appointed by Vienna.)

Cazan and Atzwang learned of the decision two days later during a visit with Baron Sumerau. He told them that the Wine Deputation's affairs, like any other individual grievances (that is, grievances not general to the land), were being referred to the *Gubernium*, that the emperor had already received three reports on the wine situation, and that nothing further was required from them. However, Sumerau did suggest that they think the wine matter over again and perhaps try to propose a remedy that had not been previously suggested.[64] The wine deputies were not at all happy about their grievances being sent to the *Gubernium*. Cazan later complained to diPauli and Unterrichter about the decision and proposed that a provisional arrangement at least be made "because *Spolitus ante omnia* is to be restored." He suggested that while the final decision was pending, no changes be made in the *Umgeld* or in the sums already collected and in the Wine Deputation's treasury and that all wines passing over the Nevis Bridge be recorded. DiPauli, who did not entirely agree with Cazan, termed the suggestion "nothing other than a complete return to the previous condition." He and Unterrichter told Cazan that Tyrol's wine commerce could not return to the old basis, that another solution had to be found—perhaps making *causam communum* with the Confinants. The two Estate deputies advised Cazan to be prudent to avoid being blamed for "trespassing" on the Welsch Tyroleans. Clearly, at least two Tyroleans now understood and to a large extent accepted the emperor's stance on the Italians. Cazan decided to think everything over and talk with them again later.[65]

Just before the New Year, Leopold had ordered Tyrol's Estate deputies to get their grievances in order, cut their deputation back to the traditional four, and send the others home. The deputies themselves had decided who should stay and who should go. In doing so, they found themselves in trouble again. On 15 February they heard from the Innsbruck *Aktivität*, reprimanding them for making the decision without preliminary discussions with Innsbruck. The deputies were also informed that after the final concertation with the grievance commission, not four but six of them should return home; only two were to wait for the emperor's final decisions to be issued. By now they had been in Vienna for three full months, and cutting the deputation would avoid running up unneeded costs. At their audience with the emperor on the evening of 17 February, they rendered their thanks, delivered their final petition, and reported that Wolkenstein and diPauli would be the two deputies to stay on. The emperor told them that they had made a good decision and that he hoped the protocols would be finished in about ten days so that the remaining two could also be on their way home.[66] Unterrichter (on his own decision and expense), Gumer, and the wine deputies Cazan and Atzwang also remained in Vienna.

On 4 March the emperor finished, for the time being, with most of Tyrol's grievances. He referred the wine matter to the Innsbruck *Gubernium* and also issued a Rescript on other grievances. Some matters, such as the emigration patent and recruiting (at that point suspended but not yet repealed) were sent to the summer *Ausschuss* for deliberation. He reserved to himself the right of legislation, but he promised to consider the Estates' suggestions and representations on all ordinances concerning Tyrol and to submit to them for deliberation the draft of the future civil law code and other laws. The Rescript also confirmed the Estates' ancient right to have tax requests submitted to them and granted their request to have the

Ausschüsse and *Steuercompromiss* meet in the summertime, when they could best take time from agricultural pursuits and still navigate the Alps with some degree of certainty. In addition, the Estates could now bring their petitions directly to Vienna instead of going through the *Gubernium*, and each Estate was granted the free election of its representatives to the *Aktivitäten*. But Leopold kept for himself alone the right to convoke the *Ausschüsse* and review the Estates' accounts.[67]

A few days before leaving, on 10 March, diPauli called on *Hofrat* Haan, a member of the grievance commission, as part of his final round of visits. Haan heaped praise on Sumerau for expediting Tyrol's business and sent a message to the Tyroleans: return to Tyrol, keep peace in the land, and try to restore harmony between Welsch and German Tyroleans. He had, said Haan, known both nations from youth, and he was aware "that you have never had an attachment for one another, yet you did not hate each other, and only in the past couple of years have you come into such conflagration against one another. I hope you will now bring the thing again into balance."[68] That Italian and German Tyrol would never quite be "in balance" again and would soon find themselves partitioned among Bavaria, Napoleon's Illyrian Province, and his Kingdom of Italy, no one could foresee in 1791.

Optimistic words also came from Baron Kressel, the vice-chancellor and extraordinary inventor, when diPauli paid his final visit. The baron said that because there were reasonable people in Tyrol, they would find a way to solve the wine problem, which he saw as the only remaining source of trouble. But Tyrol's new governor, Baron Waidmannsdorf, was not so supportive. He told diPauli that he did not believe the Confinants should be allowed to bring their wines freely into German Tyrol, but the territory should not be entirely closed to them either. The new governor added that although the Confinants insisted there was no smuggling, he for one did not believe it, especially because he knew it had happened in similar circumstances elsewhere.[69] Even more negative was Franz Gumer, who informed diPauli that the Etschland wine matter would "be settled by the right of the fist." Gumer also replied negatively to diPauli's suggestion that Italians be accepted into the Wine Deputation so that they and the Etschlanders could make common cause against the Trentines. Finally, Gumer reported that the Wine Deputation envoys would stay in Vienna and would have to obtain their goals by underhanded means.[70]

On 15 March 1791 diPauli left Vienna to return home. Some problems involving the Italian Tyroleans still existed; but the intense politicking was over. The Confinants had been granted the *Reciprolum* they sought on their daughters' inheritance rights; resolution of voting, language, and economic rights would come more slowly. And before all the loose ends were tied up, a new emperor would be on the throne, with new ideas and goals.

The Outcome:
Two Emperors and
Their Policies

The Estate deputies returned to Tyrol with many, though not all, of their problems resolved. But the Confinants still awaited seat and vote in the provincial assemblies; their wine dispute with the Etschlanders was yet to be resolved; more needed to be done on their language grievances; and the decree was still to be issued on their daughters' inheritance rights. Most of this unfinished business would be completed within the year, but a new sovereign would resolve the rest; on 1 March 1792 Leopold II died and was succeeded by his son Francis.

Contemporary observers and historians have attributed to Francis a stubbornness or inflexibility unknown in his father. Francis's biographer Viktor Bibl wrote of this emperor, "He learns nothing and he forgets nothing."[1] The British ambassador to Vienna at the beginning of Francis's reign wrote that the young emperor's life during the reigns of his uncle and father had been so much confined within the walls of the imperial palace and his communication with men in public life so restricted to the narrow line of conventional duty "that perhaps no heir of the crown arrived at the age of manhood, [who] was ever less known to the higher classes of his father's subjects or to the corps diplomatique."[2] Descriptions such as these abound; yet Francis was not as inflexible or as afraid of innovation as he has been portrayed.

Francis shared with his father certain personal qualities and ideas of government. They were both deeply suspicious; both believed firmly in absolute monarchy within the rule of law, or the *Rechtsstaat*; and they both honored the constitutions of their lands as these political systems had been restored under Leopold. Both rulers therefore worked through and with the Estates rather than around, against, or without them.

THE OUTCOME

Father and son differed, for example, in their economic philosophies. Leopold was as favorable to free trade as circumstances permitted, abolishing tariffs and other commercial taxes wherever he could; Francis, on the other hand, was willing to restore some of these tariffs and taxes, including some on wine. Although Leopold and his predecessors had supported legal restrictions on the use of land and especially on converting arable land into vineyards, Francis took a laissez-faire approach; he believed that the most profitable and therefore the wisest use of land would be determined by the market for its products. It was a growing belief at the end of the eighteenth century and one that Francis adopted as he ended a centuries-old agricultural policy by permitting Tyrol's grain growers, whose product was badly needed at home, to turn their efforts to growing grapes for exportable wines. Francis was clearly not afraid of opposition or innovation.

Francis's positions vis-à-vis his father's would affect his policies for Italian and German Tyrol. In 1790 and 1791 the Confinants' first concern was their quest for seat and vote and therefore political (and resultant economic) influence in the princely county. If that political equity was not attainable, then they requested separation from German Tyrol. Leopold would resolve this dispute, and in this his son would honor his father's decisions.

Seat and Vote

Rovereto had requested seat and vote on the *Ausschüsse,* and other parts of the Confines had asked for seat and vote at the open Diet and *Ausschüsse.* While the Chancellery was considering the matter in March 1791, another petition came in from the wine deputies Cazan and Atzwang, still in Vienna. The petition, devoted primarily to *Umgeld* and wine (see discussion below under Wine), also asked that the question of voting rights at the Diet and *Ausschüsse* be investigated and that no changes be made in Tyrol's political institutions while the investigation was in progress.[3] There was no further investigation, however. On 25 March 1791 the emperor accepted advice from the Chancellery and grievance commission: under all circumstances and without regard to the old constitution, the Confines were to have proper representation at the open Diets (which at this point no one, except perhaps a few diehards, disputed any longer), and the Italian burghers and peasants were to be allotted seats and votes at both the large and small *Ausschüsse.* Specifically, Rovereto and Arco were to have separate votes on the large *Ausschuss* and to share a vote on the small one. The countryside too was to have representatives voting in both bodies. Leopold also ruled that this decision was to be presented for consideration and approval at the summer *Ausschuss* sessions in Innsbruck.[4]

When the Estate *Ausschuss* met in July, however, it refused to grant all that the emperor had requested. The deputies protested especially against full votes for the Confinants on the small *Ausschuss*, the members of which also made up the *Steuercompromiss*. The Estates also petitioned Vienna for confirmation of their privileges. All the petitions and protests were in the *Staatsrat's* hands and ready for the emperor on 19 July and 20 July. But Leopold, displeased that the Estates had still not approved what he wanted for the Italians, sent a message to the Chancellery that "the drawing up of the confirmation of privileges, as the Tyrolean *Gubernium* proposes, is to be treated in a dilatory fashion *(dilatorisch zu behandeln)*."[5]

During the first week in August, the large *Ausschuss* met to hear Leopold's resolution of 4 March on their land's grievances (see chapter 6) and to elect a new *Landeshauptmann* since Count Lodron, selected with so much effort at the Diet, had died. They chose Count Joseph Spaur, scion of another prominent *Dynast* family of Tyrol, one member of which was the Prince-Bishop of Brixen. Then, after nine days in session, the large *Ausschuss* adjourned, turning over to the small *Ausschuss* the election of the members of the Innsbruck and Bozen *Aktivitäten* and other unfinished business.[6] The small *Ausschuss*, in its turn, sat from 10 August to 13 August, deliberating primarily on matters submitted by the emperor for review and acceptance. The stickier points, such as the *Umgeld*, were referred to special commissions; that was the fate, after a lively debate, of Leopold's decree ordering the Estates to grant the Confines seats and votes at the land's assemblies.[7] Perhaps the Estates, too, were being *dilatorisch.*

The *Ausschuss's* special commission on the Confinants deliberated for almost a month, then on 6 September sent its representations to the emperor. In response to Leopold's earlier order, the commission declared that the Confines' admission to the large *Ausschuss* was indeed feasible, but that admission to the small *Ausschuss* was not possible because it included granting the Confinants two seats, one for the cities and one for the jurisdictions. The Estates' commission, however, was ready with its own substitute solution: on the large *Ausschuss* the cities of Rovereto and Arco should share one alternating vote or decide between themselves which city would represent both; and the Confinants' jurisdictions should be represented on this *Ausschuss* by being joined to the cities of Arco and Rovereto. That would mean the Italians would have a total of one seat on the large *Ausschuss* and none on the small. The Estates' commission said it would be entirely inadmissible for the Confinants to participate in the *Steuercompromiss*, which was, in reality, the small *Ausschuss* by another name and with another function. But, said the commission, the Italians' representatives could examine accounts and criticize documentary evidence because the tax congress "did not fear openness, but only the increase of quarrels and costs."[8] There was also a clear, though unstated, reluctance to give the Italians a say in the allocation of the taxes they now had to pay along with everyone else in Tyrol. The commission therefore offered a small concession, the seat on the large *Ausschuss*, which was not even half of what Leopold wanted.

THE OUTCOME

The Estates' decision concerning the Confinants was in the emperor's hands by early October, and toward the end of the month (25 October) Leopold issued his decree. Emphasizing the positive comments and ignoring the negative ones, he expressed his satisfaction with the Estates' willingness to give the Welsch Tyroleans a political role in their land. He then enacted into law his own earlier decision: the cities of Rovereto and Arco each received seats on the cities' bench at the large Ausschuss and the Confinants' jurisdictions one seat on the peasants' bench; the two cities were given a combined vote on the small Ausschuss and the jurisdictions a vote alternating or rotating with the Burggrafenamt, the Wipptal, and the Lower Inntal. The Estates' special commission had also referred to a possible expansion of the prelates' bench; Leopold again stressed the positive and interpreted this as their acceptance of the admission of the Collegiate Abbey at Arco. So, despite all the maneuvering by the Estates and especially the Etschlanders, the Confinants were granted representation at all the assemblies of the land; by 1791 the rural jurisdictions and the county of Arco were in the Matricle.[9] But Leopold then committed a tactical error: he let the Estate congress select which participants should begin the new rotation of jurisdictions (the Confines, Wipptal, Burggrafenamt, or Lower Inntal) on the small Ausschuss.[10] In the process he gave the Estates a final opportunity for maneuvering and foot-dragging.

The decree granting the new seats and votes to the Confinants took effect at the next meeting of the small Ausschuss at the beginning of February 1792; Count Antonio Alberti di Poja appeared as the shared representative of the cities of Rovereto and Arco. Alberti-Poja tried to extend Leopold's legislation just a bit further by seeking three more votes for the Italians on this small Ausschuss: a permanent vote on the peasants' bench, an alternating vote on the prelates' bench for the Collegiate Abbey at Arco (which Leopold had decreed), and—proposed for the first time—a statute to guarantee that a noble from below the Nevis Bridge would always be on the nobles' bench. The Ausschuss did not want to give the Confinants a permanent seat on the peasants' bench, and it also made no decision on the rotation of jurisdictions for the seat and vote they were to share. The Italians were therefore again denied seat and vote on the Ausschuss, at least for the moment. The meeting also rejected Alberti-Poja's proposals for the prelates' and the nobles' benches on grounds that "from time immemorial nobles and prelates are represented 'in cumulo, not according to cantons.' "[11]

After Leopold's death on 1 March 1792 and the succession of his son Francis II, little was done initially for the Italian jurisdictions, perhaps because of the change of rulers or of Francis's preoccupation with the course of the French Revolution and its effect on all Europe. The Ausschuss in Innsbruck remained in session until 10 March, more than a month in all; but many important matters still had to be held over until the next congress or referred to the Aktivitäten for disposition. For example, no deci-

CHAPTER SEVEN

sion had yet been made on how the deputies of the Confines' jurisdictions would rotate for the *Ausschuss* seat they shared.[12]

Not until 1795 did the Confinants finally have two representatives at the small *Ausschuss*. The communes chose Felice Baroni-Cavalcabò, who had represented them so ably in 1790; the cities of Arco and Rovereto chose a Carpentari,[13] presumably the Luigi Carpentari who had taken part in the pre-Diet assemblies of the *pretura* of Rovereto in 1790. Then in 1796 from 30 May to 3 June, the large *Ausschuss* met in Bozen rather than Innsbruck because of the military situation. The purpose of the assembly was to provide for Tyrol's defense. Alois Marcobruni of Arco sat on the cities' bench for this city and Rovereto; only three other cities were represented—Bozen, Meran, Sterzing—all of them sub-Brenner localities. No one from the Confines was among the jurisdictions' representatives. Since the war with France had made the summoning of the entire open Diet impossible, the *Ausschuss* was constitutionally empowered to deliberate and decide in its name.[14] No open Diet, in fact, was held after 1790; with the arrival of Napoleon and his armies, the ensuing wars, and the partition of Tyrol, the *Ausschüsse* also ceased. After peace and Tyrol were restored, Francis granted the princely county an entirely new constitution.

Emperor Francis's Constitutional Patent of 24 March 1816[15] restored the Estate institutions as they would exist until 1848. By 1816 Trent and Brixen, secularized in 1804, were incorporated into Tyrol; and Italian Tyrol was now a compact territory including the former Confines and the former Principality of Trent. Under the new constitution the full Diet was to be convoked only in very special cases, and in fact, it never met; the large *Ausschuss* became the de facto Diet with 52 members, 13 from each Estate (see table 7-1). Seats on the prelates' bench were assigned among others to the Bishops (no longer prince-bishops) of Trent and Brixen and to the envoys of their cathedral chapters. The thirteen noble representatives came from both titled and untitled nobility. The thirteen municipal representatives included two Italians—one for Rovereto and Arco, alternating every two years, and one for Trent and Riva, also alternating every two years. For rural representation Tyrol was divided into ten *Viertel* and three *Bezirke*, each with one representative. Two of these rural representatives were for Italian areas: one for the Welsch Confines (with new boundaries they were no longer enclaves) and one for Trent. The large *Ausschuss* as the Diet would meet only on convocation by the ruler and be dissolved by declaration of the *Gubernium*. The 1816 patent for Tyrol also reunited the offices of *Landeshauptmann* and governor, and to that extent it was a return to the absolutism of Francis's grandmother and uncle.

The *Ausschuss*, as the Diet, was convoked for the first time in 1817 and met yearly in April and May until 1848. The powers of this new *Ausschuss*-Diet, like those of the old open Diet, were the traditional ones of

THE OUTCOME

a *Ständestaat* assembly. Both Francis and Metternich wanted to be sure none of the Diets in the Habsburg lands resembled any of the revolutionary assemblies in France; so the new Tyrolean assembly had no legislative initiative, none of the powers of a modern legislative body. It could only present pleas and representations and could not sanction laws.[16]

In this new political constellation, the Italian representation was clearly inequitable: with approximately half the population and territory, they had only eight of fifty-two representatives (assuming that at least two of the nobles were Italian). The Welsch Tyroleans would continue to register their dissatisfaction; and with the increased assertion of national rights, the problem would prove insoluble within the Habsburg Monarchy, even though the call for political rights was no longer closely intertwined with the Confinant-Etschlander wine competition, as it had been in 1790.

TABLE 7-1

Representation of Estates in Tyrol according to the 1816 Constitutional Patent

Prelates	Nobles	Cities	Jurisdictions
1. Bishop of Brixen	(Six from the "Herren- and Ritterstand" and six from the "Adelstand")	Meran	Viertel Etsch
2. Bishop of Trent		Bozen	Viertel Eisack
3. Cathedral Chapter of Trent		Innsbruck	Viertel Upper Inntal
4. Cathedral Chapter of Brixen		Hall	Viertel Lower Inntal
5. Innsbruck Damenstift		Sterzing	Viertel Vintschgau
6. Abbot of Stams		Lienz	Viertel Pustertal
7. Abbot of Wilten		Glurns with Vils	Viertel Burggrafenamt
8. Abbot of Marienberg		Rattenberg	Viertel Wipptal
9. Abbot of Fiecht		Kufstein	Jurisdiction of Landeck
10. Probst of Neustift		Kitzbühel	The five Lower Inntal jurisdictions: Rattenberg, Kufstein, Kitzbühel, Pillersee, and Hopfgarten
11. Probst of Innichen		Rovereto with Arco	Jurisdiction of the Welsch Confines
12. Envoy of Gries		Trent with Riva	Viertel Trent
13. Envoy of Welsch-Michael		Brixen, Klausen, and Bruneck	

SOURCE: Based on information in Joseph Egger, *Die Tiroler and Vorarlberger* (Wien and Teschen: K. Prochaska, 1882), 146–47.

CHAPTER SEVEN

The Wine Problems

In mid-March 1791, when diPauli left Vienna for home, most of the wine tariff and commerce questions were still unresolved. Leopold, as Grand Duke of Tuscany, had been an avowed advocate of free trade; but on assuming power as sovereign of all the Habsburg lands, he found he had to relax his position so that he would not further inflame the domestic situation that he now faced. Several of Joseph's economic measures had had disruptive effects, and Leopold therefore reinstated or granted some limitations on commerce, especially many of those that his new subjects were seeking as vital to their well-being. But wherever he could, he continued to favor free trade, turning back petitions for tariffs and taxes on individual items. And whenever strict import and export regulations could be eased with no apparent disadvantage to the Monarchy's agriculture or industry, Leopold, with the *Staatsrat's* support, loosened and at times totally abolished these regulations. Furthermore, Leopold rejected out of hand and flatly refused even to negotiate any attempt by the Estates to reacquire their former private tolls and road rights *(Strassenrechte)*.[17] But the import of luxury items, such as foreign wines, were another matter; Leopold II retained the 60 percent tariff even if it led to higher prices on such luxuries since "these articles were demanded only by the privileged and domestic wines lose nothing."[18]

On 4 March 1791 the emperor had ordered that Tyrol's wine problems be sent back to the *Gubernium* for resolution. That order, which had disturbed the wine deputies Cazan and Atzwang, was received in Innsbruck on 15 March, and work was begun on it. But Vienna was not yet totally free of the princely county's wine concerns. On 18 March the Chancellery reported to the *Staatsrat* on two other petitions: yet another one delivered by Cazan and Atzwang for the Etschland's Wine Deputation, again asking for a ban on the import of foreign wines and for confirmation of the deputation's former tax-collecting privileges; and a petition from the Confinants again seeking a guarantee of their right to import their wines into the rest of Tyrol. The *Staatsrat* and the emperor deliberated, and on 25 March Leopold decided to take the Chancellery's advice, which favored the Confinants.[19]

In the meantime, the Etschland wine envoys drafted still another appeal dated 21 March; they again asked for preservation of their ancient rights and objected to Leopold's 4 March order that had sent the wine question to the *Gubernium*. The Diet, argued the Etschlanders, had by its vote recognized the importance of their complaint, supported it, and sent it to Vienna for remedy; nevertheless, the ruler had ignored the Diet's decision and had sent the whole matter back to the *Gubernium* for review. Then, playing the emergency card they had decided on earlier, Cazan and Atzwang asked that a record be kept of all wines coming up over the Nevis

THE OUTCOME

Bridge, Trentine and Confinant, until the question was entirely settled. They concluded: "In sorrow and anguish, we Etschlanders, waiting on the brink of ruin, most humbly and faithfully commend ourselves to all-highest grace and justice."[20]

Within two months, the Innsbruck *Gubernium's* report was back in Vienna, through the bureaucratic channels, and in the emperor's hands for decision by 21 May. The wine interests all along had been asking for economic relief of one sort or another, and as the decrees would show, their pleas had not gone entirely unheeded. Before the *Ausschuss* assembled for the summer meeting, new wine taxes favoring the Etschland (but not tariffs at the Nevis) were a reality. At the 8 July 1791 meeting, the *Steuercompromiss* decided that there was not further need to consider the Etschland's wine grievances because "in the meantime the wine taxes had again been introduced."[21] The wine interests, both German and Italian, won another point: a 17 August decree, which again permitted the hereditary lands to import foreign wines, did *not* apply to Tyrol, nor did another decree of 25 November on the same matter.[22]

With the change of emperors in March 1792, other, more pressing matters took the new ruler's attention, and Tyrol's wine problems apparently rested until the following summer. Then on 30 June 1792 Francis ruled on Tyrol's wine tariff, undoing some of what his father, uncle, and grandmother had done. For all the hereditary lands, he reintroduced the ban against importing foreign wines in order to favor domestic wine production. However, private persons could still bring wines in for their own use if they had the proper permits, paid the customs tax established in the tariff of the year 1788, and did not import the wines for trade.[23]

But problems persisted. In a 4 May 1793 bill of particulars sent to the *Staatsrat* by the *Directorium*,[24] the new central institution that Francis had created, wine deputy Ignatz Atzwang delivered what he considered legal proof for the Etschland's point of view in the dispute with the Welsch Confines. Three days later Francis took this and other points in the bill of particulars "as information" and decided he would await further reports. He did, however, recognize that Tyrol's grain situation was precarious. In April 1793 he confirmed the existing ban on the export of any of the princely county's grains or grain products and declared the import of these goods to be free.[25] By 4 November Francis was ready to make some decisions on the free movement of wine between German and Welsch Tyrol and on the continued conversion of land to vineyards. For the most part he accepted the *Staatsrat's* proposals, but in one point his ruling constituted a major departure from the view of the Council and of his predecessors. He could not, he said, agree with point 5 of their opinion, which would restrict wine cultivation. The state should not decide these matters, "since it lies in the natural order and fairness, that each proprietor use his land in the way that would yield the greatest profit; and the state would benefit by obtaining the highest taxes on that greatest profit." Although Francis's decision pleased those converting their land into vineyards, it displeased almost everyone else, especially the established vineyard owners and their colleagues.[26]

The Etschland wine growers were totally dissatisfied with their sovereign's philosophical and economic position, and they continued to seek limitations on how much grain-producing land could be converted into growing grapes. Early in 1794, along with some other concerns, they again asked for relief from the unrestricted expansion of vineyards. Francis's decision of 8 March 1794 showed that he still had not changed his mind. His resolution said that if wine cultivation expanded so much that wine became worthless and the vines yielded no more or even less than grain fields, "the farmer (Landmann) will of his own accord abandon the cultivation of wine and give preference to that cultivation which benefits him." But until then, Francis concluded, he wanted the proprietor to be able to use his land as vineyards or grain fields, as he wished.[27]

With the new freedom Francis had given them, the owners of arable land continued, now legally, converting it to vineyards; and the wine-producing Etschland continued to seek relief. By the end of October 1794, there was yet another plea for restrictions. About two weeks later in a lengthy resolution of 17 November, Francis again refused to alter his position. Nothing stood in the way, he said, of the more established vineyard owners expanding their own cultivation; or if growing grain proved more profitable, they could transfer as much of their vineyards as they chose to grain cultivation. There was no need to press them legally to one or the other. Francis now admitted, however, that Tyrol had special circumstances that deserved special attention. The princely county had to import a substantial quantity of grain yearly from foreign lands and pay for it with scarce cash. He therefore asked for "mature consideration and a most judicious debate . . . removed from all pressure" on how to encourage the farmer to cultivate grain. Francis, willing to use a carrot if not a stick to keep Tyroleans growing grain, now ordered his officials and the Estates to examine the matter and to report their advice to him "in good time."[28]

At least one, and perhaps only one, reply to Francis's request still exists: that of 24 November 1794 from the Staatsrat-Chancellery director, Hofrat Vogel. Vogel's response is especially valuable, both because it is one of the few documents of this kind from the period that has not been destroyed and because it gives some indication, through his use of direct quotations, of what the Directorium's and hence the Chancellery's position was on this question. Vogel started by pointing out that the ban against converting arable land to vineyards had been a long-standing one arising from Tyrol's need for grain and the equal need to stem the outflow of cash. Wisely not mentioning any names, Vogel said that the ban had been abolished despite protests from subjects, the Gubernium, and even Francis's Directorium, which attributed the change to a concern "in modern times . . . for the freedom and the capricious use of proprietary things."

THE OUTCOME

Repeated appeals to restore the ban had been turned down, said Vogel, because of the assumption that a cultivator knew best how to use his land to greatest advantage. But the argument was valid, he continued, only from the individual's point of view; if the welfare of the entire land was taken into account, then the result would be different. Except for some owners of newly cleared land, there was general agreement that grain fields were needed more than additional vineyards. If a grain shortage occurred in a neighboring province where Tyrol obtained its grain, then the princely county—no matter how much wine it produced—would be unable to sell or exchange that wine for grain and would therefore be "laid open to unavoidable misery and famine, or to the highest degree of living cost."[29]

The government, said Vogel, had a duty to remedy this situation and to ensure that Tyrol produced enough for its own needs. He said the emperor was considering two alternatives then before him: either to permit the individual the freedom to dispose of his land as he wished; or to support the *Gubernium*, the *Directorium*, the *Staatsrat*, and the Etschlanders and reinstitute the ban. But another possibility did exist, urged Vogel, seconding a suggestion made by a *Staatsrat* colleague, Baron Reischach. The state might offer special rewards to those who expanded grain cultivation and levy a special tax on any arable land turned into vineyards. That would be a compromise between the total freedom the emperor favored and the reintroduction of the ban against new vineyards that almost everyone else preferred. But by 1795 Francis's attention was on France and Napoleon, and the laws from this part of his reign show no change in the regulations on new vineyards.

The Etschlanders did not get much of what they sought, but they did get something. Even though the tax on the Confinants' wines at the Nevis Bridge was not reimposed, new vineyards continued to be planted. But these German vintners were given some relief when Francis decreed new taxes on wine. Two 1793 measures were aimed at the relationship between German and Welsch Tyrolean wines; and in one of these measures, the Etschlanders won a point. First, on 22 November the *Gubernium* in Innsbruck published an order for wine taxes. The order stated that after preliminary, careful deliberation with the *Viertel* representatives on the Etsch and the representatives from other non-wine-growing localities (but not with the Confinants), a decision had been made that circumstances warranted the following wine tax, or *Kammer* tax, for 1793 and 1794.

Per Ihren*		**Per Eimer***	
(in florins and kreuzers)		(in florins and kreuzers)	
Wine 1st class	9 fl. — kr.	Wine 1st class	6 fl. 32 8/11 kr.
_____ 2nd class	8 fl. 30 kr.	_____ 2nd class	6 fl. 9 10/11 kr.
_____ 3rd class	7 fl. 45 kr.	_____ 3rd class	5 fl. 38 2/11 kr.

*An ihren is approximately 77.5 liters.   *An eimer is approximately 70 liters.

CHAPTER SEVEN

Wine of the first class included Bozen, Griess, Aichholz, Kurtatsch, Traminer, and "fit Vergenner" wines. The second class included "the worse but still stable Vergenner." And the third class was those wines from areas "lying below Botzen" and places not named in the list above, that is, the Welsch Tyrolean wines. The proclamation then pointed out that "thereby freedom of trade and commerce are in no way restricted, but present taxes shall be taken as a guideline only in the case of no actually concluded or provable contract of sale," or a case in which legal opposition was raised.[30]

The second tax measure on wines issued in 1793 also gave the Etsch-landers at least one part of what they had asked for: the wines coming from Welsch into German Tyrol were to be declared and entered into a book at the first *Intrinseco* toll station. The decree, to take effect 31 December, also reestablished Joseph II's 1786 and 1789 *Intrinseco* assessment that put German and Welsch Tyrolean wine-producing areas on an equal footing by assessing each six kreuzers per eimer of wine and 30 kreuzers per eimer of brandy. The decree also said that anyone caught smuggling Venetian wines would be punished "not only with the *Kommissum*, but with the *Dupplum* of the same," that is, with a double tax or fine. However, if the smuggler was poor and could not pay the *Dupplum*, then he could pay the *Kommissum* and undergo corporal punishment instead of further fines.[31]

When in December 1794 Francis's new wine taxes, or *Kammer* taxes, for 1795 and 1796 in Tyrol were published, the Etschlanders were favored even more.

Per Ihren
(in florins and kreuzers)

	1793 and 1794	1795 and 1796
Wine 1st class	9 fl. — kr.	8 fl. 45 kr.
_____ 2nd class	8 fl. 30 kr.	8 fl. 15 kr.
_____ 3rd class	7 fl. 45 kr.	7 fl. 45 kr.

Per Eimer
(in florins and kreuzers)

	1793 and 1794	1795 and 1796
Wine 1st class	6 fl. 32 8/11 kr.	6 fl. 21 9/11 kr.
_____ 2nd class	6 fl. 9 10/11 kr.	6 fl. —
_____ 3rd class	5 fl. 38 2/11 kr.	5 fl. 38 2/11 kr.

The tax was lowered on all but the Confinants' wines, which were included in wines of the third class; all the other wines were taxed 15 kreuzers less per ihren, which made German Tyrolean wines slightly cheaper than they had been.[32]

The Confinants were therefore not quite as successful with their wine *domande* as they had been with their request for seat and vote in the assemblies. They could still bring as much wine into German Tyrol as they wished, and the tariff at the Nevis Bridge was not reimposed, but the excise tax was higher. And as they had with wine, they also won some points and lost some points on their language grievances.

Language

Leopold had issued several ordinances on language shortly after he ascended the throne. In general, he had eased but not repealed what his mother and brother had done. Language regulations primarily affected those who entered state service and the schools that prepared them, and Leopold too preferred that all his state servants use the same language, at least in communicating with one another and with the central government. His early changes had relaxed or changed the requirements for local language use (see chapter 4). Now that he had all the Estate grievances in hand, he made further changes.

On 15 April 1791, a month after the last Tyrolean Estate deputy left Vienna, Leopold declared that only those who were graduated from German-language universities in the hereditary lands were eligible to become advocates, or lawyers.[33] "The exercise of advocacy in all the German hereditary lands without exception of the city of Vienna shall be granted to all those who have received the Gradum Doctoratus at one of the German hereditary land universities, after the prescribed examination." Attending a university but not receiving a degree (the frequent practice of the nobility) or receiving a degree from any other university was not sufficient to attain the advocature. However, a grandfather clause admitted to the further examination for the advocature those who had already attended a non-German university in the hereditary lands and had satisfied other requirements.[34]

The implications of this law were enormously disadvantageous to the nobility and to areas that were not German speaking in the otherwise German hereditary lands, areas such as Italian Tyrol. Leopold had apparently not intended to injure these national groups, at least not the Italians, and within three months he provided a remedy. A court decree that took effect in Tyrol on 12 July 1791 provided relief specifically for Habsburg subjects who had attended the University of Pavia. In the future, said the decree, degrees earned by such students at Pavia "shall give to the same all rights and privileges belonging to the other students who have been graduated at the universities in the hereditary lands."[35] Francis II expanded the rights of Pavia degree holders even further. In response to an inquiry of 9 April 1796, he ruled that Pavia graduates, if they wanted to receive their doctoral dignity in the hereditary lands, could not be further examined on those subjects that they had been taught at Pavia. But for subjects not taught there and required for a doctorate in the German universities of the hereditary lands, they would need to undergo rigorous examination.[36]

Easing of the language regulation, like many other laws, also had unintended effects. Leopold had removed the requirement that students have a knowledge of German before they could attend a gymnasium. By 1794 the prefect of Rovereto's gymnasium, Giovanni Battista Socrella (appointed by Maria Theresa and renounced by Clementino Vannetti for being a Ladin) reported that while the earlier imperial order requiring the language had convinced many students to apply themselves seriously to German, Rovereto's young of both sexes were now thronging to study French. That, he said, worked to the benefit of only a few and the detriment of many. And the students of the normal school, who were training to teach at the gymnasium, preferred Italian to German. Yet the government's intentions had not changed. In 1794 and 1795 a special study commission worked out a "Plan to Promote the German Language in the Italian Confines," a plan that remained without much effect because Francis II's government was "less feared than that of Joseph II."[37] The gymnasium professors continued using and promoting the Italian language. Ultimately, the language question was pushed aside and then became temporarily moot when Napoleon partitioned Tyrol and the Confinants found themselves in his Kingdom of Italy; here their own language was the official language. But with their return to Habsburg rule, the language problem returned. That problem was, in effect, insoluble not only in Tyrol but in almost all the Habsburg lands. It remained until the end of the Monarchy in 1918, and it still exists in many of the successor states today, including the former Etschland, now the Alto Adige Region in northern Italy.

The only loose end remaining from Italian Tyrol's 1790 grievances was to issue the decree on the inheritance rights of their daughters.

Daughters' Inheritance Rights

Leopold's decree on Tyrol's grievances in matters of justice was published in Innsbruck on 17 May 1791 and included his decision on the inheritance rights of daughters; it was essentially what the deputies had heard at their early 1791 concertation with the grievance commission. For those Tyrolean women who married in a territory that had laws limiting the inheritance and property rights of daughters, the Habsburg inheritance law would not apply in full. These Tyrolean women would have only those rights that provably belonged to the daughters in the district or country into which they had married. The full provisions of the Habsburg inheritance law would apply only where daughters had equal rights with sons.[38] On this grievance the Confinants were without opposition from any source, except perhaps prospective foreign bridegrooms. The Italians were therefore quickly and completely successful in obtaining what they sought for their daughters and for control of their family property.

CONCLUSION

Upon their accession Maria Theresa, her sons, and her grandson each faced different situations and brought with them varying philosophical views toward the task of governing. Their attitudes toward centralization and the competing demands made by the Estates, their attitudes toward the nationalities and national minorities, and their use of the traditional divide-and-conquer methods are all amply illustrated in their approaches to governing eighteenth-century Tyrol, both Italian and German.

After Maria Theresa's comparatively gentle absolutism and Joseph II's more forceful approach to reform, Leopold II found that he could not be as unswerving in pursuit of *Gesammtmonarchie* as they had been; he had to back down and give in on some policies to prevent the collapse or breakup of his inheritance. In addition, for philosophical and political reasons, he preferred to work with and through the Estates even if they did not readily comply with his wishes. And although his revocation of certain language requirements and easing of others did help the Monarchy survive for another 130 years, these steps did not contribute to the unified state that his predecessors and forebears had been working so hard to build. From the point of view of participatory government, increasing the role of the Estates was admirable, but it also strengthened the particularistic tendencies of his peoples. Francis II continued Leopold's constitutional and cultural policies, but he departed from many long-standing economic policies.

Francis II was, in fact, a superb constitutional monarch, much closer to his father than to this grandmother and uncle in dealing with the Estates and lands. For example, Maria Theresa never convoked the Estates of Tyrol despite her repeated promises, and she convoked others only when she absolutely had to or when she was assured of their compliance. Joseph was even less willing to deal with the Estates in most of his lands, convoking no Diets in Hungary or Tyrol and assembling others only when their compliance was assured. Leopold, however, preferred politically and philosophically to work with the Estates and reestablished the constitutions of his many lands. Francis adhered to constitutional requirements, convoking the Diets as often as required and otherwise adhering to the laws of his lands—respecting, almost to a fault, the rule of law in a *Rechtsstaat*.

CONCLUSION

Perhaps the biggest surprise in Francis's approach and policies was his abandonment of centuries-old economic controls in favor of a market-oriented agriculture and economy—surprising because of his reputation epitomized in Viktor Bibl's statement, "He forgot nothing and he learned nothing." The view of Francis as a ruler unwilling to innovate clearly must be reexamined. As noted before, Francis was closer to the centralizing policies of his grandmother or his uncle in attempts to strengthen central influence. After the defeat of Napoleon when Francis took control of a restored Tyrol, he reunited the offices of *Landeshauptmann* and governor, undoing what his father had done; the occupant of the office was appointed by Vienna, and the Estates again lost their independent spokesman.

Italian Tyrol in the second half of the eighteenth century and Habsburg policies toward it also show clearly pre-Napoleonic national feeling as well as some early indications of separatism and irredentism. Vienna's actions contributed to the growth of *italianità* in Tyrol and of national feeling in other lands. The rulers supported the establishment of all kinds of cultural institutions—academies, learned societies, patriotic or agricultural improvement societies (at the beginning, these societies were the same), national theaters, and the studies of local languages and even their use in some universities (such as in the Italian or Czech lands). In the eighteenth century the fostering of national cultures did not seem so contradictory to the parallel attempt to force the use of German in higher schools, courts, and government administration. The Habsburgs were not attempting to Germanize all aspects of life in the lands they ruled and were quite willing to have children educated in their own languages; indeed, Maria Theresa's General School Ordinance provided for instruction in local languages in the primary schools, or *Volksschule*. But in their support of non-German languages and cultural institutions, the Habsburgs undermined the attempt to have German used in higher schools and government. They also laid the foundation for future problems arising from nationalist and separatist sentiments and the resultant pulling of the Monarchy in directions that none of the eighteenth-century rulers would have endorsed.

The close examination of Italian Tyrol has provided both a window on how the Habsburgs approached and handled these national developments and the local or internal sources of such movements in the pre-Napoleonic period. Much that is here can be applied to understanding other parts of the Monarchy. Leopold inherited situations that were growing increasingly worse in each of his lands, and where national minorities or other disadvantaged groups were available for him to turn to, he did. The Princely County of Tyrol and its Italians provide an interesting example since Leopold ruled long enough to accomplish most of what he sought there. And although he did not have enough time to complete what he started else-

CONCLUSION

where, applying the example of Tyrol may give a good indication of what he wanted or intended in other Habsburg lands.

Leopold used similar techniques not only with national minority groups, but also with other disadvantaged or "out" groups in the Monarchy. He encouraged them and supported their efforts for a fairer, more equitable role in their lands, at the same time making use of their demands to quiet incipient rebellions being led by dominant groups in some of his lands. He therefore gave his support to these "out" groups based on self-interest and because he believed their cause, in most instances, to be fair and just.

For example, in 1790 the Hungarian nobles, the only real political force in the kingdom, were rebelling against the half-century or more of innovation and loss of power and were threatening to dethrone the Habsburgs and turn to a new dynasty. Armed now with a knowledge of events in Tyrol, it should come as no surprise that Leopold marshalled several sources of discontent to help him pacify the Magyar nobility. The burghers of Hungary's royal free towns, essentially excluded from the kingdom's government and Diet,* now advanced a claim inter alia to a political role in their land. There is no question that the burghers were directed by Vienna and "no doubt that the sole moving force behind the burgher movement was Leopold II."[1] The rebellion-minded Hungarian nobles were quick to perceive what was happening, to realize the potential danger of an active and organized burgher movement, and to negotiate more willingly with Leopold—exactly the effect he hoped to achieve. The Magyars were further encouraged to cooperate when Leopold used a discontented national minority, the Serbs, as additional leverage. Against the protests of the Magyar nobles, he permitted the Serbs to hold a national congress (which opened on 1 September 1790), and he gave them their own Illyrian Court Chancellery (which his son subsequently abolished). By these and other maneuvers and by promising to uphold their traditional constitution, Leopold was able to pacify the Magyars and on 15 November 1790 to be crowned King of Hungary.

In the Grand Principality of Transylvania, Leopold also had to deal with the effects of Joseph II's reforms—especially that of concivility. Participation in the principality's public life, according to the system established after the Reformation, was limited to those who belonged to an official nation and a "received" religion.[2] Offices were traditionally filled by apportioning them equitably among these groups. Joseph, in an early nondiscrimination law, forbade awarding offices on the basis of nationality, thereby totally disrupting the carefully balanced Transylvanian system and presenting Leopold with another incipient rebellion. Here too, to dampen rebellious spirits, Leopold encouraged the "enemies of his enemies"—in this instance the Wallachians, or Romanians. Mostly Orthodox in religion and peasant in

---

*All the royal free towns together were entitled to only one vote at the Diet.

CONCLUSION

social origin, they constituted neither an official nation nor a "recognized" religion; they therefore had no role in the political life of the principality. And it is among the Romanians of Transylvania that the closest parallels with Italian Tyrol can be found.

In the last years of Joseph II's reign, after the academies were founded in Tyrol, the Romanians founded several literary societies in the grand principality. These societies had the express purpose of promoting the general welfare of their nation and of dealing with strictly literary matters, but just what part these societies may have played in organizing the 1790–91 Romanian movement is unclear. They probably provided informal meeting places for discussion as well as the leadership and membership of that movement. In any event, in the spring of 1790 after Leopold had ascended the throne, a protest movement swept across Transylvania's Romanians and, as Keith Hitchins wrote, "the uniformity of the demands made in the numerous local meetings . . . *suggests some central coordination*."³ Hitchins did not speculate on the nature of that central coordination; but he showed clearly that the priests of both the Orthodox and the Unitate churches led the Romanians at the local level in their quest for equal rights. That Leopold was also at the center, though not the *prima causa*, here too is more than possible.

Like the Serbs in Hungary, the Romanians in Transylvania requested the right to hold a national congress with both lay and ecclesiastical delegates from both Romanian confessions to discuss matters of general concern to their nation. At the grand principality's 1790 Diet in Klausenburg (Kolozsvár, Cluj, Napoca, Claudiopolis), the Romanians and the responses they evoked often have a familiar ring to someone knowledgeable about the situation of the Italians in Tyrol. The Transylvanian Diet opened on 21 December 1790, after Leopold had been crowned King of Hungary and the Tyrolean assembly had long been adjourned. In Klausenburg, the Romanians presented language grievances, asked that they be recognized as an official nation with political representation and participation in the institutions of the principality, and that the Orthodox religion be a received religion. Leopold considered the Wallachian bishops' petition for participation in the Diet to be "fair and beneficial."⁴

As he had with Tyrol, Leopold turned the Romanians' petition back to the Transylvanian Diet for deliberation—with the instruction that they assure to the Transylvanian Romanians "an equitable role and share of the offices among the nations" and "other freedoms through a public law without difference of religion."⁵ And again as in Tyrol, the matter bounced back and forth between Vienna and Klausenberg. The Romanians, too, drafted and redrafted their petition; the final *Supplex Libellus Valachorum*, as it is known, was sent to the emperor on 28 March 1791. The Transylvanian Chancellery and chancellor completely rejected the petition, their arguments echoing those in Tyrol: that the Romanians had been conquered by

CONCLUSION

war and were therefore not entitled to such equality; that if they were made into a fourth nation and admitted to participation in political life, it would disrupt the constitutional life of the grand principality; that there was no need of this anyway because the Romanians' interests were represented by those in whose midst they lived; that they should not be allowed a national congress because they were not a nation; and that if they were allowed to become a nation, this too would disrupt constitutional life and cause social and political turmoil. But the chancellor did recommend a guarantee of their "civil rights and freedom of worship."[6] The Romanians of Transylvania, however, were not as fortunate as Tyrol's Italians and did not achieve most of their 1790 goals; Leopold did not live long enough to ensure that the Romanians would receive equitable treatment in their land no matter how they may have become part of it.[7] Nevertheless, by applying the Tyrolean example and with knowledge of what Leopold did urge on the Klausenburg Diet, we can assume that he intended to support the Romanians in Transylvania as he had the Italians in Tyrol.

Leopold's role in advancing the Italian movement in Tyrol, the burgher and Serbian movements in Hungary, and the Romanian national movement in Transylvania seems clear. But equally interesting, if somewhat less evident, is his attempt to control and lead those who were threatening rebellion and who opposed these movements. In Tyrol when Leopold's plenipotentiary, Count Franz Enzenberg, arrived in Innsbruck, he immediately joined the Etschlanders. The count was acting with Leopold's consent since the emperor most assuredly ascertained Enzenberg's personal views and intentions and felt assured of the count's ultimate loyalty before the appointment was made. In Klausenburg the court commissar to the Transylvanian Diet (Enzenberg's counterpart) was an Italian Tyrolean, Baron Giovanni Nepomuco Cristani di Rallo; he played a role similar to Enzenberg's, siding openly with those who opposed the Romanians and who were the leaders of the threatening revolt.[8] Leopold, at least in these two instances, had his representatives or agents working on both sides of the fence. In Tyrol, diarist Benedetto Sardagna, who had kept one of the accounts of the Diet's proceedings, became a police official in Vienna almost immediately after the Diet ended and continued his career in police service at least through the decade of the 1790s. Sardagna, too, was apparently working for Leopold. There is also some evidence, yet to be investigated, indicating that Leopold may have pursued similar activities in Galicia between 1790 and the second partition.

A double role of this kind is very much in keeping with Leopold's personality, his political abilities, his propensity for wholesale information gathering, and his general distrust of others. To assume that his operatives also worked within and even at the head of opposing parties and factions at other of the 1790 Diets is not unreasonable. An investigation of Leopold's involvement in these Diets would be warranted, worthwhile, and obviously

CONCLUSION

interesting. It would also contribute much to understanding the politicization of the early national movements in the Monarchy.

The politicization of Italian sentiments in Tyrol, a process to which Leopold contributed, also had its own native soil in which to grow. The Confinants, especially their upper strata, had been very much a part of the Italian humanistic tradition and of the Italian and European Enlightenments, including the central European emphasis on such concerns as defining and cultivating nationality and national languages. By the second half of the eighteenth century, Tyrol's Italians were deeply involved in questions and debates about *italianità*, especially their own. This intensification of national awareness grew from its own cultural and intellectual roots in their area and as a response to the Habsburgs' reforms in the eighteenth century. The Welsch Tyroleans, or Confinants, expressed their sentiments in pro-Italian and anti-German histories, poetry, essays, and speeches and petitions at the 1790 Diet. In that year as they sought fairer treatment in the princely county, their primary support came from the emperor, his bureaucracy, the governor Leopold inherited in Innsbruck, and the small group that followed Governor Sauer. The opposition came from Tyrol's Estates, controlled by the Etschlanders who felt their economic well-being threatened by the Confinants and therefore fought them with all the means at their command—at least on two of the four grievances for which the Italians sought remedy.

The Etschlanders wanted no part of the Confinants' request for seat and vote at the Diet and other assemblies, although gradually they did back down as Leopold urged fairer treatment. The sub-Brenner Germans, however, continued to oppose free movement of the Confinants' wines within Tyrol or treatment of those wines as Tyrolean rather than foreign products. In the Confinants' *domande*, therefore, the Etschlanders saw a direct threat to what remained of their political and economic dominance after the reforms of Maria Theresa and Joseph II. And these German Tyroleans gave way only gradually as Leopold pushed, nudged, threatened, and commanded that the Italians have more equitable treatment. Francis II in general followed through on Leopold's plans for seat and vote for Tyrol's Italians. But the Etschlanders' delaying tactics did have one positive result from their point of view: although the Confinants' wines continued to move freely in Tyrol, a tax that Francis placed on all Tyrolean wines was higher on Confinant than on Etschland wines. Francis also made other adjustments in wine policy. He disappointed both the Etschlanders and Confinants when he ignored the advice of almost everyone around him and reversed the centuries-old ban against turning new land into vineyards without permission. He was willing to see competition increase for both the Confinants and the Etschlanders and to leave regulation of grape growing and wine production to the vicissitudes of a market economy. Both the Confinants and Etschlanders therefore won on some points

CONCLUSION

and lost on others when it came to economic questions, especially those related to wine.

On the language question, too, the Italians of Tyrol gained some ground and lost some. They were no longer forced to know German for admission to their gymnasium or normal school; but they were strongly encouraged to master that language if they wanted to enter public service in any way. The people of the Confines could henceforth use their own language in bringing cases to court and were to be kept informed in that language of judicial proceedings and decisions. But the judicial and court officials and the lawyers had to know both German and Italian as preparation for taking the advocates' examination. Graduates of the university at Pavia were put on an equal footing, after a temporary disability, with those who earned their degrees at German-language universities in the hereditary lands. However, the Italians in Tyrol were denied the right to use their own language at the Diet, in 1790 and in the next century. Tyrol was therefore prevented, for better or worse, from becoming a truly bilingual province.

Finally, the Confinants' complaint on the inheritance rights Joseph II had given their daughters, especially when those daughters married foreigners, was immediately and simply resolved. A reciprocal arrangement was decreed, requiring that a Tyrolean woman's rights be the same as those legally granted to women in her husband's homeland. Since this solution disturbed no Tyrolean or Habsburg interest, it was accepted without opposition.

Tyrol's Italians—despite the opposition of the German Etschland and with the strong support of Leopold II—sought and attained a great deal through their 1790 efforts. What had begun as a linguistically and historically based nationalism was by the time of the 1790 Diet a political movement with well-developed grievances to present and alternatives to put forward. Leopold and then Francis, preferring not to heed the alternative appeal for separation from German Tyrol, worked toward equitable treatment for these Italians. That effort continued even after 1804 when the incorporation of the Brixen and Trentine principalities greatly increased the number of Italians and the proportion of Tyrol that they inhabited. But despite the gains, Welsch Tyrol never achieved a truly equitable role in the land. Nevertheless, many of the arguments used by both sides in 1790 would resound again and again, one of the loudest resonances coming with the 1848 revolutions.

The linguistic border at Salurn just below Bozen was and is an acknowledged dividing line between Italian-speaking and German-speaking areas; that line became a rallying point in 1848. The Innsbruck Diet of that year was the first modern assembly of Tyrol, with people, not Estates, represented. But the Italian Tyroleans were not allowed to participate in any way comparable to their numbers and refused entirely to attend the Innsbruck assembly. They did, however, attend the parliaments at Kremsier and

CONCLUSION

Frankfurt, where many of them sought their own crownland within the Monarchy. At Kremsier a Welsch Tyrolean referred to the Salurn border as a dividing line on the language map between Germans and Italians. That line, he said, was evidence "that here no mixing exists as in Galicia, Bohemia or Moravia. In Tyrol the German element stops where the Italian begins."[9] And at the Frankfurt Paliament one of his compatriots pointed to Salurn as the place where "nature has created a dividing wall between two nations. The peoples have respected it and national policy will heed it in the future."[10]

In fact, the Italians never again attended Tyrolean provincial assemblies in any number. They demanded instead—at the very least—their own crownland, an alternative they had first proposed in 1790. After the formation of the Kingdom of Italy in 1860, irredentist voices began to be heard. These voices became increasingly vocal and persuasive to their fellow Italians, although even through World War I there were Italians who merely sought their own Habsburg crownland. With the border changes following World War I, not only did Italian Tyrol become part of Italy, but sub-Brenner German Tyrol did as well. That border adjustment brought with it a mirror image of the problem in the eighteenth and nineteenth centuries: there is a now a sizable German minority in an Italian state. That situation was further complicated in the 1930s when the Fascist government transferred Italian population from the south into the Bolzano/Bozen area. Now it is the Italians who must deal with a minority population.

As for Leopold II, he was an essential mover, if not a prime mover, for Tyrol's Italians in 1790, as he was for disadvantaged groups and national minorities in other of his lands. He himself, personally and through his agents and confidants, had a hand in encouraging and politicizing Welsch Tyrol's grievances, for his own reasons and because of his sincere belief in the fairness and justice of what Italian Tyrol wanted. The Italian Tyroleans themselves were more fortunate than some of the other groups because Leopold lived long enough to see to it that most of their grievances were favorably resolved or were on the way to resolution. But other groups, such as the Romanians in Transylvania, were not as fortunate; although many aspects of their 1790 movement for national political and other rights paralleled those of Tyrol's Italians, Leopold's reign was not long enough for him to resolve the grievances of the 1790–91 *Supplex Libellus Valachorum.* Nevertheless, while he reigned, he helped stimulate the national consciousness that was beginning to grow among his peoples. Many of the measures he enacted, therefore, had the effect of arresting the long march toward building a *Gesammtmonarchie*, begun by Maximilian I. By giving the Estates a greater role, by fostering those 1790 national movements, and by making possible a greater use of languages other than German, he also contributed, albeit unwittingly, to those forces that within a little more than a century would help put an end to the Habsburg Monarchy.

APPENDIX A

The Habsburg Bureaucracy

A fringe benefit of this study has been the journey involved through the eighteenth-century central bureaucracy of the Habsburg Monarchy and the feeling thus gained of how that bureaucracy functioned. Most of the *Hofstellen* (main parts of the central administration) that existed at the end of the eighteenth century had been created or reshaped by Maria Theresa, then rearranged by her and by each of her successors. They were all trying to cope not only with organizing the administration of their many lands into that elusive *Gesammtmonarchie*, but also with establishing some kind of clearing house or funnel, or both, through which all matters would pass on their way to the monarch. These attempts resulted in Maria Theresa's *Directorium*, which she herself dismantled; Joseph II's *Vereinigte Hofstelle* (established in 1782 by uniting the Bohemian-Austrian Court Chancellery, the *Hofkammer*, and the *Ministerial-Banco-Deputation*); Leopold II's ungluing of the *Vereinigte Hofstelle* into its separate parts; and finally (for this study), the *Directorium* of Francis II (established 1793).

Not all the central bureaucracy is pertinent to this study. But several *Hofstellen* do play an active role: the Bohemian-Austrian Court Chancellery (or occasionally the *Vereinigte Hofstelle*), the *Oberste Justizstelle*, the *Hofkammer*, and the *Hofrechnungskammer* (or *Hofrechenkammer*). What follows is a kind of road map, or guide, through that bureaucratic maze.

The *Oberste Justizstelle* (established 1754) was, for the German hereditary lands and Galicia, both a supreme court of appeal in criminal and civil matters and a ministry of justice; it also had a role in drafting legislation.

The Bohemian-Austrian Court Chancellery (*Böhmisch-Österreichische Hofkanzley*) was established in 1760 by uniting the Bohemian and Austrian Court Chancelleries. It was concerned with all publico-political matters, contribution and tax decisions, and ecclesiastical concerns. Petitions, problems, and grievances on these matters were sent to this chancellery from the *Gubernia* or *Regierungen* (see below) in the regional administrative capitals. Here, questions were discussed, pertinent documents examined, and a report made to the sovereign through the *Staatsrat* (see below) with accompanying recommendations and dossier. Sixteen *Hofräte* or court councillors were at the Chancellery, six of whom had responsibility for one or more provinces. Each *Hofrat* was also responsible for one of the main concerns of the state, for example, ecclesiastical matters and tariffs. Each *Hofrat* was assigned four or five rooms in the Chancellery to accommodate all his areas of concern.

The *Staatsrat* (or State Council) was established in 1760 by Maria Theresa. It was the link between the ruler and the rest of the bureaucracy. The flow of paperwork from the periphery toward the center went, first, from the local level to the *Gubernium* in the regional capital, then to the Chancellery (or *Oberste Justizstelle*, or *Hofkammer*) in Vienna, then to

APPENDIX A

the *Staatsrat* to be prepared for the ruler. When a matter arrived, it was assigned to a councillor—or, as he was sometimes called, a *Staatsminister*—and summarized by his *Conzipist*. The councillor then reviewed the summary and circulated it among the other members of the *Staatsrat*, beginning with the most recently appointed and moving up in seniority; each added his *Votum* with supporting arguments. If the vote was unanimous, a draft decree was submitted to the ruler along with the summaries and recommendations. If the vote was not unanimous, the monarch received extracts of the individual *Vota* and, if needed, the documents themselves. The ruler then made the final decision, or "resolution," sometimes accepting the recommendations, sometimes rejecting them in part or as a whole. When necessary, consultations were held with the chiefs of the *Hofstellen*. Each member of the *Staatsrat* was sworn to give his true opinion, and from the records that still exist, apparently did. The emperor's candor was also evident. By the end of Joseph's reign, the members of the *Staatsrat* were Count Karl Friedrich Hatzfeld, Prince Kaunitz (who was usually busy elsewhere), Baron Kressel, Baron Reischach, Baron Carlo Antonio Martini, Friedrich Eger, and Baron Izdenczy. The first three were Bohemian nobles, the fourth a Swabian, the fifth a Tyrolean, the sixth an Austrian, and the seventh a Hungarian. Most of these "state ministers" appear—at least briefly—in this study, especially during the post-Diet politicking in Vienna.

The *Hofkammer* (established 1527) collected and administered the crown's own financial assets. Subordinated to it were all the regional or provincial *Kammern*, or treasuries, except for those of Lombardy and the Austrian Netherlands; but the *Hofkammer* also received the surpluses from these areas too.

The *Hofrechnungskammer* (also called the *Hofrechenkammer*) (established 1760) served essentially as the Monarchy's auditors and accountants, examining the accounts for all state incomes and expenses. Joseph II subordinated to the *Hofrechnungskammer* the bookkeeping and auditing of the individual lands, Estates, cities, and the two *Rechenkammern* in the Austrian Netherlands and Lombardy. He also assigned to its supervision the accounting in Hungary and Transylvania.

On the provincial or regional level were *Gubernia* or *Regierungen* (governments). Each *Gubernium* had a "Gouverneur" and each *Regierung* a "Präsident" at its head; he was named by the ruler and represented the ruler. Otherwise, the *Gubernium* and *Regierung* were exactly the same institutionally. During the eighteenth century, as the *Gubernia* expanded their range of activities, they gradually displaced the role of the Estates in governing the lands; this was especially so in Tyrol. Often, more than one land was included in a *Gubernium*. In the sixteenth century the Habsburg's German hereditary lands had been divided administratively into Upper Austria (or sometimes Upper and Anterior Austria), that is, Tyrol, Vorarlberg, and the Vorlande; Lower Austria, or Austria above the Enns

APPENDIX A

and Austria below the Enns; and Inner Austria, or Styria, Carinthia, Carniola, then Trieste, Görz, and Gradisca. These divisions persisted through the eighteenth century and were part of the accepted and used *Kanzleisprache*. But by the end of that century, the expressions Upper Austria and Lower Austria also began to be used to indicate Austria above the Enns and below the Enns (present-day Upper and Lower Austria).

Other elements of the bureaucracy existed, but because they do not enter into this study, they are not discussed here.

APPENDIX B

Alternate Geographical Names

Form Used in This Study	Other Forms
Arco *(Italian)*	Arch *(German)*
Bozen *(German)*	Bolzano *(Italian)*
Brenner *(German)*	Brennero *(Italian)*
Brixen *(German)*	Bressanone *(Italian)*
Chur *(German)*	Ciora *(Italian)*; Coire *(French)*
Eisack *(German)*	Isarco *(Italian)*
Etsch *(German)*	Adige *(Italian)*
Folgaria *(Italian)*	Filgereut, Vilgreit *(German)*
Flavon *(Italian)*	Flaum, Pflaumb *(German)*
Graubünden *(German)*	Grigioni *(Italian)*; Grisons *(French)*
Gresta *(Italian)*	Agrest *(German)*
Grigno *(Italian)*	Grimb *(German)*
Innsbruck	Oenipons *(Latin)*
Ivano *(Italian)*	Ivan *(German)*
Klausenburg *(German)*	Kolozsvár *(Hungarian)*; Cluj, Napoca *(Romanian)*; Claudiopolis *(Latin)*
Lemberg *(German)*	Lvov *(Russian)*; Lwów *(Polish)*; Léopol *(French)*
Levico *(Italian)*	Levig *(German)*
Meran *(German)*	Merano *(Italian)*
Nevis *(German)*	Lavis *(Italian)*
Nonsberg *(German)*	Val di Non *(Italian)*
Passeiertal *(German)*	Val Passiria *(Italian)*
Pressburg *(German)*	Pozsony *(Hungarian)*; Bratislava *(Slovak)*
Primiero *(Italian)*	Primör *(German)*
Pustertal *(German)*	Val Pusteria *(Italian)*
Riva *(Italian)*	Reif *(German)*
Rovereto *(Italian)*	Rovereit *(German)*; Roboretum *(Latin)*
Sacco *(Italian)*	Sack *(German)*
Salurn *(German)*	Salorno *(Italian)*
Sterzing *(German)*	Vipiteno *(Italian)*; Vipitenum *(Latin)*
Sulzberg *(German)*	Val di Sol *(Italian)*
Telvano *(Italian)*	Telfan *(German)*
Transylvania *(English; Latin)*	Erdély *(Hungarian)*; Ardeaul *(Romanian)*
Trent *(English)*	Trento *(Italian)*; Trient *(German)*; Tridentum *(Latin)*
Valsugana *(Italian)*	Valsugan *(German)*
Vintschgau *(German)*	Val Venosta *(Italian)*
Welschmichael *(German)*	San Michele *(Italian)*

APPENDIX C

Thumbnail Biographies

Antonio **ALBERTI di POJA** (?–?), a count, was the first representative of the cities of Rovereto and Arco on Tyrol's small *Ausschuss*, the one that met in February 1792. The family traces its origins to the House of d'Albret, Duke of Luines, in France. During the Guelf-Ghibelline struggle, the Albertis moved from upper Italy into Tyrol. In 1774 three brothers were elevated to counts of the Empire: Alberto Vigilio, a councillor of the Prince-Bishop of Trent; Francesco Antonio, canon at Trent; and Antonio Clemente, then a *Kammerrat* in Salzburg.

Joseph Vincenz von **ASCHAUER** (?–?) came from a family that owned a very productive brass works in Kramsach-Achenrain, one that produced for markets all over Europe. Ennobled in 1675 with the predicate von und zu Achenrain, the Aschauers expanded their industrial activity, began moving into state service and were immatriculated in Tyrol in 1772. Joseph Vincenz von Aschauer first served in the *Gubernium* in Innsbruck and under Joseph II became syndic of the Estates, where as a loyal supporter and implementer of the emperor's policies he earned the undying enmity of the Estates. Aschauer was forced from office in August 1790, went to Vienna, and later returned as *Kreishauptmann* in Imst, then was made a baron, and subsequently transferred to the diplomatic service. After Napoleon's defeat, Aschauer played a role in the return of Tyrol to Austria. A freemason, he belonged to the lodge "Zu den drei Bergen" in Innsbruck.

Ignatz **ATZWANG(er) von und zu Reiglheim** (*1744–1800*). In 1613 Adam Atzwanger was accepted as a burgher of Bozen on payment of 15 florins; in 1682 he became *Bürgermeister*, and in 1667–68 another Atzwanger (Franz) occupied the same office. The Atzwang family's home in Bozen became the locus of an Illuminati or Rosicrucian lodge founded there in 1780 and an Egyptian-rite Cagliostro lodge in 1789. Atzwang was one of the two deputies sent to Vienna by the Wine Deputation tax farmers in 1790–91.

The **BARONI di CAVALCABÒ** family, along with the Fedrigotti family, grew wealthy from the monopoly they were granted on the transport of goods along the Etsch between Sacco and Branzoll.

Clemente **BARONI di CAVALCABÒ** (*1726–96*) studied Latin, Italian literature, logic, metaphysics, and mathematics with his brother Cristoforo (1712–86). Clemente became a member of the Agiati shortly after it was founded and a leader of the area's intellectual life—in some eyes, replacing Girolamo Tartarotti after Tartarotti's death. Baroni was a judge in the *pretura* of Rovereto, a prolific writer, a historian, and a close friend of Clementino Vannetti and Carlo Rosmini. His interests ranged from local history to political and natural philosophy, religion, sericulture, and hydraulics. His works include *Idea della storia e delle consuetudini antiche della*

APPENDIX C

Valle Lagarina ed in particolare del Roveretano, published anonymously and without date or place in 1776.

Felice BARONI **di** CAVALCABÒ (?–?) was a deputy for the Welsch Confines at the 1790 Innsbruck Diet and in Vienna after the Diet ended. In 1795, he became a representative to the small *Ausschuss*. He was a member of two Masonic lodges in Innsbruck, "Zu den drei Bergen" and also "Zur wahren Eintracht." When Cagliostro established his Egyptian-rite lodge in Rovereto in 1788, the installation ceremony was held at Felice Baroni's home.

Giovanni Battista BARONI *(1751–1808)*, a priest, was born in Rovereto. He was enrolled as a member of the Agiati in 1770. Under Leopold II he was a court agent, and he died in Vienna in 1808.

Georg Adalbert von BEEKHEN *(1741–1801)*, a baron. The family was originally Swabian, lived in lands of the Holy Roman Empire over the centuries, then settled in Styria at the beginning of the eighteenth century where they were immatriculated in 1720. The Beekhens held the rank of baron. In 1762 Georg Adalbert became a *Hofconcipist*, worked at departments of the *Hofrechenkammer*, and in 1773 was named a *k. k. Truchsess*. Circa 1778–82 he became a *Gubernialrat* in Lemberg, the capital of the Habsburg share of the first partition of Poland. In 1783 he was transferred back to Vienna to become a *Hofrat* at the *Hofrechenkammer*, where, as director of the *Stiftungen-Hofbuchhalterei*, he was active in drafting Joseph II's church and monastic reforms and in administering the Religion Fund that resulted from the sale of former ecclesiastical properties. In 1789 he was sent to Milan to learn about Lombardy's finances; a year later, Leopold II called him back to Vienna as director of two departments of the *Hofrechenkammer*. Beekhen became a Freemason in 1778 and ultimately master of the lodge "Zu den weissen Adlern" in Lemberg; in Vienna he was a member of the lodge "Zur wahren Eintracht."

Giovanni Battista BETTA **dal** TOLDO *(1701–65)*, an abbot, enrolled as a member of the Agiati in 1751. The family origin was Spanish; in 1580 Archduke Ferdinand gave them the predicate dal Toldo. Giovanni Battista was born in Brentonico, studied in Rovereto and then Verona for three years; in 1721 he entered the seminary and was ordained in 1725, after which he returned to Rovereto. His testamentary bequest was one of the main factors in the establishment of the Theresianum in Innsbruck.

Carlo BETTA **(dal Toldo)** *(1774–1816)*. At the 1790 Diet he first represented the communes of the *pretura* of Rovereto; but when he asked for immatriculation as a Tyrolean noble and therefore his own seat and vote, he was replaced by Felice Baroni-Cavalcabò. The Betta family, claiming the inheritance of the Betta dal Toldos who had died out in midcentury, first petitioned Maria Theresa in 1767, then Joseph II in 1776. During the 1790 Interregnum in the Holy Roman Empire, the *Reichsvikar* for the western part of the empire, Karl Theodor of Palatinate-Bavaria, ennobled and

APPENDIX C

made barons of the empire the three Betta brothers and gave them the predicate of the old Betta dal Toldo family. This ennoblement was not recognized by Tyrol or the Habsburgs until 1840; the ennoblement was, however, confirmed by the Prince-Bishop of Trent, Pietro Vigilio Thun, in 1790.

Franz Johann von Bieschin (Běšín) *(1742–1802)*, a baron, was from an old and large Bohemian noble family. He studied law at Prague and began his state service in Bohemia. In 1765 he became a councillor on the knights' bench (*Ritterbank*) of the Bohemian Appeals Court and subsequently served in several other provincial judicial offices. In 1782 Joseph II brought Bieschin to Vienna and to the *Oberste Justizstelle*; in April 1790 Leopold II named him a member of the reorganized court legislative commission and a *Kämmerer*. Bieschin also served on the 1790–91 commission for Estate grievances and in the latter year was made a baron. Under Francis II in 1792, Bieschin was named Vice-President of the Bohemian Appeals Court (where he had begun his career 25 years earlier) and six months later was promoted to *Landrechtspräsident* and chief *Landrichter* in Prague. Bieschin belonged to the Masonic lodge "Sincerité" in Pilsen and Klattau in 1775–76 while he was *Kreiskommissar* in Ellbogen; then in Prague he was among the Masonic founders of a boarding house for poor children, established by the Scottish-rite Masons of the lodge "Karl zu den drei gekrönten Sternen."

Giuseppe Rinaldo Carli *(1720–95)*. Of an old noble Istrian family, Carli wrote dramas at age 12 and had an essay on the northern lights and some poems published at age 18. In 1744 the Senate of Venice invited him to teach navigation and astronomy; he also worked in the arsenal where he designed and had built a new kind of warship with 74 cannons. He also wrote on literature, numismatics, archeology, and especially economics. When a collegium of national economy and trade and a Higher Studies Council were established in Milan, Carli became president of both, then in 1771 president of Milan's new Finance Collegium. His two main historical works were a history of Italian antiquity (Milan: 1788–91) and a history of Verona up to 1519 (Verona: 1796), the latter published posthumously.

Luigi Carpentari *(1733–1808)*. The family was made knights of the Holy Roman Empire by Leopold I in 1700 with the predicate de Mittenberg. Luigi Carpentari became a codirector of Rovereto's new theater in 1783. He attended the pre-Diet meetings of the *pretura* of Rovereto in 1790 and in 1795 was the joint representative of the cities of Rovereto and Arco on the small *Ausschuss*. He was enrolled as a member of the Agiati in 1759.

Marx Cazan zu Griessfeld *(1708–?)*, a baron, was from a family ennobled by Maximilian I, immatriculated in Tyrol in 1646 or 1647, and made heredi-

APPENDIX C

tary Austrian barons in 1708. Marx Cazan was a court councillor of the Prince-Bishop of Brixen, and he was a Freemason.

Andreas Alois DIPAULI *(1761–1839)*, the son of an educated and prosperous peasant-farmer, was born in Aldein southeast of Bozen. Both his parents died when he was six, within eight days of one another. In 1772 his guardian sent him to nearby Cavalese to learn Italian and study agriculture, but he had no real interest in agriculture. So his guardian entrusted him to a priest to learn Latin. A year later he entered the gymnasium at Brixen, spent two years there, then finished at Innsbruck, where in 1782 he entered the university for juridical studies. But at the end of that academic year, Joseph II converted the university into a lyceum; diPauli continued to study privately and in 1784 entered the university at Pavia, where he earned a doctorate. In 1786 he entered service at the Fiscal Office at Bozen and was soon elected a *Magistratsrat*. In 1790 he was entered into the Bozen *Bürgerbuch* gratis, was chosen a burgher representative from Bozen to the Innsbruck Diet, and was a member of the deputation that brought the Diet's grievances to the court at Vienna. During the 1796–99 war, diPauli was a member of the southern Defense Deputation at Bozen and for his service was ennobled in 1797 with the predicate von Treuheim. In 1803 he was appointed a councillor at the Innsbruck Appeals Court; he remained in this position when Tyrol was transferred to Bavaria and when it was returned to Austria in 1814. In 1816 diPauli was appointed *Hofrat* at the *Oberste Justizstelle* in Vienna. Along with Archduke Johann and several others, diPauli was a founder of the *Sammler für Geschichte und Statistik von Tirol*, the first scholarly journal in Tyrol, which appeared from 1806 to 1808. In 1824 diPauli was a founder of the Landesmuseum Ferdinandeum, the library of which has about 1,400 volumes that he collected (Biblioteca Tirolensis Dipauliana); diPauli for many years was director of the Ferdinandeum. In 1836 he was awarded the Commander-Cross of the Order of St. Leopold to commemorate his fifty years of service and was made a baron the following year. In 1823 he joined the Agiati in Rovereto.

Friedrich von EGER *(1734–1812)* was born in Vienna, son of an Austrian *Regierungsrat*. He entered the Court Chancellery in 1751 as a probationer, advanced through the ranks, and in 1769 went to Trieste as a Commerce *Hofrat*. In 1770 he was commissioned to compile and systematize all the commercial regulations, a task he completed in Vienna. In 1779 he was accepted into the Carniolan Estates and in 1780 into the Carinthian Estates. In 1785 Joseph II named him to the *Staatsrat*, and in 1789 he was made a privy councillor. In 1796 he was raised to baron, a rank he acquired on his own merits for elevating and protecting Austrian industry by his work on legislation.

APPENDIX C

Markus II EGLE (*?–?*) was abbot of the Premonstratensian Abbey of Wiltau/ Wilten from 1784–1820, succeeding Norbert von Spergs, brother of Joseph Sperges (see entry and chapter 2). Egle was a thoroughly conservative cleric who opposed many of Joseph II's monastic reforms. During his tenure as abbot, many convents and monasteries were closed, and his abbey appeared to be threatened. But the Abbey of Wiltau survived Joseph's reign, and under Leopold II the existence of the Abbey was no longer threatened. During the Coalition Wars, troops were quartered there and Egle became an enthusiastic participant in the Defense *Ausschuss*—so much so that he had his bed brought to the *Landhaus*. When Tyrol was annexed by Bavaria in 1807, Egle remained loyal to Austria and the House of Habsburg. After the 1809 Hofer uprising, Bavaria abolished the Abbey; in 1813 Egle himself leased whatever property the Abbey still had so that it would not be sold. With the reoccupation by Austria, Egle went to Vienna as an Estate deputy to work for the restoration of Tyrol and of his Abbey—which was restored along with four others. Egle then worked to have his Abbey's art collection returned to it.

ARCHDUCHESS Maria ELISABETH Josephina (*1743–1808*) was the fifth child and fourth daughter of Maria Theresa and Franz Stephan. As the sister of Leopold II, she stood in for him and received the Tyroleans' oath of hereditary homage in 1790. Before smallpox destroyed her beauty in 1767, she was considered as a possible spouse for, among others, the King of Poland, Stanislaus Poniatowski; Louis XVI of France; and the Duke of Pfalz-Zweibrücken. After 1767, she was named abbess of the Innsbruck *Damenstift*, which her mother had established. Elisabeth was well liked in Tyrol, where she personally attended every public celebration from 1781 to 1805—from the Diet, to reopening the university, to a *Schützfest*.

Franz Joseph von ENZENBERG (*1747–1819*), a count, came from a family that first appeared in Tyrol in 1495, became knights of the empire in 1628 and barons in 1671. His father, Cassian Ignaz (1709–72), was elevated to count by Maria Theresa, and in 1764, when the *Gubernium* was established in Innsbruck, he became Tyrol's first governor. The emperor and empress were Franz Enzenberg's godparents. In 1754 at age 8, he entered the Theresianum in Vienna. He later entered state service, and from 1766 to 1771 he held his first positions: in Milan with the Governor of Lombardy, Count Carl Firmian; then with the Governor-General of the Austrian Netherlands, Count Karl Johann Kobenzl; then a year at Wetzlar learning about the administration of justice in the Holy Roman Empire. In 1770 he was appointed to the Bohemian *Gubernium;* from February until April 1771, he was at the *Intendenza* in Trieste learning about commerce and maritime affairs. Enzenberg was then named to the Upper Austrian Gubernial and Revision Council in Innsbruck; he took the oath of office from his father (who died the following year) and served in this position for eleven years. In 1781 he was named *Obristhofmeister* at the Klagenfurt court of the emperor's sister, Archduchess Marianne. In 1782 when Joseph II combined the Inner and Upper Austrian Appeals and Criminal Courts with a seat in Klagenfurt, Enzenberg was named vice-president; then, in 1791, when Leopold II separated the courts again, Enzenberg was named president of the Inner Austrian Appeals Court. From Klagenfurt he was involved in planning the Tyrolean uprising of 1809 and gave asylum to those fleeing Tyrol. He was a member of the Agiati, of many other learned societies all over Europe, a Freemason in Innsbruck and Vienna, and, along with many others of his time, an alchemist. He wrote his own epitaph: "If posterity can say no more of him / Than what it is able to learn from this stone, / Regret not his death, Wanderer,—/ He lived too long!"

Wenzel EPPSTEIN *(1757–1824)* was born in Prague and was a baptized Jew. Before entering state service, he was employed by the Henikstein business house, where his service earned him shares of the business. He entered state service and became secretary to the governor of Tyrol, Count Wenzel Sauer; when the count left Tyrol, Eppstein accompanied him to Vienna. In the capital Eppstein became a court secretary at the *Hofkammer* and was ennobled with the predicate von Ankerberg. He was a Freemason in Innsbruck and in Vienna joined the lodge "Zur gekrönten Hoffnung im Orient," where his lodge brothers included Mozart, Franz Gumer, Count Sauer, and the vice-chancellor, then chancellor, of Transylvania, Samuel Teleki.

Gottardo Antonio FESTI *(1716–75)*, one of the founders of the Agiati, attended the University of Padua from 1744 to 1746, where he earned a doctorate of law. He took sacerdotal orders, then returned home to Rovereto to teach humane letters at the gymnasium. He also gave private music lessons and was Clementino Vannetti's tutor. He wrote both Italian and Latin; the Agiati's archives hold a number of his manuscripts, and the BCGT has the manuscript of Clementino Vannetti's biography of Festi. When Cagliostro came to Rovereto, he stayed at Festi's home.

Francesco Giuseppe FRISINGHELLI *(1691–1758)* was from a family that settled in Isera near Rovereto in the sixteenth century and became nobles of the Holy Roman Empire in 1620. Francesco, the last of his family, studied for the priesthood and was ordained. In 1726 he became a member of Trento's Academy of the Accessi, and later, in 1751, he joined the Agiati where he delivered his famous lecture the following year. He was a collector of antiquities for the Marchese Scipione Maffei of Verona.

Giuseppe Matteo Felice GIVANNI *(1722–87)* was born in Rovereto, studied logic and metaphysics at Rovereto's gymnasium, and dedicated himself to the priesthood. He wrote poetry in Roveretan dialect and translated several historical works. He taught at the gymnasium and was a founder of the Agiati. His published works include a translation into Italian of L. Curzio's *Dei Fatti di Alessandro il Grande* (1829).

Franz GOLDEGG von und zu Goldegg und Lindenburg *(1754–1804)*. The family was elevated into the Knights of the Empire in 1563; their primary land holdings were in Tyrol. Franz Goldegg was a court councillor and a Freemason; he defended the Masons at a session of the 1790 Diet, which he attended as a representative of Bozen. After the Diet, he resettled in Vienna.

Franz GUMER *(1731–94)* was from an extremely successful commercial and banking family. In 1765 Emperor Franz Stefan obtained a loan of 200,000 gulden in gold ducats from the family. From the beginning of the eighteenth century on, this family held a leading position in the Bozen Mercantile Magistrate and helped the city keep its importance as a transit place and market until the end of the century. From 1771 to 1776 Franz was *Bürgermeister* of Bozen; in 1783 he was entered in the Tyrolean nobles' Matricle. In May 1778 he funded and opened a workhouse for Bozen's unemployed. Because Bozen's businessmen as a whole usually backed Gumer, he had a great deal of influence in the affairs of the princely county. He was a zealous Freemason and belonged to several lodges: in 1777 he was a founding member of the Innsbruck lodge "Im Gebirge Moria" and later had the rank of master in another Innsbruck lodge, "Zu den drei Bergen." He was also a founding member of a Bozen Rosicrucian group that met at the Atzwang home. After the local populace (for reasons unstated) stormed the house, the gatherings were temporarily discontinued. Gumer was also connected to a lodge in Venice, and belonged to the Vienna lodge, "Zur gekrönten Hoffnung im Orient." After the 1790 Innsbruck Diet, he went to Vienna and settled there, returning to Bozen twice a year to confer with foreign merchants. At the center of many intrigues, Gumer was about to be banned from Vienna by Leopold II, but the emperor's death intervened. In 1794 a secret denunciation of Gumer was sent to the Vienna police authorities, but it arrived two weeks after his death; it described him as "a man of extraordinary talents and great knowledge, but of a 'bad heart.'"

Joseph Anton GUMER *(?–?)* was an older brother of Franz Gumer (see entry). He was a prosperous banker, and was *Bürgermeister* of Bozen from 1741 to 1749.

Mathias Wilhelm Virgilius von HAAN *(1737–1816)* was of an old Alsatian family that had been ennobled in 1566 and that had migrated to Austria at the end of the seventeenth century. He studied with the Jesuits, then concentrated on law at the University of Vienna. After a brief career in diplomatic service, in 1761 he was named a *Regierungsrat* on the Scholars Bench *(Gelehrtenbank)* of the Lower Austrian Government. In 1775 he became a *Hofrat* at the *Oberste Justizstelle* (essentially following the career

APPENDIX C

of his father) and took part in the judicial reforms of Joseph II. In 1779 Haan was elevated to the hereditary Austrian nobility as a knight. In 1790 and 1791 he served on the commission for Estate grievances; from 1790 to 1792 he took part in the work of the codification commission and served on the *MildeStiftungs-Commission*. In 1792 Francis II named Haan vice-president of the Lower Austrian Appeals Court and in 1795 president of the Lower Austrian *Landrecht*, granting him the dignity of privy councillor. In 1797 he became vice-president and in 1809 president of the court commission in political and juridical matters. Together with Joseph von Sonnenfels, he issued *Specimen juris germanici de remediis juris, juri romano incognitis* (Wien 1757). Haan was awarded the grand cross of the Order of St. Stephen in 1811. His son Josef Georg Haan (1786–1839) continued the family tradition, following in his father's and grandfather's footsteps.

Joseph Ignaz Veit von HORMAYR-Hortenburg *(1703–78)*, a baron, was the last Tyrolean chancellor (1759–78). He was born in Innsbruck of an old Bavarian-Tyrolean noble family; he entered service early with positions in Vienna, Wetzlar, Regensburg, and Swabian Austria. He was among the first group of men awarded the Royal Hungarian Order of St. Stephen. In 1777, he was elevated to baron of the hereditary lands and of the Holy Roman Empire. He was an untiring researcher and collector and a friend and benefactor of the arts and sciences, compiling an imposing 22-folio-volume subject register on civil and criminal law. During travels in Germany, the Netherlands, and Italy, he collected many unpublished and until then unknown documents on the history of the Habsburgs and especially Tyrol. He awakened a feeling for the history of his fatherland and also for natural science. He was a member of the Agiati and obtained a charter for the academy from Maria Theresa.

Franz Georg von KEESS *(1747–99)* was among the most important jurists of eighteenth-century Austria. He finished his legal studies at the University of Vienna and immediately entered state service in 1768 with a councillor's position on the knights' bench of the Lower Austrian *Landrecht*. Two years later, in 1770, he became a Lower Austrian *Regierungsrat* and in 1774 a *Commissionsrat* with the Illyrian Court Deputation. In 1777 Maria Theresa appointed Keess to the *Oberste Justizstelle*; Joseph II promoted him to head of that *Hofstelle* and put him on the codification commission. In 1772 he was awarded the Order of St. Stephen. Leopold II abolished the compilation commission and replaced it with another headed by Martini, excluding all previous members, including Keess. But Keess stayed at the *Oberste Justizstelle* and took part in the commission on Estate grievances in 1790 and 1791. When Francis II came to the throne, he restored Keess's 2,000-florin-yearly personal allowance and added him to the new legislative commission. In the following year Keess was assigned to work on Galician affairs at the *Oberste Justizstelle* and was instrumental in drafting the 1795 Ordinance for West Galicia. He wrote and published several works and compiled the collection of laws in matters of justice (see Bibliography, "Published Collections of Austrian Laws").

Joseph von KOLLER, Herr zu Trestorf und Teutsch-Proderstorf *(1731–1800)* was from a family in Austria above the Enns. In 1773 he became director of the *Staatsrat's* Chancellery and remained in this office until 1785 when he was transferred to the Bohemian-Austrian Court Chancellery. In 1783 he was elevated to Knight of the Hereditary Lands. In 1790 and 1791 he served on the commission on Estate grievances; in 1791 he became a *Hofrat* at the *Hofkammer* and in 1794 a member of the Lower Austrian Estates.

Leopold von KOLOWRAT-KRAKOWSKY *(1727–1809)*, a count, rose through the upper ranks of the bureaucracy to become supreme chancellor *(Oberste Kanzler)* at the head of the Bohemian-Austrian Court Chancellery. His family's origins are far enough back in Bohemian history that no extant documents show them, and only a few legends describe them. Only eight of the great old Czech land owning families survived the Counterreformation with themselves and their possessions intact; the Kolowrats were one of them. In the eighteenth century the family had two branches; the senior line established at Brzeznitz, and the line at Radienin. Count Leopold Kolowrat belonged to this second branch, which was established by his father, Count Philipp (d. 1763, Knight of the Golden Fleece). Leopold Kolowrat-Krakowsky was president of the *Hofkammer* from 1774 to 1782. When Joseph II created the *Vereinigte Hofstelle,* Kolowrat became its supreme chancellor; when Leopold dissolved the *Vereinigte Hofstelle* into its component parts, Kolowrat headed the Bohemian-Austrian Court Chancellery and remained supreme chancellor. He also served on the commission hearing Estate grievances in 1790 and 1791. In 1801 he became Interior Minister *(dirigender Staats- und Conferenzminister* in domestic affairs). He was a Knight of the Golden Fleece and a member of the Order of St. Stephen and of the Order of St. Leopold. He also belonged to the Masonic lodge "Zur wahren Eintracht" in Vienna, where his lodge brothers included Georg Adalbert Beekhen, Joseph von Sonnenfels, Joseph Haydn, and Franz Enzenberg.

Franz Karl KRESSEL von Gualtenberg *(1720–1801)*, a baron, was from an old Bohemian noble family. He studied at Prague and at foreign universities, then returned home and entered state service as assessor of the Commission on the Land's Borders. In 1754 he became director or first referent of the juridic faculty at Prague. In 1760 he and his brother Johann were elevated to baron. In 1772 Maria Theresa called him to Vienna and named him *Hofrat* on the *Staatsrat;* he was also put on the compilation commission, which was made up of the *Staatsrat's* newest members. He became a privy councillor; and in 1781 or 1782 he left the *Staatsrat* and became President of the *Geistliche Hofkommission* to oversee Joseph's church reforms and the dissolution of the cloisters and monasteries. In 1790 and 1791 he served on the commission hearing Estate grievances and became vice-chancellor for Bohemia on the Bohemian-Austrian Court Chancellery when Leopold dissolved the *Vereinigte Hofstelle* in 1791. Kressel was an active Freemason in Prague, where he was involved with the orphanage run by the lodge there. In Vienna he was a member of the Masonic lodge "Zur wahren Eintracht." He was provincial grand master for the Austrian (mother) lodge of St. Johannis and with a Prince Dietrichstein drafted the statutes. At age 40 Kressel began to learn Greek and was subsequently able to read Homer in the original language. He received the Commander-Cross of the Order of St. Stephen from Joseph II.

Franz Joseph von LODRON-Laterano *(1745–91)*, a count, was born in Innsbruck of one of the old and large feudal families, or "dynasts," of Tyrol. His family traces its roots back at least to the year 1050, and they were counts of the Holy Roman Empire. The Lodron family also had lines in Bohemia, Styria, and Bavaria. Franz Joseph Lodron was the brother-in-law of Count Franz Enzenberg (see entry). In 1790, when he was elected *Landeshauptmann* of Tyrol, Lodron was serving as *Kammer-* and *Revisionsrat* at the Court of Elector Karl Theodor in Munich; Lodron served only one year as *Landeshauptmann* before he died at age 46.

Antonio MALANOTTI da Caldés *(?–?)* was a deputy to the 1790 Diet from the jurisdiction of Stein-unter-Lebenberg. In 1809, he commanded the Sulzbergers in the uprising against Napoleon. The family belonged to the nobility of the Nonsberg (Val di Non) and Sulzberg (Val di Sol). In 1552 at Innsbruck, Emperor Charles V confirmed their nobility; in 1648 they were entered into the Tyrolean Matricle on command of the land's prince.

Francesco MANFRONI da Caldes *(?–?)* drafted the map that caused such a stir in Trento and Rovereto in 1778 (see chapter 2). He also contributed to Antonio Chiusole's *Compendio di geografia antica e moderna* (Venezia: 1755).

Giovanni MARCHETTI *(?–1806)* was a teaching priest in Rovereto beginning in 1774 and became normal school director there until circa 1806. He was from the Nonsberg and was enrolled in the Agiati in 1775. A contemporary called him "Ludi litterarii Rectorem optimum" (the best guide for the education of the young).

Carlo Antonio di MARTINI zu Wasserberg *(1726–1800)*, a baron, was one of the most important Austrian jurists of the eighteenth century. Born at Revo in Italian Tyrol, he studied at Trent, then Innsbruck, from 1741 to 1747, studying law and government. At the University of Vienna, he attended theology lectures and gave lectures himself as he earned his juridical doctorate. He was at the imperial embassy in Spain for a year

APPENDIX C

and then traveled all over western Europe. In 1754 he was at the University of Padua and was then appointed a professor of national law, history, Roman law, and institutions at the University of Vienna; he also taught law at the Theresianum in Vienna. From 1760 to 1773 he was a member of the *Studienhofcommission*; and in 1764 he became a *Hofrat* at the *Oberste Justizstelle*. Ten years later, in 1774, he was named to the Bohemian-Austrian Court Chancellery to oversee matters related to the dissolution of the Jesuits. Joseph II entrusted Martini with introducing judicial reforms in Milan and the Austrian Netherlands. In 1779 at his own request, he returned to the *Oberste Justizstelle* and in 1788 became its vice-president, then also vice-president of the new court commission on legislative matters. Leopold II promoted Martini to the presidency of the new court commission in legislative matters and in 1792 to second president of the *Oberste Justizstelle*, where he worked on the civil law code and on the new code for Galicia. From 1797 until his death in 1800, he led the administration of justice. Martini became a member of the Agiati in 1755 and a Knight of the Order of St. Stephen in 1773. He was elevated to baron in 1780 and in 1785 received the dignity of privy councillor. His list of published works is far too long to mention here.

Sigmund von MOLL *(1759–1826)*, a baron, came from a family originally of the Netherlands that moved to Tyrol and Salzburg. They became Austrian nobles in 1580 and barons in 1789. Sigmund Moll was appointed *Gubernialrat* in Innsbruck, then *Kreishauptmann* of the Welsch Confines in April 1790.

Antonio MORROCCHESI *(1768–1838)* was a dramatic actor who achieved fame above all for his interpretations of Shakespeare and of the Italian dramatist Vittorio Alfieri. For many years, Morrocchesi performed at the theaters of Ognissant and of San Maria in Florence. A school of declamatory acting formed around him, with a style described as "a little thundering, a little asthmatic, a little exaggerated." (See Manzi, "Clementino Vannetti tra i comici," 450). In 1811 Morrocchesi left the theater for the chair of dramatic declamation at the Academy of Fine Arts of Florence, where he published his two famous *Lezioni di declamazione d'arte drammatica* (1832). He was also a dramatist and wrote comedies and tragedies, frequently drawing from themes of the "pathetic and lacrimose" repertory. His *Memorie* were published posthumously in 1869.

Giuseppe PEDERZANI *(1740– or 1749–1837)*, a priest and man of letters, was born at Villa Lagarina near Rovereto. He was a tutor to children of noble families and was inscribed as a member of the Agiati in 1784. Pederzani wrote both prose and poetry well, but most of his work remained unpublished during his lifetime, primarily because of Pederzani's modesty about his own productions. He was a colleague and friend of Clementino Vannetti, who corresponded with him about the sonnet addressed to Morrocchesi.

APPENDIX C

Carlantonio Pɪʟᴀᴛɪ *(1733–1802)* was from a family ennobled in 1360. Beginning in 1749 he studied at Salzburg and Leipzig, then Göttingen, where he also taught. In 1760 at Trent he began teaching civil law at the legal lyceum, a position created just for him. When the French invaded the Trentino in 1796, Pilati was asked to take part in that Napoleonic government; but he refused because he did not want to serve foreigners in his homeland. However, in 1801 after the third French invasion and because his fellow citizens elected him, he accepted the presidency of the *Consiglio superiore del Tirolo meridionale* in Trent; he said the office enabled him to mitigate as best he could the effects of the occupation on the population. After the Peace of Luneville, Pilati returned to his home Tassullo, helped the poor of the area, and died there in 1802. He was inscribed as a member of the Agiati in 1758; his published works, in addition to those mentioned in the text (chapter 2), include *Storia dell'Impero germanico e dell'Italia dai tempi Carolingi alla pace di Vestfalia* (Stockholm [Chur]: 1769–72).

Simon Thaddäus von Rᴇɪꜱᴄʜᴀᴄʜ *(1728–1803)*, a baron, was from an old Swabian family. In 1776 he entered state service in Vienna as a privy councillor, a *Kämmerer*, and Bohemian-Austrian court chancellor. And in 1778 he was named to the *Studienhofcommission* and also was named Transylvanian court chancellor, which he remained until 1781. In 1782 he was appointed to the *Staatsrat*. Reischach was awarded the Grand Cross of the Order of St. Stephen and remained a *Staatsminister* on the *Staatsrat* until his death in 1803.

The Rᴏꜱᴍɪɴɪ family was reported to be the richest family in Rovereto. They were invested by the emperor with half the customs tariffs imposed on the timber transported on the Leno beyond Vallarsa and a third of the decima on agricultural produce (including grapes) of the *pretura* of Rovereto. The family was ennobled by Leopold I in 1672.

Angelo Rᴏꜱᴍɪɴɪ *(?–?)* studied theology at Pavia in 1772–73. He became a city magistrate at Rovereto and in 1787 was chosen *Podestà* of Rovereto. In 1790 he was Rovereto's deputy to the Innsbruck Diet, and both he and Felice Baroni took the Confinants' grievances to Vienna when the Diet rebuffed them. Angelo was the brother of Carlo Rosmini (see entry).

Carlo Rᴏꜱᴍɪɴɪ *(1750–1827)* was educated by private tutors in Rovereto and then studied philosophy in the Collegium Nobilium at Innsbruck. His closest friends were Clemente Baroni-Cavalcabò and Clementino Vannetti. Rosmini became a member of the Agiati in 1782. He was much interested in erotic poetry and poets and together with Vannetti published a small collection of such poetry under their combined academic names in 1783: *Versi d'Erotico e di Cimone Doriano*. His two closest friends, Vannetti and Baroni, died within a year of one another (1795–96), and Rosmini wrote commemorations of both of them. In 1803, the year after his mother died, Rosmini moved to Milan, where he remained for the rest of his life—and where he produced his main work, a four-volume *Istoria di Milano* (Milan: 1815–20), tracing the duchy from the beginnings to 1535 and including a volume of documents. It was so well received that he wrote a supplement, taking the history up to 1740.

Francesco Antonio SAIBANTE *(1731–96)*. The family was ennobled by Emperor Charles V in 1521, and the descendants settled in Verona and Rovereto. Francesco studied at home with Girolamo Tartarotti, who lived with the family, and at the gymnasium in Rovereto. Saibante and his sister, Bianca Laura, were founding members of the Academy of the Agiati. Because of his urging, a public library was built in Rovereto in 1764, in which Girolamo Tartarotti's personal collection formed the core of the initial holdings.

Bianca Laura Felicita Gioseffa Anna SAIBANTE-VANNETTI *(1723–97)* was a founder of the Agiati, wife of another founder, Giuseppe Valeriano Vannetti, and mother of Clementino Vannetti. She was born in Rovereto and was educated in the Ursiline convent in Trent, where she learned the things conventional for a gentlewoman of that day: embroidery and drawing, the German and French languages, and literature. At home, she and her brother Francesco were tutored by Girolamo Tartarotti in literature, dialectics, and philosophy. She was also a member of academies elsewhere, for example, the Occulti in Rome and the academy in Brescia. After her husband's death in 1764, she devoted herself to her literary endeavors and to educating her son Clementino, whom she outlived by two years.

The SARDAGNA family settled in Trent in the fifteenth century and became part of the city's patriciate. In 1572 they were inscribed as citizens of Trent. In 1579 they became nobles of the Empire. Under the *Reichsvikar* Karl Theodor of Palatinate-Bavaria, during the 1790 interregnum, they were made counts of the Empire. The family was large and prominent outside Tyrol and Trentino: in the eighteenth century it included a bishop of Cremona, a rector of the University of Vienna, and a member of the *Oberste Justizstelle*.

Benedetto di SARDAGNA *(1766–1812)* was the son of Carlo Pompeo; his manuscript diary of the 1790 Diet served as a primary source for this study. Both Benedetto and his father were Freemasons in Tyrol. In 1786, Benedetto became *Kreis* secretary in the Lower Inntal *Kreis*; in 1790 after the Diet, he became a "Police Commissar" in Vienna, and in 1794, when he was "Polizey-Sekretair," he was considered for a possible mission to Venice. Subsequently, Benedetto Sardagna became police director in Trent. He left not only his diary, but also his manuscripts on typography, history, and statistics, all of which are in the Ferdinandeum in Innsbruck.

Carlo Pompeo di SARDAGNA *(1720?–?)* was a noble who spoke in behalf of the Confinants at the 1790 Innsbruck Diet. He was a *Kämmer-Procurator* and in 1790 was appointed to the Upper Austrian *Gubernium* in Innsbruck, then in 1792 to the *Gubernium* at Klagenfurt.

Wenzel von SAUER *(1742–99)*, a count, was born in Graz, the son of count Kajetan Sauer and Countess Kajetana von Purgstall. In 1744 Wenzel Sauer entered public service as a councillor with the Cameral Administration in the Banat of Temesvár. Eight years later, in 1782—during Pope Pius VI's stay in Vienna—Sauer caught his sovereign's attention: he made a long speech in which he praised Joseph's church reforms and condemned the times "where the darkness of ignorance still prevailed" and, in a skillful turn of speech, managed to portray the Pope as hurrying to Vienna to greet Emperor Joseph and to acknowledge the ruler's outstanding piety. Joseph's appreciation was expressed in Sauer's rapid promotion. In 1783 Sauer became a *Hofrat* in Tyrol and in 1786 or 1787 governor and *Landeshauptmann* in the combined office. He was a Freemason in Tyrol and in Vienna's lodge "Zur gekrönten Hoffnung im Orient," where his lodge brothers included his former secretary Wenzel Eppstein von Ankersberg; Franz von Gumer; Mozart; the Hungarian vice-chancellor and then chancellor, Samuel Teleki; and at least one Siegmaringer-Hohenzollern. Sauer was named president of the Lower Austrian Government in January 1791. He retired in 1795.

Franz Michael SENN *(1759–1813)* became a judge in Pfunds in the Upper Inntal in 1787. He apparently had absorbed ideas from nearby Switzerland, with deep feelings of concern for the peasantry. He took part in the defense of Tyrol against the French in 1796–97. He took part in the 1809 uprising and had to flee to Vienna, where he became a *Magistratsrat*.

Karl Joseph von SEYDEL *(?–?)* was born in Troppau; he became a member of the Agiati in 1767. In 1789, he was made a *Concipist* at the *Staatsrat's* Chancellery. After serving as court secretary at Tyrol's Diet, he served in 1791 and 1792 as a court secretary at the Bohemian-Austrian Court Chancellery in Vienna and then in the latter year was sent to a post in Venice as a representative of the Empire. In 1815 he became a *Rathsprotokollist* at the *Oberste Justizstelle.*

Giovanni Battista SOCRELLA *(1737–1819)*, a Ladin and ex-Jesuit, was a teacher of grammar; he was named vice-prefect of Rovereto's gymnasium in October 1779 and took office in June 1780; he later became prefect and held the post for thirty years. Socrella had almost policelike functions in carrying out the government's school policies. Clementino Vannetti, as he fought Socrella and the school reforms, referred to the prefect as Corvo Socrello, or Crow Socrella, who adhered rigorously to the new regulations. In 1813 he became a member of the Agiati.

Johann Nepomuk von SPAUR *(1724–93)*, a count, was from one of the great dynast families of Tyrol. In 1772 when the governor of Tyrol formed a 53-man "Poor Deputation" to take care of the poorhouse, Spaur was

APPENDIX C

named president of the deputation. He was also president of the *Landrecht* in Innsbruck and a *Kämmerer* and privy councillor. He was selected as *Landeshauptmann* in August 1791 after the death of Count Franz Lodron. His own term of office was not much longer than Lodron's one-year term.

Joseph von SPERGES auf Palenz und Reisdorf *(1726–91)*, a baron who was born Spergs in Innsbruck, was a statesman, scholar, classicist, historian, and cartographer. He adopted the spelling Sperges because he felt it was easier for the Italians, with whom he dealt so much, to pronounce. He studied in Innsbruck and entered state service. As secretary to the border commission in Rovereto working out disputes with Venice, he made his famous map (see chapter 2); as a reward for this service, which ended in 1756, he was awarded the further predicate auf Palenz und Reisdorf. He joined the Agiati while he was in Rovereto, the Taxiana in Innsbruck, and in 1759 the Electoral-Bavarian Academy of Sciences at Munich. Sperges, who loved architecture, also had a part in the rebuilding and enlarging of the University of Pavia. In 1768 in Vienna be became a member of the Academy of Plastic and Graphic Arts, in 1769 a member of its academic council, and in 1783 its president. In December 1756 he became an adjunct of the Court and State Archives in Vienna; in 1759 Kaunitz had him installed as archivist at the *Staatskanzlei*, and in 1765 Sperges became head of the *Staatskanzlei*'s Dipartimento d'Italia. Also in 1765 he was enrolled as a Tyrolean noble and his *Tyroler Bergwerksgeschichte* appeared in Vienna. In 1771 he was named a Knight of the Order of St. Stephen. From youth on, Sperges collected copies of archival materials, inscriptions, and other papers; the collection is now in the Ferdinandeum in Innsbruck.

Joseph Thaddäus von SUMERAU *(?–1817)*, a baron, was from a family that originated in Altsumerau; they were elevated to hereditary Austrian barons in 1745 and barons of the Empire in 1765. Joseph Sumerau served as Tyrolean referent in the Bohemian-Austrian Court Chancellery and worked to settle the grievances brought to Vienna by the Tyroleans after the 1790 Diet. In 1791 he was promoted to president of the Anterior Austrian Government. In 1801 he became vice-president and in 1804 president of the *Polizei Hofstelle* in Vienna; in 1802 he also became president of the Lower Austrian Government. He requested release from the Lower Austrian presidency in 1804 but continued at the *Polizei Hofstelle* until 1808. He was a member of the Masonic lodge "Zur edlen Aussicht im Orient" in Freiburg-im-Breisgau.

Pietro Vigilio/Peter Vigil THUN-Hohenstein *(1724–1800)* belonged to one of the dynast families of Tyrol, a family that supplied many bishops and cardinals to the Church of Rome. Pietro Vigilio Thun studied in Trent, then Rome, and was a canon of Salzburg when he became Prince-Bishop of Trent in 1776. He remained prince-bishop until his death in 1800.

APPENDIX C

Girolamo TIRABOSCHI *(1731–94)*, an ecclesiastic, was the son of a businessman and was born at Bergamo. He attended the Collegium at Monza, at age 15 entered the Jesuit Order at Genoa, then taught in the lower schools. During this period Tiraboschi edited Carlo Mandosio's *Nuovo Vocabolario* and began to assemble material for what would be his magnum opus on the history of Italian literature. He became a member of the Agiati in 1776. In 1770 he became director of the ducal library at Modena and remained there until his death. His greatest contribution, *Storia della letteratura italiana*, in its first edition (1771–82) comprised fourteen volumes and began with Etruria; he presented as complete a picture as he could of Italian civilization from its origins through the seventeenth century—tracing the development of sciences, schools, libraries, academies, the press, and other institutions. In reality, the work is more of a cultural than a literary history. The *Storia* was translated into German and French and went through several editions.

Giovanni Battista TODESCHI de Eschfeld *(1730–99)*, a baron, was a great traveler, a cultivated man of letters, a most amiable citizen, and a devotee of his *patria*, Rovereto. He attended the University of Padua in 1745 and the University of Bologna in 1750. He and three of his brothers were ennobled in 1751 with the predicate of von or de Eschfeld and were elevated to barons. When Wolfgang Mozart and his father Leopold traveled through Rovereto in 1770, Baron Todeschi hosted a concert in his home for the notables of the area. In 1785 a council of the nobility in Innsbruck commissioned Todeschi to compile a catalog of Rovereto's noble families; the catalog was approved in 1794 and published in February 1795. As president of Rovereto's City Council during the 1796 French invasion, Todeschi officially surrendered the city to the French. In 1806, under Bavarian rule, he became *Podestà* of the city. Todeschi and several other Roveretans and Veronans founded one of Cagliostro's Egyptian-rite lodges; before he died in 1812, Todeschi renounced this lodge. In 1751, he was enrolled as a member of the Agiati, and his many manuscripts on Rovereto, a valuable historical source for the period, are in the Agiati archives in Rovereto.

Federigo TARTAROTTI von Eichenberg *(?–?)* was elevated into the hereditary Austrian nobility in 1743 by Maria Theresa with the predicate von Eichenberg. He was chancellor of the castle at Rovereto. In 1790 he became a deputy to the Innsbruck Diet for the city of Rovereto, and with Felice Baroni and Angelo Rosmini, he went to Vienna to present the Welsch Tyroleans' case to the emperor.

Girolamo TARTAROTTI *(1706–61)* attended lower school and gymnasium in Rovereto. German- and Italian-language sources differ on his personality and where he studied theology (Wurzbach discusses this discrepancy in vol. 43, 98). The most recent twentieth-century Italian scholars say Tartarotti studied at Padua and that he also spent time in Verona, Venice, Rome, and Turin. He collected rare books and amassed a valuable personal library, which he donated to the new public library in Rovereto—which now bears his name. Tartarotti wrote poetry in Italian and Latin; it was published posthumously in 1785 in a collection made by Clementino Vannetti.

Johann Wenzel von **UGARTE** *(1748–96)*, a count, was from a Bohemian noble family that came originally from Spain, then the Netherlands. In the seventeenth century Emperor Leopold I elevated them to counts of the Empire. They had large estates in Moravia and received the Incolat in both Bohemia and Moravia. Ugarte attended the Theresianum in Vienna, finished in 1770, and received the dignity of *Kämmerer*; he then entered state service. Later he was named a councillor at the Lower Austrian government; in 1782 he was named to the Lower Austrian Appeals Court and then, in the same year, to the *Oberste Justizstelle*. In 1787 he became vice-chancellor of the Bohemian-Austrian Court Chancellery, in 1790 a privy councillor and member of the commission Leopold II established to hear Estate grievances. In 1794 Ugarte was named Lower Austrian *Oberstlandrichter* and president of the *Landrecht*, the next year president of the Appeals Court in Vienna. He was only 48 when he died in 1796. In 1775, he joined the Masonic lodge "Zu den drei Adlern," in Vienna.

Johann Christof von **UNTERRICHTER** von Rechtenthal *(?–?)*, from a family ennobled in 1575, was elevated by Charles VI into hereditary Austrian knighthood with the predicate von Rechtenthal. In 1789 Unterrichter was displaced from his post as estate referent at the *Gubernium* in Innsbruck by a favorite of governor, Count Sauer.

Clementino **VANNETTI** *(1754–95)*, the son of two of the founders of the Academy of the Agiati, was educated by private tutors. At age 15 he wrote a comedy in Latin, *Lampadaria*; only at age 30 did he begin to write in Italian. He also had some knowledge of French and Greek, but he never learned German. He spent his entire life in and around Rovereto, mostly on his landed estates. Here he wrote poetry and carried on a vast correspondence with other men and women of letters. In 1764 his father died; his mother saw to his education, then administered the family property, permitting Clementino to devote himself to his literary pursuits. He became a member of the Agiati in 1771 at age 17 and its permanent secretary from 1776 until his death. Under his secretaryship, the academy flourished; but he was apparently not very adept at keeping or preserving records: most of the academy's documents from that period are lost. He died in 1795 at the age of 40, two years before his mother died.

Giuseppe Valeriano **VANNETTI** *(1719–64)*, a founder and first president, or *Agiatissimo*, of the Academy of the Agiati and father of Clementino, was from a family of Veronese merchants that moved to Rovereto in 1660. His

APPENDIX C

uncle Giuseppe Benedetto was ennobled in 1721. Giuseppe Valeriano studied in German-speaking Meran and Brixen, then Innsbruck. In 1736 he went to Siena to study at the Collegio dei Nobili, returning to Rovereto in 1739 when his father died. There he studied with Adamo Chiusole, a Roveretan historian who would also be a member of the Agiati. In 1758 Vannetti was elected councillor and *provveditore* in Rovereto, positions that he held until his death at age 45. He wrote Italian poetry, made translations from German, and wrote about the Roveretan dialect.

Maximilian Christoph von WAIDMANNSDORF *(1742–1811)*, a baron, was born in Graz. Maria Theresa appointed him second assessor for the Inner Austrian *Geheim-Stelle* in Graz. He later became a councillor at the Bohemian-Austrian Court Chancellery. In 1791 he was named governor of Tyrol after the office was separated from that of *Landeshauptmann*. He served as governor until 1796, when he became fearful—in the face of an imminent French invasion—of arming the population, which the Tyrolean constitution required; a court commissar was sent to replace him. He died in Graz in 1811.

Franz von WOLKENSTEIN-TROSTBURG *(?–1821)*, a count from one of the dynast families of Tyrol, was *Landmarschallamtsverwalter* up through the 1790 Diet, where he lost the office of *Landeshauptman* to Count Franz Lodron in a questionable election. In 1791 he was named councillor at the Lower Austrian government in Vienna.

ABBREVIATIONS

Archives and Archival Funds

AVA	Allgemeines Verwaltungsarchiv, Vienna
BC di Trento	Biblioteca Comunale di Trento, Trento
BCGT	Biblioteca Civica Girolamo Tartarotti, Rovereto
Dip.	Dipauliana, Ferdinandeum, Innsbruck
HHStA	Haus-, Hof- und Staatsarchiv, Vienna
Kabinetskanzley	Kabinetskanzleyakten, HHStA
KFA	Kaiser Franz Akten, HHStA
SRP	Staatsrat Protocolle, HHStA
SRP Index	Staatsrat Indexen, HHStA
VA	Vertrauliche Akten, HHStA

Journals and Series

AÖG	Archiv für Österreichische Geschichte
Atti	Atti del'Accademia degli Agiati Roveretana (title varies)
MIÖG	Mitteilungen des Instituts für Österreichische Geschichtsforschung
MÖStA	Mitteilungen des Österreichischen Staatsarchiv
ST	Studi Trentini di Scienza Storiche

NOTES

CHAPTER ONE

1. The term "Welsch" derives from a Celtic root that meant foreigner, especially one speaking a Romance language. Walloon and Wallachian derive from the same root. For a brief account of how and when the Italian enclaves and communes became part of Tyrol, see Michael Mayr, *Die politischen Beziehungen Deutschtirols zum italienischen Landestheile. Eine geschichtliche-staatsrechtliche Studie* (Innsbruck: Marianische Vereinsbuchdruckerei, 1901), 39–44.

2. Nikolaus Grass, "Alm um Landstände in Tirol," *Anciens pays et assemblées d'états/Landen en Standen*, vol. 32 (Louvain, 1964), 139. Also see A. E. Alcock, *The History of the South Tyrol Question* (London: Joseph, 1970), 5; Nikolaus Grass, "Aus der Geschichte der Landstände Tirols," in *Studies presented to the International Commission for the History of Representative and Parliamentary Institutions*, vol. 24: *Album Helen Maud Cam* (Louvain: Publications Universitairès and Paris, Éditions Béatrice-Nauwelaerts, 1961), 306–7; Otto Stolz, *Grundriss der österreichischen Verfassungs- und Verwaltungsgeschichte* (Innsbruck-Vienna: Tyrolia, 1951), 115; Hans Voltelini, "Die territoriale Entwicklung der südlichen Landschaften Österreich-Ungarns im Mittelalter und in der Neuzeit und die Entstehung der heutigen Südgrenze Österreichs," *Mitteilungen der k. k. Geographischen Gesellschaft in Wien*, Nos. 8 and 9 (1916): 481–519; Franz Huter, "Die historische Entwicklung Tirols," in *Alpenländer mit Südtirol* (Stuttgart: Alfred Kröner, 1966), 433.

3. On Tyrol's constitutional development see, e.g., Hermann Baltl, *Österreichische Rechtsgeschichte* (Graz: Leykam, 1972); Alfred Wretschko, "Zur Geschichte der Tiroler Landesfreiheiten," in *Festschrift zu Ehren Emil von Ottenthals* (Innsbruck: Wagner, 1925): 309–34; Otto Stolz, "Das Land Tirol als politischer Körper," in *Tirol, Land und Natur, Volk und Geschichte, Geistiges Leben* (Munich: Deutscher und Österreichischer Alpenverein, 1933): 1:337–89; Rudolf Granichstaedten-Czerva, *Die Entstehung der Tiroler Landesverfassung (1790–1861)* (Innsbruck, Vienna, Munich, Bozen: Tyrolia, 1922); Joseph Egger, *Die Tiroler und Vorarlberger* (Vienna: K. Prochaska, 1882); on the 1720 Diet and the Pragmatic Sanction, see Nikolaus Grass, "Die pragmatische Sanktion und Tirol," *Der Donauraum* (1964), 15–17; Ferdinand Hirn, "Die Annahme der pragmatischen Sanktion durch die Stände Tirols," *Zeitschrift des Ferdinandeums*, Series 3, 47 (Innsbruck, 1902): 115–59; Ulrich G. Schaaf, "Die Tätigkeit und der Einfluss der Tiroler Landstände in der Regierungszeit Kaiser Karl VI (1714–40)," Innsbruck diss., 1953.

4. On these restrictions see chapter 3 on grievances. Also see Raffaele Zotti da Sacco, *Storia della Valle Lagarina* (1862–63; reprint Bologna: Forni, n.d.).

5. The five duchies were Styria, Carinthia, Carniola, Austria above the Enns, and Austria below the Enns.

6. Granichstaedten-Czerva, *Entstehung*, 4, 6–7.

7. Ibid., 8–9.

8. See Alois Mages von Kompillan, *Die Justizverwaltung in Tirol und Vorarlberg in den letzten hundert Jahren. Festschrift zur Eröffnung des neuen Justizgebäudes in Innsbruck* (Innsbruck: Wagner, 1877), 17–19, 22; Mayr, *Die politische Beziehungen*, 52–53; Otto Stolz, *Geschichtliche Beschreibung der ober- und*

vorderösterreichischen Lande (Karlsruhe: Südwestdeutsche Druck- und Verlags-Gesellschaft, 1943), 353.

9. There were some legal and traditional differences between the *Gericht* and *pretura*, but they are not of significance here. For more information on the origins and history of the jurisdictions, see: Hans Voltelini, *Erlauterungen zum historischen Atlas der österreichischen Alpenländer*, Abteilung 1: Die Landgerichts-karte, Part 3, "Das welsche Südtirol," (Vienna: Adolf Holzhausen, 1919); Otto Stolz, "Geschichte der Gerichte Deutschtirols," AÖG, 120 (1912): 83–334; Emil Werunsky, *Österreichische Reichs- und Rechtsgeschichte. Ein Lehr- und Handbuch* (Vienna: Manz, 1894–1938).

10. Maria Theresa created six *Kreise*, which Joseph II reduced to five: Upper Inntal, Lower Inntal, Pustertal, Etsch (and Eisack), and the Welsch Confines. The sixth Theresian *Kreis* was divided up, the Vintschgau going to the Upper Inntal and the Burggrafenamt to the Etsch *Kreis*. In the discussion that follows, the Etschland generally refers to the entire area of Joseph II's Etsch *Kreis*. There were also other, less dramatic border changes in the *Kreise* from their inception in 1755 until 1804 when the incorporation of Brixen and Trent changed the political geography of the princely county. See Fridolin Dörrer, "Probleme rund um die theresianische Kreiseinteilung Tirols," in *Beiträge zur geschichtlichen Landeskunde Tirols. Festschrift zum 60. Geburtstag von Prof. Dr. Franz Huter*, Schlern-Schriften, vol. 207 (Innsbruck: Wagner, 1959), 57–85; also see idem, "Die Verwaltungs-Kreise in Tirol und Vorarlberg (1754–1860)," in *Festschrift für Universitätsprofessor Dr. Franz Huter anlässlich der Vollendung des 70. Lebensjahres* (Innsbruck: Wagner, 1949), 25–68 plus maps.

11. See census data for 1781 and for previous and succeeding years, published in Helmut Reinalter, *Aufklärung—Absolutismus—Reaktion. Die Geschichte Tirols in der 2. Hälfte des 18. Jahrhunderts* (Vienna: A. Schendl, 1974), 49. After the secu-larization and incorporation of the principalities of Trent and Brixen in 1804, Italians constituted approximately half of Tyrol's population.

12. On inheritance laws and customs, see chapter 3.

13. Rudolf Granichstaedten-Czerva, *Beiträge zur Familiengeschichte Tirols*, 2: 229.

14. Eric R. Wolf, "Cultural Dissonance in the Italian Alps," *Comparative Studies in Society and History. An International Quarterly* 5 (The Hague: October 1962–July 1963): 13.

15. On the nobility and their position and prerogatives, see Hans Ho-chenegg, *Der Adel im Leben Tirols. Eine soziologische Studie*, Veröffentlichungen der Universität Innsbruck, No. 70 (Studien zur Rechts-, Wirtschafts- und Kulturge-schichte, No. 8) (Innsbruck: Kommissionsverlag der Österreichischen Kommis-sionsbuchhandlung, 1971).

16. At one time or another parts of the princely county were under the following "foreign" bishops: Brixen, Trent, Salzburg, Chur, Constance, Augsburg, Freising, Chiemsee, Aquileja, Görz, Feltre, Padua, and Venice. Until 1772 the bishop of Trent was under the ecclesiastical authority of the Patriarch of Aquileja;

when the Patriarchate was abolished in that year, the Trentine diocese was made directly subject to the papal curia; the rest of the Patriarchate became the diocese of Görz.

17. Johannes Hofer, "Zur Geschichte des Toleranzpatentes Josefs II. in Tirol," *Historisches Jahrbuch der Görres-Gesellschaft* 47 (1927): 500.

18. John Owen, *Letters on Holland, France, Switzerland, Germany and Italy* (London, 1796), 256, Letter 138, 30 April 1792.

19. Henry D. Inglis, *The Tyrol; with a Glance at Bavaria* (London: Whittaker, Treacher, and Co., 1834), 1:200–21.

20. The focus here is on Italian Tyrol and therefore on the princely county's relationship with Trent. For further information on Brixen, see, for example, Walter Tappeiner, "Die Beziehungen des Fürstentums Brixen zum Landesherrn und zu den Landständen Tirols von 1665–1803," Innsbruck diss., 1975.

21. See Hans Voltelini, "Ein Antrag des Bischofs von Trient auf Säcularisierung und Einverleibung seines Fürstentums in die Grafschaft Tirol vom Jahre 1781–82," *Veröffentlichungen des Museums Ferdinandeum*, Jg. 1936, No. 16 (Innsbruck 1938); idem, "Die territoriale Entwicklung der südlichen Landschaften Österreich-Ungarns im Mittelalter und in der Neuzeit und die Entstehung der heutigen Südgrenze Österreichs," *Mitteilungen der k. k. Geographischen Gesellschaft in Wien*, Nos. 8 and 9 (1916): 481–519; and Joseph Durig, *Ueber die staatsrechtlichen Beziehungen des italienischen Landestheiles von Tirol zu Deutschland und Tirol*, Jahres-Bericht der k. k. Ober-Realschule zu Innsbruck, Studienjahr 1863–64 (Innsbruck: Wagner, 1864), 29.

22. The cities and jurisdictions of the principalities did not generally send independent envoys to the Diets; the city of Trent did send deputies to the 1790 Diet.

23. On the Ferdinandean Transaction, see the section on wine in chapter 3; on the interdict of Rovereto's church, see chapter 2.

24. See Aldo Stella, "Riforme trentine dei Vescovi Sizzo e Vigilio di Thun (1764–1784)," *Archivio Veneto*, Anno 85, Series 5, vol. 54 (1954), 91.

25. Otto Stolz, *Geschichte des Zollwesens, Verkehrs und Handels in Tirol und Vorarlberg von den Anfängen bis ins XX. Jahrhundert*, Schlern-Schriften, vol. 108 (Innsbruck: Wagner, 1953), 29–30. For a copy of the 1777 treaty, see BC di Trento, Ms. No. 290. Also see Giulio Rizzoli, *Il Trentino nella sua condizione politica dei secoli XVIII e XIX* (Feltre: G. Sanussi and Co., 1903), 15; Durig, *Ueber die staatsrechtlichen Beziehungen*, 29 ff; and Joseph Egger, *Geschichte Tirols* (Innsbruck: Wagner, 1880), 3:92–93.

26. Thun maintained that his predecessor, Cristoforo Sizzo, had made a similar offer to Maria Theresa, but no documents exist to support his contention, and it does not appear as part of the 1777 treaty negotiations; see Voltelini, "Ein Antrag des Bischofs," 399–403. Documents concerning Thun's offer are in the same work, 399–412, and in Reinalter, *Aufklärung*, 404–5, 408–12.

27. Herbert Hassinger, "Der Aussenhandel der Habsburgermonarchie in der zweiten Hälfte des 18. Jahrhunderts," in *Die Wirtschaftliche Situation in Deutschland*

und Österreich um die Wende vom 18. zum 19. Jahrhundert (Stuttgart: Gustav Fischer, 1964), 77–78. Also see Otto Stolz, *Geschichte des Zollwesens,* 169–70.

28. "Cis-Leithania" refers to the lands and provinces that made up the Austrian half of the monarchy after the 1867 *Ausgleich* with Hungary; the primary parts of Cis-leithania were the German hereditary lands, the lands of the Crown of St. Wenceslas, Galicia, and the Littoral.

29. Stolz, *Geschichte des Zollwesens,* 88–89. Businessmen who brought their wares to the Bozen markets paid only the lower *Transito* tariff unless they sold to a Tyrolean, in which case they paid additionally the difference between the *Transito* and *Consumo.* On tariff studies and regulations of the 1750s and 1760s for Tyrol, see Adolf Beer, "Die Zollpolitik und die Schaffung eines einheitlichen Zollgebietes unter Maria Theresia," MIÖG, 14 (1893):237–326; Egger, *Geschichte,* 3:54–57; Hans Kramer, "Die Zollreform an der Südgrenze Tirols 1777–1785," in *Festschrift Hans v. Voltelini zum siebzigsten Geburtstage, 31. Juli 1932,* Veröffentlichungen des Museum Ferdinandeum, No. 12 (Innsbruck: Wagner, 1932), 240.

30. HHStA, SRP, 1783, No. 3528; the imperial Resolution to this *Staatsrat* Protocol is a lengthy discussion of the Tyrolean tariff; also see SRP, 1783, Nos. 494, 1929, 2826, 3444, 3709, and Paul Mitrofanov, *Joseph II. Seine politische und kulturelle Tätigkeit* (Vienna and Leipzig: C. W. Stern, 1910), 2:450–51; Beer, "Zollpolitik und Schaffung," 237–326; Kramer, "Zollreform," 260–61; Eduard Vehse, *Geschichte des österreichischen Hofs und Adels und der östreichischen Diplomatie* (Hamburg: Hoffman und Campe, 1852), 2:308; Stolz, *Geschichte des Zollwesens,* 92.

31. Thomas Nugent, *The Grand Tour; Or, a Journey through the Netherlands, Germany, Italy, and France,* 3rd ed. (London: J. Rivington and Sons, et al., 1778), 2:347–48.

32. George Waring, Jr., *Tyrol and the Skirt of the Alps* (New York: Harper & Brothers, 1880), 68.

33. Ibid., 71–72; also see Maximilien Misson, *Voyage d'Italie* (Amsterdam and Paris, 1743), 1:163.

34. Montaigne, writing from Bozen in 1580, as quoted in Nikolaus Grass, "Fragmente zur Geschichte der Tiroler Weinkultur," in *Festschrift für F. Ulmer,* Tiroler Wirtschaftsstudien No. 17 (Innsbruck, 1963), 158. Wolkenstein's comments are in Marx Sittich v. Wolkenstein, *Landesbeschreibung von Südtirol, verfasst um 1600. Festgabe zu Hermann Wopfners sechzigsten Lebensjahr,* Schlern-Schriften, vol. 34 (Innsbruck: Wagner, 1936), 47; and Stephan Keess, *Darstellung des Fabriks- und Gewerbswesens in seinem gegenwärtigen Zustande . . . ,* 2 volumes in four (Vienna: Mörschner and Jasper, 1834), Anhang, 7.

35. Nugent, *Grand Tour,* 2:347.

36. Hermann Ignaz Bidermann, *Die technische Bildung im Kaiserthum Österreich. Ein Beitrag zur Geschichte der Industrie und des Handels . . .* (Vienna: C. Gerold, 1854), 33. Also see Anton Baldauf, *Beiträge zur Handels- und Zollpolitik Österreichs in der zweiten Hälfte des XVIII. Jahrhunderts insbesondere unter Joseph II.* (Halle: C. A. Kaemmerer & Co., 1898), 59.

37. The plans for the silk-throwing machine were later smuggled into England and a huge throwing mill set up at Darby. See David S. Landes, *The Unbound Prometheus. Technological Change and Industrial Development in Western Europe from 1750 to the Present* (Cambridge University Press, 1970), 81.

38. Monsieur de Blainville, *Travels through Holland, Germany, Switzerland, But especially Italy, by the Late Monsieur de Blainville, Sometime Secretary to the Embassy of the States-General, at the Court of Spain* (London: John Noon, 1757), 1:427.

39. Nicolò Cristani de Rallo, *Breve Descrizione [sic] della Pretura de Roveredo del 1766* (Rovereto: G. Grigoletti, 1893), 9. Cristani was an official of the *Gubernium* and his *Descrizione* an official report; it was originally submitted in German and translated into Italian (translator unknown) for this publication in the following century.

40. Ibid, 37; also see Keess, *Darstellung*, Anhang, 61. In 1723, Charles VI established the "Kaiserliche Tabakmanufaktur," the precursor of the Habsburg tobacco monopoly; both Tyrol and Hungary were excluded. Joseph II set up a new tobacco monopoly in 1784, but it was not extended to Tyrol until the nineteenth century. On tobacco, see, for example, M. N. Farini, "Come è sorta la manifattura tabacchi di Sacco un secolo fa," *ST*, 32 (1953): 240–45; Hassinger, "Der Stand der Manufakturen," 126; Johann Retzer, *Tabakpachtung in den österreichischen Ländern von 1670 bis 1783* (Vienna, 1784); Antonio Soini, "Ala," *Der Sammler für Geschichte und Statistik von Tirol* 4 (Innsbruck, 1809), 94–98; *150 Jahre Österreichs Tabakregie, 1784–1934* (Vienna, 1934).

41. The first monoply privilege went to the inhabitants of Sacco in 1584, and was renewed several times, before being granted to the Fedrigotti and Baroni families. For information concerning this transport company, see Guido Canali, "I trasporti sull'Adige da Bronzolo a Venezia," *Archivio per l'Alto Adige* 24 (1929): 277–402, and an unpublished history by Dr. Franz v. Plattner, a Bozen mercantile official, in Innsbruck, Bibliothek des Landesmuseum Ferdinandeum, Dip. 972 II. Also see Richard Staffler, "Das Holzmonopol der Sacco'schen Speditionskompagnie," *Der Schlern*, 23(9–10) (1949): 51–57; and Richard Staffler, "Die Speditionskompagnie von Sacco," *Der Schlern*, 23(9–10) (1949): 371–75.

CHAPTER TWO

1. Lodovico Muratori to Girolamo Tartarotti, as quoted in Ferruccio Trentini, "Duecent'anni di vita dell'Accademia degli Agiati," *Atti*, Servies 5, 1 (1952): 6.

2. Muratori's ideas on church reform had a great influence on Joseph II and his church policies. See Eleonore Zlabinger, *Lodovico Antonio Muratori und Österreich*, Veröffentlichungen der Universität Innsbruck, No. 53 (Studien zur Rechts-, Wirtschafts- und Kulturgeschichte, ed. Nikolaus Grass, vol. 6), (Innsbruck: Österreichischen Kommissionsbuchhandlung, 1970).

3. Muratori received much support for his *Rerum*, some of it from very high places. In 1721 a group of mostly anonymous benefactors consisting of influential Lombard nobles formed the *Società palatinà* to help finance the *Rerum*'s publication. Some of these nobles turned to Emperor Charles VI and also enlisted his aid since after the Treaty of Utrecht in 1713 he became the ruler of Lombardy. The emperor's assistance sometimes took the form of a veiled threat aimed at territorial princes reluctant to make manuscripts available to Muratori; access to the documents and their inclusion in the *Rerum* usually followed. On the society of nobles, see Luigi Vischi, "La Società palatinà di Milano," *Archivio storico lombardo* 7 (1880): 391–566.

4. See Ferruccio Trentini, "Duecent'anni di vita dell'Accademia degli Agiati," *Atti*, Series 5, 1 (1952): 6–7; also see Trentini's "La figura e l'opera di Girolamo Tartarotti nel bicentenario della morte," *Atti*, Series 6, 2 (1960): 47; and Ettore Zucchelli, *Il Ginnasio de Rovereto in duecentocinquant'anni di vita (1672–1922)*, Annuario del R. Ginnasio-Liceo "Vittorio Emanuele III" di Rovereto, new series, Anno IV, scholastic year 1921–22 (Rovereto: Ugo Grandi, 1923), 12.

5. Franco Venturi, *Italy in the Enlightenment. Studies in a Cosmopolitan Century* (London: Longman Group Limited, 1972), 107. Begun in 1744 and finished in 1747, *Del Congresso* appeared in 1749 in Venice although it was marked "Rovereto."

6. As quoted by Venturi, *Italy in the Enlightenment*, 109.

7. Ibid., 108.

8. On this witchcraft debate, see Ludwig Rapp, *Die Hexenprozesse und ihre Gegner in Tirol*, 2nd ed. (Brixen: A. Wagner, 1891). Maria Theresa finally put an end to witch trials in Habsburg territory by making it a state crime and removing it from the jurisdiction of the church; she felt the phenomenon was the result of sickness and not possession by the devil.

9. See Trentini, "Figura," 58; also see Francesco Vigilio Barbacovi, *Memorie Storiche della Città di Trento e del Territorio di Trento* (Trent: Monaui, 1821), 1:180; also Cesare Ravenelli, "Memorie originale. Un Interdetto per una polemica. Contributi per una storia di Girolamo Tartarotti e i suoi tempi," *Tridentum* 5 (1902): 302.

10. See Trentini, "Figura," 60–63; Ravenelli, "Interdetto," 310–20, for details of the attempt to have the interdict lifted.

11. As quoted in Filippo Largaioli, "Un gruppo di lettere inedite di Girolamo Tartarotti a G. M. Mazzuchelli (1748–1758)," *Tridentum* 4 (1901): 162.

12. The Academy of the Accesi was not in Habsburg territory but in the confederated principality ruled by the prince-bishop. This academy was established in 1628 or 1629 with the blessings and patronage of the prince-bishop and was essentially a literary society; it existed more or less continuously until 1732.

13. Christian Schneller, *Südtirolische Landschaften. Zweite Reihe. Das Lagerthal—La Valle Lagarina* (Innsbruck: Wagner, 1900), 228. This academy was so short-lived and left so few traces that some historians have questioned whether it

existed at all. After examining what evidence is available, Ettore Zucchelli concluded that the Dodonei were primarily friends meeting together for purposes of study; see Ettore Zucchelli, "Iacopo Tartarotti (1708–1787)," *LVI Annuario del'i.r. Ginnasio superiore di Rovereto* (Rovereto, 1908), 32–33.

14. As quoted in Schneller, *Lagerthal*, 227; Schneller also translated it into German on 440, n. 44.

15. Cesare Beccaria's *Dei delitti e delle pene* (Livorno, 1764), Pietro Verri's *Meditazioni sulla economia politica* (Livorno, 1772) and his two-volume *Storia di Milano* (Milan, 1783–98), and his brother Alessandro's *Le Notti romane al sepolcro dei Scipione* (Rome, 1792). The name Pugni apparently came from the pugnacious attitude of the academy's members in their disputes with established academies in Milan and rumors that they were so intense and serious about their work that they came to blows over it.

16. Carli's essay is reproduced in S. Romagnoli, ed., *Il Caffè* (Milan: Feltrinelli, 1960), 297–303, and in Ettore Rota, *Il Problema italiano dal 1700 al 1815 (L'Idea unitaria)* (Milan: Istituto per gli Studi di Politica internazionale, n.d.), 44–51. Also see Emiliana Pasca Noether, *The Seeds of Italian Nationalism 1700–1815* (1951; reprinted New York: AMS Press, Inc., 1969), 102,104–5, 121–22; and Giuseppe Ricuperati, "Zeitschriften und Gesellschaften im Italien der Reformen. Enzyklopädie und Aufklärung in den Zeitschriften der zweiten Hälfte des 18. Jahrhunderts," in Friedrich Engel-Janosi, Grete Klingenstein, and Heinrich Lutz, eds., *Formen der europäischen Aufklärung* (Munich: R. Oldenbourg, 1976), 207, 211.

17. Gian Rinaldo Carli, "Della patria degli italiani," reproduced in Rota, "Il Problema," 45.

18. For additional information on the Academia Taxiana, see Andreas Alois diPauli, "Anton Roschmann und seine Schriften," *Beiträge zur Geschichte, Statistik, Naturkunde und Kunst von Tirol und Vorarlberg* 2 (1826): 37–61; Nikolaus Grass, "Benediktinische Geschichtswissenschaft und die Anfänge des Instituts für österreichische Geschichtsforschung," MIÖG 68 (1960): 478; Nikolaus Grass, "Die Innsbrucker Gelehrtenakademie des 18. Jahrhundert und das Stift Wilten," *Tiroler Heimatblätter* 23 (1948), passim; and Zlabinger, *Muratori*, 24, 40–45.

19. Composizioni delgi Agiati—Anno I, Tornata VII del 30 giungo 1751, No. 55, Archivio Accademico, BCGT, quoted in Trentini, "Agiati," 8.

20. On Muratori's "I primi disegni della repubblica letteraria d'Italia," which appeared in his *Delle riflessioni sopra il buon gusto nelle scienze e nelle arti*, see Noether, *Seeds*, 116–17; Zlabinger, *Muratori*, 21–22; and Carli, *Muratori*, 55–56, 61. Also see Antonio Zieger, *Bagliori unitari ed aspirazioni nazionali 1751–1797* (Milan: Pallade), 1933, 16, on the Agiati and the literary republic.

21. On the linguistic disputes and the academies, see Noether, *Seeds*, 111–25.

22. Composizioni degli Agiati—Anno I, vol. 1, No. 2, Archivio Accademico, BCGT, quoted in Trentini, "Agiati," 13. This speech was later published as *Lezione sopra il dialetto roveretano* by G. Valeriano Vannetti (Rovereto: F. Antonio

Marchesani, 1761), as noted in [M. Manfroni], *L'Accademia de Rovereto dal 1750 al 1880* (Rovereto: Grigoletti, 1882), 14–15. Also see Fausta Regina Rossi, "Adamo Chiusole, Scrittore d'Arte e Pittore 1729–1787," *ST* 19 (1938): 77. For some works by early members of the academy, see Irene Tuma-Holzer and Josef Jacob Holzer, "Die 'Accademia degli Agiati' von Rovereto. Aspekte ihrer Tätigkeit im Zeitalter der Aufklärung," *Österreich in Geschichte und Literatur* 21 (November/December 1977): 353–63.

23. Trentini, "Agiati," 12.

24. Francesco Frisinghelli, "Che questo nostro paese di Rovereto è parte della vera Italia," Ms. 3005, f. 2, 6, 8v–9, BC di Trento; the Trent library also has another copy, Ms. 2439; the memoir is also reproduced in Adriano Rigotti, "Francesco Giuseppe Frisinghelli d'Isera, Prete, letterato e poeta (1690–1758)," *ST* 53 (1974): 30–59, 127–45; lengthy sections in Zieger, *Baglioni*, passim. Some local scholars disagreed with Frisinghelli's arguments, though not with his conclusion. *Agiatissimo* Vannetti sent the professor one such critique from someone who preferred to remain anonymous—perhaps Vannetti himself. Frisinghelli replied to each objection in a lengthy letter that formed a supplement to his original memoir; for the letter-supplement of 12 September 1752, see Ms. 48.21, No. 123, BCGT.

25. Sperges' map was published as *Tyrolis Pars Meridionalis episcopatum tridentum (olim ducatem et marchiam) finitimasque valles complexa . . .* (Innsbruck, 1751; reissued 1762). On Sperges, who later became head of the Dipartimento di Italia in Vienna, see Andreas A. DiPauli, "Der Freiherr Joseph von Sperges," *Neue Zeitschrift des Ferdinandeums für Tirol und Vorarlberg*, Series 2, 3 (1837): 1–57; Franz Pascher, "Joseph Freiherr von Sperges auf Palenz und Reisdorf 1725–1791," *Österreich in Geschichte und Literatur* 10 (1966): 539–49; Hans (Hermann) Lentze, "Joseph von Spergs und der Josephinismus," *Festschrift zur Feier des 200-jährigen Bestand des Haus-, Hof-, und Staatsarchivs*, 2 (Vienna, 1952): 392–412, repr. in Hans (Hermann) Lentze, *Studia Wiltinensia*, Forschungen zur Rechts- und Kulturgeschichte, ed. Nikolaus Grass (Innsbruck: Wagner, 1964), 1:165–93.

26. See chapter 1. The Manfroni map bore the title *Tyrolis pars meridionalis Episcopatum et Principatum Tridentum continens*. For the objections and protests of the Trentine cathedral chapter, see Ms. No. 233, f. 41, 42v, BC di Trento. These documents are also published in B. T., "Una questione per una carta geografica," *Archivio Storico Lombardo*, Series 2, Anno XI, 1 (Milan 1884): 533–47.

27. Ms. 408, Miscellanea, f. 53, 55v, BC di Trento; the article appeared anonymously in the *Giornale Enciclopedico* of Vicenza, No. 9, 3–8; also see Rota, *Il Problema italiano*, 54–55.

28. Vannetti to Tiraboschi, 21 April 1780, Letter XXVI in *Carteggio fra Girolamo Tiraboschi e Clementino Vannetti (1776–1793)*, G. Cavazzuti and F. Pasini, eds. (Modena: Giovanni Ferraguti and Co., 1912), 46. On Vannetti, see, for example, Vittore Vittori, *Clementino Vannetti. Studio del secolo passato* (Florence: Elzeviriana, 1899).

29. Vannetti to Tiraboschi, 20 May 1780, Letter XXVII in *Carteggio*, 49. Also see Livio Marchetti, *Il Trentino nel Risorgimento* (Milan, Rome, Naples, 1913),

1:19; and Alberto M. Ghisalberti, *Gli albori del risorgimento italiano (1700–1815)* (Rome: Paolo Cremonese, 1931), 88. For an in-depth view of Vannetti's anti-Germanism, see Ferdinando Pasini, "Memorie originali. Di alcuni giudizi di Clementino Vannetti sulla letteratura contemporanea," *Tridentum* 4 (1901): 433–57 and 5 (1902): 57–85.

30. Tiraboschi to Vannetti, 14 August 1782 and 6 April 1783, Letters LXXI and LXXXIV in *Carteggio*, 113, 128; Vannetti to Tiraboschi, 30 March 1783 and 10 August 1782, Letters LXXXII and LXX in *Carteggio*, 127, 110.

31. Marchetti, *Il Trentino*, 1:16. Also see Michael Mayr, *Der italienische Irredentismus. Sein Entstehen und seine Entwicklung, vornehmlich in Tirol* (Innsbruck: Tyrolia, 1917), 6.

32. Vannetti to Tiraboschi, 4 July 1789, Letter CCIV in *Carteggio*, 250; this letter includes the sonnet.

33. Tiraboschi to Vannetti, 12 July 1789, Letter CCV in *Carteggio*, 253.

34. Vannetti to Tiraboschi, 17 July 1789, Letter CCVI in *Carteggio*, 254. On the new regulations and other resulting grievances, see chapter 3.

35. Alberto Manzi, "Clementino Vannetti tra i comici," *Nuova Antologia* vol. 353, Fasc. 1414, Anno IX, Series 7 (Rome, February 1931), 454–55; this article contains excerpts from Morrocchesi's diary, which he kept while in Rovereto.

36. Translated with the assistance of Victoria deGrazia. Several versions of this sonnet are published, with very minor variations; see Mayr, *Der italienische Irredentismus*, 7; Giuseppe Borghetti, *Trento italiano* (Florence, 1903), 26.

37. The correspondence with Pederzani is Ms. 47.27, No. 32, BCGT; for the changes made, see this correspondence and Ms. 210, f. 133, BC di Trento; also see Manzi, "Comici," 461; and Vittori, *Vannetti*, 15.

38. Carlo Rosmini to Clementino Vannetti, 16 January 1791, Ms. 7.33, fol. 18, BCGT; also see Ms. 7.34, fol. 34, BCGT. Also see Mayr, *Der italienische Irredentismus*, 6, and Ghisalberti, *Gli albori*, 88.

39. See Trentini, "Agiati," 14, 15.

40. Enrico Broll, "Carlo Antonio Pilati (28 decembre 1733–27 ottobre 1802)," *Archivio Trentino* 17 (1902): 197; also see Adam Wandruszka, *Österreich und Italien im 18. Jahrhundert* (Vienna: Verlag für Geschichte und Politik, 1963), 97.

41. Franco Venturi, "Carlantonio Pilati," in *Illuministi italiani*, vol. 3: *Riformatori Lombardi Piemontesi e Toscani* (Milan and Naples: Riccardo Ricciardi, [1958], 565, 569. Also see Alfred Noyer-Weidner, *Die Aufklärung in Oberitalien*, Münchener Romanistische Arbeiten, vol. 11 (Munich: Max Hueber, 1957), 90.

42. The other work is *Riflessioni di' un italiano sopra la Chiesa in generale e sopra il clero si regolare che secolare sopra i Vescovi ed i Pontifici romani e sopra i diritti ecclesiastici de' Principi.*

43. Franco Venturi, "Da illuminista a illuminato: Carlo Pilati," in *La Cultura illuministica in Italia*, Mario Fubini, ed. (Torino, 1957), 237–39; also see Meta von Salis Marshlins, "Ein genialer Abenteurer," 68. *Jahresbericht der Historisch-Antiquarischen Gesellschaft von Graubünden*, Jg. 1938 (Chur, 1939): 126.

44. Pilati was quite myopic.

45. Maria Rigati, *Un illuminista trentino: Carlantonio Pilati* (Florence: Vallecchi, 1923), 242, 245.

46. See Ms. 14.5.(10), BCGT.

CHAPTER THREE

1. Since the Italians were, for the most part, excluded from participation in the Estates' assemblies, German Tyrol is often used synonymously, here and elsewhere, with the Estates.

2. Not all the changes were unwelcome. Joseph decreed a tariff more favorable to the Bozen markets and transit trade, which provided a large part of Tyrol's income. Maria Theresa began and Joseph continued road improvements throughout the Monarchy; and Joseph dismantled still further the by then almost negligible power of the guilds and continued to charter guild-free manufacturing enterprises. Except among the members of the few vestigial guilds, these moves were popular, but not popular enough to offset the discord caused by the other, more far-reaching changes.

3. Otto Stolz, "Die Bestätigung der alten Tiroler Landesfreiheiten durch die Landfürsten," in *Beiträge zur Geschichte und Heimatkunde Tirols. Festschrift zu Ehren Hermann Wopfners*, Schlern-Schriften, vol. 52 (Innsbruck: Wagner, 1947), Part 1, 323.

4. See Johannes Hofer, "Zur Geschichte des Toleranzpatentes Josefs II. in Tirol," *Historisches Jahrbuch der Görres-Gesellschaft* 47 (1927): 502,506, and 510, n. 19.

5. Helmut Reinalter, *Aufklärung—Absolutismus—Reaktion. Die Geschichte Tirols in der 2. Hälfte des 18. Jahrhunderts* (Vienna: A.Schendl, 1974), 87–88, 89–90.

6. Joseph Egger, *Geschichte Tirols* (Innsbruck: Wagner, 1876–80), 3:107. Joseph even provided for ex-monastics and ex-nuns to reclaim a share of the family inheritance; see *Justizfache*, Joseph II: Nr. 30, 9 Nov. 1781; Nr. 72, 30 Aug. 1782; Nr. 215, 26 Nov. 1783; Nr. 593, 6 Nov. 1786; Nr. 607, 28 Dec. 1786; Nr. 939, 22 Dec. 1788.

7. Paul Mitrofanov, *Joseph II. Seine politische und kulturelle Tätigkeit* (Vienna and Leipzig: C. W. Stern, 1910), Part 1, 377; also see Reinalter, *Aufklärung*, 68.

8. Joseph also banned emigration from other Habsburg lands; see Anton Taffner, "Die bisher unbekannten Auswanderungspatente des Kaisers Joseph II," *Südostdeutsche Vierteljahrsblätter*, 23 (1) (1974): 1–5.

9. During Maria Theresa's reign, some sort of perpetual congress for Tyrol was also discussed. See SRP Index entries under Tyrol for 1771 with reference to SRP Nos. 261, 517, 328, 707, and 3553; and for 1773 with reference to SRP No. 2876.

10. Egger, *Geschichte*, 3:122; also see Rudolf Granichstaedten-Czerva, *Die Entstehung der Tiroler Landesverfassung (1790–1861)* (Innsbruck, Vienna, Munich, and Bozen: Tyrolia, 1922), 10.

11. The second of "Zwo Relationen des Graf. Sauer vom 5. März 1787 u. 4. 7ber üeber die Verbesserungen in Tyrol," KFA, alt 1, neu 1, "Miscellanea von verschied. Prov. 1783–1787," No. 7, fol. 284–302; also KFA, alt 9, neu 7, Tirolo No. 7.

12. Sauer charged Unterrichter with badly mismanaging Estate funds and using his influence to his own advantage. Joseph ordered Count Sauer to be specific in his charges so that an orderly investigation could be conducted and so that if Unterrichter was found guilty, he might be suitably punished; Unterrichter's pension was withheld until the matter was resolved. Unterrichter presented his own case; Joseph acquitted him and reinstated his pension. See SRP, 1789, No. 874; Ferdinandeum, Dip. 1239/1240, "Tagebuch von A. A. diPauli über die Verhandlungen des offenen Landtages vom J. 1790," vol. 1, "Beylagen und Urkunden," "Erklärendes Verzeichniss" (hereafter this diary is cited as diPauli, Diet Diary); Egger, Geschichte, 3:130; also Reinalter, Aufklärung, 97.

13. For more on Welsch Tyrol's early representation, see Hermann Ignaz Bidermann, Die Italiäner im Tirolischen Provinzial-Verbande (Innsbruck: Wagner, 1874), 90, 153. For more information on this sixteenth-century Roveretan tax revolt, see Joseph Hirn, Erzherzog Ferdinand II. von Tirol. Geschichte seiner Regierung und seiner Länder (Innsbruck: Wagner, 1888), 2:41–43.

14. Bidermann, Italiäner, 158–60; and Ulrich G. Schaff, "Die Tätigkeit und der Einfluss der Tiroler Landstände in der Regierungszeit Kaiser Karl VI (1714–1740)" (Innsbruck diss., 1953), 17.

15. Clemente Baroni-Cavalcabò, "Ragioni dei Distretti del Tirolo Italiano austriaco per essere ammessi alle Diete tanto generali che particolari della Provincia con Voto e Sessione," as published in Savino Pedrolli, "I manoscritti del Barone G. B. Todeschi," Atti, Series 2, 16 (Rovereto, 1909): 10–11.

16. Ibid., 12–13.

17. It was legal to import some foreign wine, for example, "for the needs of the court, and of the military and the treasury," provided that the required patent or license could be produced. But even this limitation was often a loophole, since the number of permits or licenses often reached a level that was most unsettling to the South Tyroleans. Officials made extensive use of this privilege, some to the extent of carrying on formal trade in foreign spirits. See Hirn, Ferdinand II, 1:411; Joseph Egger, Die Tiroler und Vorarlberger, Die Völker Oesterreich-Ungarns, vol. 4 (Vienna: K. Prochaska, 1882), 237; Otto Stolz, "Zur Geschichte des Landwirtschaft in Tirol," Tiroler Heimat, New Series, 3 (1,2), (Innsbruck, 1930), 95.

18. Ferdinand Tremel, Wirtschafts- und Sozialgeschichte Österreichs (Vienna: Franz Deuticke, 1969), 111, 214; Otto Stolz, "Zur Geschichte des Weinbaues in Tirol," Der Schlern, 222 (9), (September 1948), 330–37; also Otto Stolz, Geschichte des Zollwesens, Verkehrs und Handels in Tirol und Vorarlberg von den Anfängen bis ins XX. Jahrhundert, Schlern-Schriften, vol. 108 (Innsbruck: Wagner, 1953), 75. The ordinance is published in Ausgewählte Urkunden zur Verfassungs-Geschichte der deutsch-österreichischen Erblande im Mittelalter, eds. Ernst Schwind and Alphons Dopsch (Innsbruck: Wagner, 1895), document no. 128, 256–57. Also see Matthias Mayer, Der mittelalterliche Weinbau im Nordtiroler Unterlande, Schlern-Schriften, vol. 95 (Innsbruck: Wagner, 1952), 63.

19. M. Mayer, *Der mittelalterliche Weinbau*, 63.

20. Emphasis added; "A Perpetua Memoria" of Maximilian I, November 1510, reproduced in Italian translation in Raffaele Zotti da Sacco, *Storia della Valle Lagarina* (1862–63; reprinted Bologna: Forni Editore, n.d.) 2:1–19; according to Zotti, the original Latin document was published in the eighteenth century in Clemente Baroni-Cavalcabò, *Idea della Storia della Valle Lagarina*, 215, No. 5. For the city council's conditions, see Zotti, 1:446, Point 11.

21. Egger, *Tiroler und Vorarlberger*, 237; also Hirn, *Ferdinand II*, 1:411.

22. Hirn, *Ferdinand II*, 1:411–12, and n. 1; and Egger, *Tiroler und Vorarlberger*, 238.

23. Guiseppe Dal Ri, *Notizie intorno all'Industria ed al Commercio del Principato di Trento dal sacro Concilio (1545) fino alla secolarizzazione (1803)* (Trento, 1888), 26–27; also Hirn, *Ferdinand II*, 1:411. The duty was 18 carantani or 18 kreuzer per orna/eimer. The old measure of 5,200 orna (about 400,000 liters) was equivalent to 325 wagon kegs. Also see the unpublished "Weingeschichte," KFA, alt 123, neu 121, No. 1, Enzenberg's Journal, section 3, which is a continuation of his history of Tyrol, "Vom Kaiser Ferdinand I., dessen zweiten Sohn Erzherzog Ferdinand, dem Landtage vom J. 1573. und darauf getroffene Landtag- und Steuereinrichtung," 3rd–8th paragraphs; also Stolz, *Geschichte des Zollwesens*, 75; and Hirn, *Ferdinand II*, 1:411.

24. BC di Trento, Ms. 1157, " 'Memoriale della città di Rovereto presentato nel 1743 alla Regina di Ungheria e Boemia,' con osservazioni. Tratta del commercio di esportazione dei vini."

25. Ibid., fol. 1v–2, 5v–6, 2v–3.

26. Ibid., fol. 6v.

27. Ibid., fol. 7v–8.

28. The Nevis (or Lavis) Bridge was eight kilometers (5 miles) north of Trent on the Etsch/Adige River. This bridge, where the duties on Welsch wines were collected, was described by an eighteenth-century traveler in Monsieur de Blainville, *Travels through Holland, Germany, Switzerland, But especially Italy: by the Late Monsieur de Blainville, Sometime Secretary to the Embassy of the States-General, at the Court of Spain*, translated into English by the late Dr. Turnbull (London: John Noon, 1757), 1:416–17.

29. See diPauli, Diet Diary, Beilage No. LII, ff. 534–34v; the old measures were 254 eimer (about 17,831,520 liters) and 56,873 eimer (about 3,981,100 liters); also see KFA, alt 123, neu 121, No. 5, Punkt 19.

30. Jürgen Bücking, *Kultur und Gesellschaft in Tirol um 1600. Des Hippolytus Guarinonius' "Grewel der Verwüstung Menschlichen Geschlechts" (1610) als kulturgeschichtliche Quelle des frühen 17. Jahrhunderts*, Historische Studien, vol. 401 (Lübeck and Hamburg, 1968), 63. For more on wine falsification and the attempts to stop it, see Nikolaus Grass, "Fragmente zur Geschichte der Tiroler Weinkultur," in *Festschrift für F. Ulmer*, Tiroler Wirtschaftsstudien 17 (Innsbruck, 1963), 159–60; *Maria Theresa Laws*, vol. 5, No. 915, 182; *Justizfache*, Franz II, 3 Sept. 1803, 499, sections 156–58.

31. "Die früheren Wein und Weinfuhrlohnstaxen," *Tiroler Bote*, 1885, Nos. 60–66, as cited in Ri, *Notizie*, 27.

32. Otto Stolz, *Quellen zur Geschichte des Zollwesens und Handelsverkehres in Tirol und Vorarlberg vom 13. bis 18. Jahrhundert* (Wiesbaden: F. Steiner, 1955), 257, No. 4. A copy of this treaty is in BC di Trento, Ms. No. 290. The 1777 treaty may have been part of the preliminaries intended to lead to secularization and incorporation of the principality into Tyrol (see discussion in chapter 1).

33. See *Joseph Laws*, vol. 9, 66–67, and cf. note 22 above.

34. Ri, *Notizie*, 25–27; also SRP, 1789, No. 1239; and Vienna, Hofkammerarchiv, Camerale, 1790, Fasc. 7, Juni, Fol. 585, Exp. 516.

35. *Maria Theresa Laws*, vol. 2, No. 366, 406; vol. 3, 333, No. 449; also see Stolz, "Zur Geschichte des Weinbaues," 331.

36. Frida Reitböch, "Die kulturellen und sozial Reformen unter der Regierung der Kaiserin Maria Theresia in Tirol," (Innsbruck diss., 1943), 88.

37. Sebastian Hölzl, "Studien zum Pflichtsschulwesen in Tirol 1774–1806. Zum 200 Jahres Jubiläum der Mariatheresianischen 'Schulordnung,' " Part 1, *Tiroler Heimat* 38 (1974): 92. On the gymnasium at Rovereto, see Ettore Zucchelli, *Il Ginnasio di Rovereto in duecentocinquant'anni di vita (1672–1922)*, Annuario del R. Ginnasio-Liceo "Vittorio Emanuele III" di Rovereto, New Series, Anno IV (Rovereto: Ugo Grandi, 1923), 15–16. When Maria Theresa ascended the throne, there were four gymnasia in Tyrol: Innsbruck (est. 1562), Hall (1573), Rovereto (c. 1670), Meran (1725). During her reign the one at Hall closed, but others opened at Lienz (1772) and Ala (1774); and the Collegium Nobilium or Theresianum was founded at Innsbruck (1775), in part through the legacy left by the Roveretan Jesuit Bartolomeo Betta dal Toldo. See Rudolf Granichstaedten-Czerva, *Innsbrucker Theresianisten. (Die Theresianische Ritter-Akademie zu Innsbruck)* (Innsbruck: Albert Ditterich, 1951).

38. Hölzl, "Studien zum Pflichtsschulwesen," Part 1, 96, 109, 116, 127; and Part 3, *Tiroler Heimat* 40 (1976): 53. Also see Zuchelli, *Ginnasio*, 29.

39. Zucchelli, *Ginnasio*, 31, 37–39.

40. Clementino Vannetti to Girolamo Tiraboschi, 23 April 1779, Letter XVII in *Cartaggio fra Girolamo Tiraboschi e Clementino Vannetti (1776–1793)*, eds. G. Cavazzuti and F. Passini (Modena: Ferraguti, 1912), 33–34. He also complained about the appointment of Giambattista Socrella as new director of the gymnasium in June 1780. Socrella, an ex-Jesuit, was neither Italian nor German, but Ladin; and Vannetti bemoaned the school's fate: "Thus education will always be betrayed: the barbarians come again to browbeat the Italians, and all plot to extinguish every germ of courtesy. A Ladin director of studies in a land of Italy! What could be more absurd?" (See Vannetti to Tiraboschi, 26 June 1780, Letter XXXII in *Cartaggio*, 57; also quoted in Zucchelli, *Ginnasio*, 46.

41. Zucchelli, *Ginnasio*, 45.

42. Ibid., 48–49 and n. 1.

43. *Justizfache*, Joseph II, first 4 years of his reign, 391, No. 329; Jakob Probst, ed., *Geschichte der Universität in Innsbruck seit ihrer Entstehung bis zum Jahre 1860*

(Innsbruck: Wagner, 1869), 126–27.

44. *Justizfache,* Joseph II, in the 7th year of his reign, 110–11, No. 655, decree of 26 March 1787.

45. *Justizfache,* Joseph II in the 8th year of his reign, 1, No. 450, decree of 30 November 1787. The *landesübliche* languages were: German in the greater part of the German hereditary lands, Italian in the Italian areas, and Latin in Galicia, Hungary, Croatia, and Transylvania. In addition, Italian and less frequently Latin, as well as French were used by the *Hofstellen* in Vienna and in correspondence with them.

46. *Justizfache,* Joseph II, in the 7th year of his reign, 99, No. 633. On the Bozen Market regulations, see Alois Mages von Kompillan, *Die Justizverwaltung in Tirol und Vorarlberg in den letzten hundert Jahren. Festschrift zur Eröffnung des neuen Justizgebäudes in Innsbruck* (Innsbruck: Wagner, 1887), 31; and Alfred Fischel, *Das österreichische Sprachenrecht* (Brünn: Friedrich Irrgang, 1910), 36.

47. *Justizfache,* Joseph II, in the 6th year of his reign, 45, No. 548, and 7th year, 6, No. 606. Also see Egger, *Geschichte,* 3:112.

48. John W. Cole, *Estate Inheritance in the Italian Alps,* Research Reports No. 10, Department of Anthropology, Univ. of Massachusetts, Amherst (December 1971), 12, 25, 28, 29. Also see Hans Voltelini, "Zur Geschichte des ehelichen Güterrechtes in Tirol," in *Festgaben zur Ehren Max Budinger* (Innsbruck: Wagner, 1898), 331–64; and Gunter Wesener, *Geschichte des Erbrechtes in Österreich seit der Rezeption* (Graz and Cologne: Herman Böhlaus Nachf., 1957).

49. Cole, *Estate Inheritance,* 42.

50. Mages von Kompillan, *Justizverwaltung,* 20; also Cole, *Estate Inheritance,* 42, 52.

CHAPTER FOUR

1. Paul Mitrofanov, *Joseph II. Seine politische und kulturelle Tätigkeit* (Vienna and Leipzig: C. W. Stern, 1910), 1:332. It would be interesting to see the following documents, if they still exist, in Pergen-Akten in the Allgemeines Verwaltungsarchiv; during research for this study, the Pergen-Akten were closed for restoration: XVIII/D 1, H 8–12 (X., XI. 1789), "Die geheime Polizeiinstruktion Wenzel Graf v. Sauer, Gouverneur von Tirol, ihn vorgelegt"; X/B,H 5, H 6 (11.21.I. 1790), "Graf von Sauer, Gouverneur von Tirol. Bericht über Unzufriedenheit in Tirol"; XVIII/8, H 4, H 7 (3., 19. II. 1790), "Graf v. Sauer, Meldung über gefährliche Zeitungsnachrichten"; and XXII/1, H 13 (12. III. 1791), "Über die Polizei-Tätigkeit Graf von Sauer." Mitrofanov had access to these documents before they were badly burned in 1927.

2. See Ferdinandeum, Dip. 1239 and 1240, "Tagebuch von A. A. diPauli über die Verhandlungen des offenen Landtages vom J. 1790," "Erklärendes Verzeichniss der Urkunden," no folio numbers; hereafter cited as diPauli, Diet Diary.

3. AVA, Hofkanzleiakten, IV M 3 Tirol, "Schreiben des Gouverneurs Graf

Wenzel von Sauer an den Obersten Kanzler Graf Leopold von Kollowrat vom 6.1.1790," as reproduced in Hans Hollerweger, "Die Zustände in Tirol am Ende der Regierungszeit Joseph II.," MÖStA 21 (1968): 124-33; also reproduced in Helmut Reinalter, *Aufklärung—Absolutismus—Reaktion. Die Geschichte Tirols in der 2. Hälfte des 18. Jahrhunderts* (Vienna: A. Schendl, 1974), 265-75.

4. AVA, Hofkanzlei, IV M 3 Tirol, "Vortrag der Hofkanzlei vor dem Kaiser von 22.1.1790 und Entschliessung"; as reproduced in Hollerweger, "Zustände," 133-40, and in Reinalter, *Aufklärung*, 276-85. Also see SRP, 1790, No. 247.

5. SRP, 1790, No. 247.

6. AVA, VII C 1, Karton 721, A. H. Resolution vom 24. Jan. 1790, as quoted in Mitrofanov, 1:381. Joseph, faced with imminent rebellion in Hungary, on 28 January 1790 also repealed his reforms for that land, except for the Toleration Patent, the Livings Patent for the clergy, and the legislation on the peasantry.

7. AVA, Altes Kultusarchiv 11 Tirol 93 ex Februario 1790, "Weiteres Schreiben des Gouverneurs an den Obersten Kanzler vom 4.2.1790," as reproduced in Hollerweger, "Zustände," 140-41; and in Reinalter, *Aufklärung*, 285-86.

8. Joseph Egger, *Geschichte Tirols* (Innsbruck: Wagner, 1876-80), 3:126.

9. His emphasis; Robert Murray Keith, *Memoirs and Correspondence (Official and Familiar) of Sir Robert Murray Keith* (London: Henry Colburn, 1849), 2:250.

10. Leopold to Marie Christine, 12 February 1790, in "Nachlass des Herzogs Albert von Sachsen-Teschen," quoted in Adam Wolf, ed., *Leopold II. und Marie Christine. Ihr Briefwechsel (1781-1792)* (Vienna: Carl Gerold's Sohn, 1867), 95.

11. Leopold to Joseph, 16 February 1790 and 24 February 1790, in Alfred Arneth, ed., *Joseph II. und Leopold von Toscana. Ihr Briefwechsel von 1781 bis 1790* (Vienna: Wilhelm Braumüller, 1872), 2:320, 321.

12. Cölestin Wolfsgruber, *Franz I. Kaiser von Österreich* (Vienna and Leipzig: Wilhelm Braumüller, 1899), 2:155.

13. Leopold to Marie Christine, 2 March 1790, in Wolf, *Leopold II. und Marie Christine*, 116, 118.

14. For the "confession of faith" letter, see ibid, 84-86.

15. Leopold to Marie Christine, 1 June 1789, in Adolf Beer, ed., *Leopold II., Franz II., und Catharina, Ihre Correspondenz* (Leipzig: Duncker & Humblot, 1874), 213.

16. Adam Wandruszka, "Die Persönlichkeit Kaiser Leopolds II.," *Historische Zeitschrift* 192 (1961): 300; and Adam Wandruszka, *Leopold II. Erzherzog von Österreich, Grossherzog von Toskana, König von Ungarn u. Böhmen, Römischer Kaiser* (Vienna and Munich: Herold, 1965), 2:279.

17. Philip Mazzei, *Memoirs of the Life and Perigrinations of the Florentine Philip Mazzei 1730-1816*, trans. Howard R. Marraro (New York: Columbia University Press, 1942), 246.

18. All during February Leopold wrote Joseph of plans to take this Tyrolean route because bad weather had made the shorter route through Venice impassable. See letters to Joseph of 16 and 24 February in Arneth, ed., *Joseph II. und Leopold*,

2:320, 321. Leopold stopped in Mantua before arriving in Rovereto. There has been some discussion in the literature about why Leopold chose this route rather than the shorter one through Venice in the spring; see Adam Wandruszka, "Leopold II., Die 'Welschen Confinen' und die Stände Tirols," MÖStA, Festschrift Richard Blaas, 31 (1978): 154-60; and a conversation with Adam Wandruszka, summer 1976, in Vienna.

19. See KFA, alt 4, neu 3, No. 1, "Doglianze generali sentite da S.M. e notate nel suo Viaggio per venire a Vienna, nel Marzo 1790 in Tirolo, Carintia e Stiria." No. 1 and No. 2 are identical in content except that the documents in No. 1 are in German (although the cover description is in Italian) and the documents in No. 2 are in Italian. For a brief summary of all the 1790 Tyrolean grievances, see Otto Stolz, Geschichte des Landes Tirol (Innsbruck and Munich: Tyrolia, 1955), 576-77.

20. KFA, alt 4, neu 3, No. 1, f. 16-17 and No. 2, fol. 44-45.

21. KFA, alt 4, neu 3, No. 1, f. 14-14v and No. 2, fol. 46-46v.

22. Antonio Zieger, "Penombre massoniche settecentesche," Archivio per l'Alto Adige, Part 1, 12 (1934), 352.

23. On Bozen's grievances see KFA, alt 4, neu 3, No. 1, f. 14-15 and No. 2, fol. 46-47v.

24. KFA, alt 4, neu 3, No. 1, f. 14 and No. 2, f. 46.

25. Egger, Geschichte, 3:130.

26. His emphasis, Keith, Memoirs, 2:304; and 254 on Leopold's arrival.

27. Leopold to Marie Christine, 15 March 1791, in Wolf, ed., Leopold II. und Marie Christine, 119-20.

28. On Aschauer, see Miriam Levy, "Leopold II, Joseph von Aschauer, and the Role of the Estates in the Habsburg Monarchy," MÖStA 38 (1985): 197-222.

29. Reinalter, Aufklärung, 97; also see Egger, Geschichte, 3:130.

30. SRP Index, 1790, entries under "Botzen, Stadt" and "Tyrol" referring to SRP No. 988. Also see [Giuseppe Pilati], Cenni su la vita e su le opere di Carlo Antonio Pilati stesi per la prima volta coll'aiuto di documenti da un Trentino (Rovereto: V. Sottochiesa, 1875), 267-68.

31. Egger, Geschichte, 3:131. The manner in which this conference was called and the fact that it was composed essentially of those who happened to be in or near Innsbruck at the time suggests that it may have been modeled on the "Little Diet" of Bohemia. But there the "Little Diet," though an ad hoc group, was a preparation for the "Big Diet" and was part of the tradition of the Bohemian Estates. In Tyrol it had no precedent. See Robert Joseph Kerner, Bohemia in the Eighteenth Century. A Study in Political, Economic, and Social History with Special Reference to the Reign of Leopold II, 1790-1792 (New York: Macmillan, 1932), 87-88.

32. Egger, Geschichte, 3:131-32. And see diPauli, Diet Diary, Beilage I, "Schreiben" by Lemmen, fol. 1-8; Beilage II, "Das Schreiben des Viertelvertretters an der Etsch Franz Spar v. Dellman," fol. 9; and SRP, 1790, No. 982.

33. KFA, alt 123, neu 121, No. 1, Enzenberg's Journal, section 1, Art. No. 1, 1st and 2nd paragraphs. Also see Sighard Enzenberg and Otto Preuschl-Haldenburg, "Franz I. Joseph Graf Enzenberg," *Carinthia I* 153 (1963): 559. These documents—Enzenberg's commission and instruction—are in the AVA in Vienna, but the fund is closed for restoration; see AVA, Hofkanzleiakten, Karton 848—Tirol, IV.H.3. Landtage, 180 ex Majo 1790.

34. Nikolaus Grass, "Aus der Geschichte des Landstände Tirols," in *Studies presented to the International Commission for the History of Representative and Parliamentary Institutions*, vol. 24: *Album Helen Maud Cam*, 311 (Louvain: Publications Universitairès and Paris: Éditions Béatrice-Nauwelaerts, 1961). Also see SRP, 1790, No. 1944; on this convent or *Damenstift*, see Ellinor Langer, *Die Geschichte des adeligen Damenstiftes zu Innsbruck*, Schlern-Schriften, vol. 73 (Innsbruck: Wagner, 1950).

35. "Andreas Aloys von di Pauli," *Taschenbuch für die Vaterländische Geschichte*, vol. 30, in New Series, vol. 12 (1841): 412–13.

36. Points 9 and 36; see Herman Ignaz Bidermann, *Die Italiäner im Tirolischen Provinzial-Verbande* (Innsbruck: Wagner, 1874), 167–68. Also see Antonio Zieger, *Bagliori unitari ed aspirazioni nazionali (1751–1791)* Milan: Pallade, 1933), 30.

37. As quoted in Savino Pedrolli, "Un capitolo di storia roveretana (1770–1801)," *Atti*, Series 3, 9 (1903): 159. For some preliminary speculation on Beekhen, see Wandruszka, "Welsche Confinen," 159. For additional information on Beekhen, see the thumbnail biography in appendix C.

38. See Wandruszka, "Welsche Confinen," 157–59; also HHStA, Vertrauliche Akten, alt 62, neu 41, No. 14, f. 339–47, which is Beekhen's August 1792 appeal to Emperor Francis II, who was then rebuking, if not threatening, Beekhen for allegedly speaking out against the government in public coffeehouses. Beekhen recounted his career as part of his appeal. On the Danzig mission, see Henrick Grossman, *Österreichs Handelspolitik mit Bezug auf Galizien in der Reformperiod 1772–1790* (Vienna: Carl Konegen, 1914), 342–49, 419.

39. HHStA, Sammelbände, Karton 16, "Relazione del Viaggio e Soggiorno farro da S.A.R. in Vienna nel Luglio 1784," 142–43, on the administration of the monastic and ecclesiastical estates, concerning Beekhen. I am indebted to Adam Wandruszka for sharing this source with me.

40. Vienna, Hofkammerarchiv, Camerale, 1790, Fasc. 5, April, Fol. 322, Exp. 164/1215, f. 488, memorandum of 19 March 1790. Beekhen became the director of the general *Rechnungs-Centralis* and the *Systemal-Affairs*. On Beekhen's official travels, see, for example, Vienna, Hofkammerarchiv, Camerale: 1791, Fasc. 27, Juli, Fol. 389, Exp. 113/727; 1792, Fasc. 27, Jänner, Fol. 170, Exp. 976/105; and 1792, Fasc. 27, May, Fol. 937, Exp. 87/932.

41. During an interregnum, two vicars administered the non-Habsburg areas of the Holy Roman Empire: the Elector of Bavaria in the western part and the Elector of Saxony in the eastern part. Nobility from a foreign prince was not to be accepted without the permission of the Habsburg ruler; Carlo Betta did not obtain

this permission—although he did have his nobility confirmed by the Prince-Bishop of Trent. But both the 1790 Tyrolean Diet and the Habsburgs (until 1840) refused to recognize his or his family's nobility.

42. Pedrolli, "Un Capitolo," 159.

43. Ibid., 159–60.

44. Zieger, *Bagliori*, 29; also see Antonio Zieger, *I Franchi muratori del Trentino* (Trento: Tipografia Editrice Mutilati e Invalidi, 1925), 219; and Biderman, *Italiäner*, 163, which also lists the deputies for all the Italian areas to the Diet on 162–63. As noted above, n. 41, the Diet rejected Betta's claim to seat and vote as a noble.

45. *Justizfache*, Leopold II, 1st year of his Reign, 2, No. 5.

46. SRP, 1790, No. 1031; *Justizfache*, Leopold II, 1st year of his Reign, 9, No. 19; also see *Leopold Laws*, vol. 3, 18, No. 356.

47. SRP, 1790, No. 1489. The AVA, which has this commission's records, was unable to find any documents dealing with this 5 May 1790 report, in part because this fund has not yet been organized or cataloged.

48. Vienna, Hofkammerarchiv, Camerale, 1790, Fasc. 7, Juni, Fol. 585, Exp. 516.

49. KFA, alt 123, neu 121, No. 1.

50. Egger, *Geschichte*, 3:134; Reinalter, *Aufklärung*, 102–3.

51. KFA, alt 123, neu 121, No. 1, Art. 1.

52. Ibid., section 2, 2nd paragraph; for Enzenberg's history of Tyrol, see ibid., No. 1, Enzenberg's Journal, section 3.

53. Ibid., 3rd and 7th paragraphs.

54. Ibid., section 10, 1st paragraph.

55. Ibid, 2nd paragraph. Seydel's reports from Rovereto were dated 11 July and 14 July.

CHAPTER FIVE

1. Ferdinandeum, Dip. 1239, "Tagebuch von A. A. diPauli über die Verhandlungen des offenen Landtages vom J. 1790," between folios 10 and 11; it is not clear what V. and X. indicate before the last two lines. Hereafter this diary is cited as diPauli, Diet Diary. (Another diPauli manuscript is his diary of post-Diet events in Vienna, which is cited below and used extensively in chapter 6 as diPauli, Vienna Diary.)

2. Kabinetskanzley, Bd. 60, No. 2, "Böhmische Hof Kanzley, 22ten July 1790"; Ref. Sumerau No. 1787.

3. Kabinetskanzley, Bd. 55, "Protokolle der von Sr. Maj. durch den Staatsrath mit Votirung S. K. Hoheit erlassenen Resoluzionen vom 19. July bis Ende Decemb. 1790," No. 2202, 17–18; and SRP, 1790, No. 2202; also see Kabinetskanzley, Bd. 53, "Circulandum den 24. July," SRP, No. 2202; and KFA, alt 158, neu 154, summary of SRP, 1790, No. 2202, no folio numbers.

4. diPauli, Diet Diary, f. 8.

5. See KFA, alt 9, neu 7, "Tirolo No. 5," for Kolowrat's letter and Sauer's response.

6. HHStA, Nachlass Kolowrat, No. 1241, 7. Nov. 1793, no folio numbers.

7. For Enzenberg's journal, see KFA, alt 123, neu 121 "Tyrolische Ständische Gegenstände," No. 1, "Journal des Gr. Enzenberg"; and No. 2, "Nachtrag desselben"; hereafter cited as Enzenberg, Journal.

8. For diPauli's entire record of the 1790 Diet, see Ferdinandeum, Dip. 1239 and 1240, "Tagebuch von A. A. diPauli über die Vernhandlungen des offenen Landtages vom J. 1790" and "Beylagen und Urkunden zum Tagebuche des offenen Landtages vom J. 1790."

9. For Sardagna's diary see Ferdinandeum, F. B. 2695 and 2696, "Tagebuch des öffentlichen Landtags in Tyrol vom Jahre 1790 entworfen von Benedikt v. Sardagna"; hereafter cited as Sardagna, Diary.

10. For these journals of Archduke Francis, which include much information no longer available elsewhere, see Kabinetskanzley Akten, especially Bd. 50, 53, 55, 57, 60, 61, 62, 63, and 65. Enzenberg's Journal, diPauli's Vienna diary (see chapter 6), and the records of Archduke Francis have not been used before.

11. Franz Goldegg's journal was published anonymously as *Journal des offenen Tiroler Landtages zu Innsbruck 1790. Aus den Papieren eines Zeitgenossen.* Hugo R. Goldegg, ed. (Bozen: J. Eberle, 1861). The Goldegg journal was compiled by Franz Goldegg's grandson and published only in 1861.

12. See the list at the end of Goldegg, Journal, 122–36. Also see Hermann Ignaz Bidermann, *Die Italiäner im Tirolischen Provinzial-Verbande* (Innsbruck: Wagner, 1874), 161; Josef Egger, *Die Tiroler und Vorarlberger* (Vienna: K. Prochaska, 1882), 147; and Joseph Egger, *Geschichte Tirols* (Innsbruck: Wagner, 1876–80), 3:134–35.

13. The champion proxy holder was Baron Karl Hippoliti, who held twenty-three; his brother Joseph held another nine.

14. Savino Pedrolli, "Un capitolo di storia roveretana (1770–1801)," *Atti*, Series 3, 9 (1903), 160.

15. diPauli, Diet Diary, f. 1v.

16. Goldegg, Journal, 3–4.

17. Enzenberg, Journal, section 6, 2nd, 4th–6th, 8th, and 9th paragraphs.

18. Kabinetskanzley, Bd. 60, No. 5, Vereinigte Hofstelle, vom 29. July 1790.

19. Goldegg, Journal, 12; Sardagna, Diary, f. 6; diPauli, Diet Diary, f. 2v.

20. Goldegg, Journal, 26; and Eliodoro Degara, *Cronaca di Arco dell'Arciprete Mons. Eliodoro Degara dall'anno 1771 al 1879 con aggiunte e complementi* (Arco: C. Emmert, 1905), especially 59.

21. diPauli, Diet Diary, f. 2v–3; also see Goldegg, Journal, 15.

22. Goldegg, Journal, 5, 12; diPauli, Diet Diary, f. 3.

23. Sardagna, Diary, f. 8–9; Goldegg, Journal, 17; also see diPauli, Diet Diary, f. 3v–4. This section of the Goldegg journal and the Sardagna diary are identical, word for word. Perhaps this is the reason why, on the title page of one copy of the

Goldegg journal in the Ferdinandeum (F. B. 2495, S. 122), a penciled-in notation attributes Goldegg's entire journal to Sardagna. Except for this one section, however, the two journals are quite different and clearly have different authors.

24. Goldegg, *Journal*, 18; Sardagna, Diary, f. 9v.

25. diPauli, Diet Diary, f. 5–5v; Sardagna, Diary, f. 9, 10v; Goldegg, *Journal*, 21–22.

26. Bidermann, *Italiäner*, 176; for information about the sixteenth-century tax revolt, see chapter 3, especially n. 12.

27. Egger, *Geschichte*, 3:138.

28. Sardagna, Diary, f. 120, 124v–125, and f. 127, first four points; diPauli, Diet Diary, f. 48v, 51–51v, 52. Either he did not know about, or chose not to mention Rovereto's sixteenth-century refusal to be part of Tyrol (see chapter 3). Also see diPauli, Diet Diary, f. 51v, the first ten points.

29. diPauli, Diet Diary, f. 52v, 54v; Sardagna, Diary, f. 128.

30. Bidermann, *Italiäner*, 170–77, passim; also see diPauli, Diet Diary, f. 58v–59.

31. Kabinetzkanzley, Bd. 60, No. 13, "Böh. Kanzley, von 19. August 1790." Also see Bidermann, *Italiäner*, 177.

32. diPauli, Diet Diary, f. 77v.

33. Pedrolli, "Un Capitolo," 161. Also see diPauli, Diet Diary, f. 87.

34. Bidermann, *Italiäner*, 177. Also see diPauli, Diet Diary, f. 87v.

35. diPauli, Diet Diary, f. 87v–88; Bidermann, *Italiäner*, 177–78; Egger, *Geschichte*, 3:145.

36. diPauli, Diet Diary, Beilage No. 11, "Marx Baron von Cazanisches *Votum* in Betreff der welschen Confinen," f. 526–28; for the full text see f. 526–37, hereafter cited as Cazan Votum.

37. Cazan Votum, f. 526–27, 529–29v, 533–34v.

38. Ibid., f. 534v–535. Also see Bidermann, *Italiäner*, 180; Antonio Zieger, *Bagliori unitari ed aspirazioni nazionali (1751–1797)* (Milan: Pallade, 1933), 32; Antonio Zieger, *Storia del Trentino e dell'Alto Adige* (Trento: G. B. Monaui, 1926), 145. Cazan, as clear proof of the brotherly feeling toward Italian Tyrol, referred to the Confinants' need for grain in 1782 when the Estates provided "the most considerable financial assistance of 84,000 f [lorins] as a loan, of which history shows no example." See Cazan Votum, f. 535–36.

39. Cazan Votum, ibid.

40. Ibid., f. 536–37. Cazan's "let them separate" statement is often quoted and, in retrospect, especially interesting. Also see Zieger, *Storia del Trentino e dell'Alto Adige*, 145; Zieger, *Bagliori*, 32; Bidermann, *Italiäner*, 180–81.

41. Sardagna, Diary, f. 175; also see Bidermann, *Italiäner*, 181.

42. Sardagna, Diary, f. 65; diPauli, Diet Diary, Beilage XIV, f. 54–56 for the Bozen burghers' instructions to diPauli; also see diPauli, Diet Diary, f. 32v.

43. diPauli, Diet Diary, f. 11v; Goldegg, *Journal*, 30; Sardagna Diary, f. 86, 89; Bidermann, *Italiäner*, 176–77.

44. diPauli, Diet Diary, f. 51v.

45. See ibid., f. 54v, 59, 61; Sardagna, Diary, f. 133; Bidermann, *Italiäner*, 170–77, passim.

46. See diPauli, Diet Diary, f. 51v, 52, "Weg der Ausfuhr der Weine von den Welschen Konfinen."

47. Bidermann, *Italiäner*, 176, 179.

48. diPauli, Diet Diary, f. 49v, point 3 and f. 48; also see Sardagna, Diary, f. 117, especially Salurn's points 2 and 4.

49. diPauli, Diet Diary, f. 43.

50. Sardagna, Diary, f. 117, 124v–125, and f. 128, first four points; diPauli, Diet Diary, f. 48v, 51–51v, 52.

51. diPauli, Diet Diary, f. 324, 52v, 54v; Sardagna, Diary, f. 128.

52. SRP, 1790, No. 2584; Kabinetskanzley, Bd. 56, No. 34. Also see KFA, alt 123, neu 121, No. 6, Protocol of 8 January 1791, Point 11, 105–7; I have seen no published version of the emperor's decision, but this KFA document refers to one.

53. diPauli, Diet Diary, f. 51–52; Sardagna, Diary, f. 65, 124v–125.

54. diPauli, Diet Diary, f. 70v.

55. Michael Mayr, *Der italienische Irredentismus. Sein Entstehen und seine Entwicklung, vornehmlich in Tirol* (Innsbruck: Tyrolia, 1917), 10–11; also see diPauli, Diet Diary, f. 6, and Goldegg, *Journal*, 23; also Zieger, *Bagliori*, 31.

56. diPauli, Diet Diary, f. 51v.

57. For details on the election see Miriam J. Levy, "Leopold II and the 1790 Italian Movement in Tyrol: A Case Study in the Politics of the Habsburg Monarchy" (Columbia University diss., 1982), 186–87, 190–92. Also see Goldegg, *Journal*, 90; Egger, *Geschichte*, 3:143–44; diPauli, Diet Diary, f. 59v–60. And see Rudolf Granichstaedten-Czerva, *Beiträge zur Familiengeschichte Tirols*, Schlern-Schriften, vol. 131 (Innsbruck: Wagner, 1954), 2:220.

58. Enzenberg, Journal, section 6, 11th and 12th paragraphs; also see Egger *Geschichte*, 3:139.

59. See Goldegg, *Journal*, 105; and diPauli, Diet Diary, f. 63.

60. diPauli, Diet Diary, f. 70v; Ferdinandeum, Dip. 1241/I, "Andreas diPauli, Tagebuch über die Verhandlungen der Deputirten des offenen Landtages vom J. 1790 in Wien, mit Urkunden, und einem erklärenden Verzeichnisse," "Erklärendes Verzeichnis"; no folio numbers; hereafter cited as diPauli, Vienna Diary.

61. This list was compiled from information in diPauli, Vienna Diary, "Erklärendes Verzeichnisse," and in the appendix to Goldegg, *Journal*, 122–36; also see diPauli, Diet Diary, f. 85v–86.

62. KFA, alt 123, neu 121, No. 1, Enzenberg, Journal, section 16 "Die Auseinanderlassung des offenen Landtages veranlasste Bewegungen betrefend."

63. For an account of the maneuvering on both sides, see Levy, "Leopold II," 203–4.

64. diPauli, Diet Diary, f. 93, 96–100; Goldegg, *Journal*, 116. On the closing speech, see diPauli, Diet Diary, f. 98v–100; Egger, *Geschichte*, 3:146; and Goldegg,

Journal, 113–16. Also see Bidermann, *Italiäner*, 178; Goldegg, *Journal*, 114, 115, 116; Hans Hochenegg, *Der Adel im Leben Tirols. Ein soziologische Studie* (Innsbruck: Österreichische Kommissionsbuchhandlung, 1971), 123.

65. For the entire instruction to the Vienna-bound deputies, see Ferdinandeum, Dip. 1242, also published in Reinalter, *Aufklärung*, Anhang XIII, 311–14; also see Goldegg, *Journal*, 117–19.

CHAPTER SIX

1. HHStA, Kabinetskanzley, Bd. 61, No. 21, Ver. Hofst. 13 Sept. 1790., Ref. Sumerau, No. 2207; and Bd. 62, No. 23, Ver. Hofstelle 20 Sept. 1790., Ref. Sumerau, No. 2262.

2. KFA, alt 123, neu 121, No. 6, Protocol of 8 January 1791, Point 11, 105–7.

3. Enzenberg's reply is in diPauli, Vienna Diary, Beilage XXV, f. 224–31. "Bericht des Herrn Franz Grafen v. Enzenberg Exc., über die von den Deputirten der wälschen Konfinen an Sr. Majt. eingerichte sogennante *Risposta* al Voto Cazan." DiPauli's summary is in his Vienna Diary, f. 36–38. For a discussion of Enzenberg's reply, see Hermann Ignaz Bidermann, *Die Italiäner im Tirolischen Provinzial-Verbande* (Innsbruck: Wagner, 1874), 182–83.

4. diPauli, Vienna Diary, f. 36v; what appears here is only a very brief summary of diPauli's entries.

5. As quoted in ibid., f. 36v–38.

6. Enzenberg's reply to the *Rispota* in diPauli, Vienna Diary, f. 224.

7. Ibid., f. 224v–25, 229, 230.

8. Ibid., f. 230–31.

9. HHStA, Kabinetskanzley, Bd. 63, "Protokolle der Böhm. Öst. Hofkanzley vom 2. bis 29. Nov. 1790, Sitzung vom 4. Nov. 1790," No. 2615, Allerhöchstes Handbillet; also see "Sitzung 2 Nov. 1790," No. 2580 and No. 2597; and SRP Index, 1790, under entries for "Sauer" and "Tyrol," especially the entry "v. Sauer Graf Gubernial Praesident in Tyrol" referring to SRP 1790, No. 4063, which has more information than the protocol itself.

10. HHStA, Kabinetskanzley, Bd. 57, 132, which summarizes SRP, 1790, No. 3487.

11. Enzenberg said of his history that it would have been better to treat it as an appendix, but that he had thought of doing so only after the whole thing had been put together. See KFA, alt 123, neu 121, No. 3, for the history.

12. All the underscores are mine. KFA, alt 123, neu 121, No. 1, section 4; translated by Christopher G. Trump.

13. The usual bureaucratic path for these decisions was from the *Gubernium*, the court commissar, or the former governor to the Chancellery or the *Oberste Justizstelle* (then perhaps to the special grievance commission), and finally to the *Staatsrat* and the emperor for decision. At each step, arguments and recommendations were made.

14. BC di Trento, Ms. 2447, "Memorie" in "Carte appartenute a Carl'Ant.

Pilati," 1; hereafter cited as Pilati, "Memorie." The Italian words referring to Franz Gumer are "*testaccia pericolosa.*"

15. Ibid., 2, 3; his underscore.

16. Ibid.

17. Ibid., 3–4, 5. Gumer told his brother this audience had taken place on a day when, in fact, Leopold was not in Vienna but in Buda-Pest being crowned King of Hungary.

18. Savino Pedrolli, "Un capitolo di storia roveretana (1770–1801)," *Atti,* Series 3, vol. 9 (April–June 1903):161–62.

19. Quotations from Unterrichter and Kolowrat, as well as other comments, are in Joseph Egger, *Geschichte Tirols* (Innsbruck: Wagner, 1876–80), 3:162. For a description of the deputies' journey to Vienna, see diPauli, Vienna Diary, "Erklärendes Verzeichnis," n.f.

20. See HHStA, Kabinetskanzley, Bd. 63, 22 Nov. 1790, XIII; for further biographical information, see the thumbnail biographies in appendix C.

21. In honor of the Hungarian coronation, the deputies found themselves treated to impressive ceremonies and spectacles, including a procession in the center of the city led by the emperor and the illumination of the entire city in the evening. See diPauli, Vienna Diary, ff. 1v–2.

22. diPauli, Vienna Diary, ff. 2–2v.

23. Ibid., f. 3–3v.

24. Ibid., f. 4–4v.

25. Ibid., f. 4v, 5.

26. Ibid., f. 5v–6.

27. Ibid., f. 8v.

28. Ibid., f. 8–13.

29. Ibid., f. 14–14v.

30. Ibid., f. 14v–15. On Leopold's view of the Tyrolean constitution, see Martha Hämmerle, "Der Staatsrat Kaiser Leopold II." (Vienna diss., 1939), 37, and n. 2; unfortunately, because of a typographical error the footnote does not refer to the proper *Staatsrat* document but to a published work on Styria, which has nothing to do with Tyrol. The documents themselves no longer exist.

31. diPauli, Vienna Diary, f. 18.

32. Ibid., f. 19–19v.

33. Ibid., f. 20–20v, 21v–22.

34. Ibid., f. 24v, 26.

35. For the chancellery report see SRP, 1790, No. 3868. For the debate on paper see KFA, alt 123, neu 121, No. 5, "Vortrag ueber die Vorstellung der welschen Tyroler, Deputiae beym Landtag zu haben," n.f.; a copy of this document is in KFA, alt 124, neu 122, between No. 10 and No. 11, and in Ferdinandeum, F.B. 8711/1, "Akten zur Geschichte der tirolischen Landtage 1790–1793." Citations are to KFA, alt 123, neu 121, No. 5.

36. Their underscores; KFA, alt 123, neu 121, No. 5, 1st point.

37. His underscore; ibid., 2nd point and Ad 2dum.

38. Ibid., 3ten Punkt, and Ad 3tum.

39. Ibid., Punkte 6, 7, 8, 9; and Ad 6tum, 7mum, 8vum, 9vum.

40. Ibid., 9ten Punkt, and Ad 9tum. The Eisack *Viertel* was part of the Etsch *Kreis.*

41. Ibid., 19ten Punkt, and Ad 19tum.

42. Ibid., 24ten and 25ten Punkte and Ad 24tum and 25tum, and Sauer's *Gutachten.* The remainder of this "debate" has no numbering of any kind.

43. Ibid., Sauer's *Gutachten.*

44. Ibid.

45. On the emperor's decision, see SRP, 1790, No. 3868; and Kabinetskanzley, Bd. 53, "Circulandum 20. Dez.," No. 3868; also see Reinalter, *Aufklärung,* 129, where this imperial decision is quoted with a citation to F.B. 8711, fol. 90.

46. Kabinetskanzley, Bd. 65, XIII—Sumerau, Sitzung, 16 Dezember 1790, No. 2916.

47. KFA, alt 123, neu 121, No. 3, with reference to section 9 of Enzenberg's Journal, *Gutachten,* 1st point and 3rd point; and SRP, 1790, No. 3954.

48. Signed by "L. G. Kollowrath" and "Baron v. Sumerau" as reproduced in Reinalter, *Aufklärung,* 127 citing Hoermann, *Tirol,* 1:385–86; also see Egger, *Geschichte,* 3:152.

49. On the note to Francis see KFA, alt 125, neu 123, No. 4.

50. On Lodron see diPauli, Vienna Diary, f. 61v.

51. On seat and vote see HHStA, Kabinetskanzley, Bd. 65 "Sumerau, B.Ö.H.K. Session, 27 Dez. 1790"; and Bd. 53, "Circulandum den 31. Dez.," No. 3954; also see SRP, 1790, No. 3954; on inheritance rights see KFA, alt 123, neu 121, No. 6, Protocol of Sessions 4., 8., 16. January 1791, *Erste Abtheilung,* Point 4, 15–18.

52. diPauli, Vienna Diary, f. 64v.

53. Ibid., f. 68–69.

54. KFA, alt 123, neu 121, No. 6, Protocol of 8 Jan. 1791, Point 11, 105–7; it is not clear where the Chancellery—which quoted a document—is quoting from, but it appears to be from a decision of the emperor. I have also been unable to find a copy of the 16 April 1789 ordinance, which is not published in the collection of Joseph's laws.

55. diPauli, Vienna Diary, ff. 74v–79.

56. KFA, alt 123, neu 121, No. 7, 18 January 1791, 1, 6–7, 54–55.

57. Handwritten note to Kaunitz, 25 January 1791, informing him of the appointments, which took effect on the last day of January; see SRP, 1791, No. 295; and *Leopold Laws,* vol. 3, No. 567, 148–149, 150, 151.

58. Sighard Enzenberg and Otto Preuschl-Haldenburg, "Franz I. Josef Graf Enzenberg," *Carinthia I,* Jg. 153 (1963), 560–61; also see Kabinetskanzley, Bd. 55, No. 3291, 107, Ad 6tum. The rescript was issued in November 1790. Also see diPauli, Vienna Diary, f. 6.

59. diPauli, Vienna Diary, Beilage XI, f. 148; for the petition see SRP, 1791, No. 296. The Napoleonic wars brought hard times to Enzenberg, who in 1810 petitioned Vienna for support; see KFA, alt 168, neu 164, Konv. 4, Nr. 7.

60. SRP, 1791, No. 441; diPauli, Vienna Diary, ff. 105–6.

61. KFA, alt 125, neu 123, No. 7, "Della Supplica umiliata a S.M. li 10. Marzo 1791."

62. KFA, alt 125, neu 123, No. 1, "Anmerkungen Wider der freye Ausfuhr der tyrolischen Confinanten Weine"; there is a copy among the documents in KFA, alt 124, neu 122, No. 7. There are no page or folio numbers on the document.

63. Ibid.; also see SRP, 1791, No. 648.

64. SRP Index, 1791, entry under "Weinen" and "Tyrol" referring to SRP No. 648; also see SRP, 1791, No. 648 and a copy of this SRP in KFA, alt 124, neu 122, No. 7; also see diPauli, Vienna Diary, f. 119v.

65. diPauli, Vienna Diary, f. 120–21.

66. Ibid., f. 107, 112v.

67. See *Leopold Laws*, vol. 4, 86 ff; for a lengthy description of the resolution, see Egger, *Geschichte*, 3:153–55; also see Otto Stolz, "Die Bestätigung der alten Tiroler Landesfreiheiten durch die Landesfürsten," in Part 1, *Beiträge zur Geschichte und Heimatkunde Tirols. Festschrift zu Ehren Herman Wopfners*, Schlern-Schriften, vol. 52 (Innsbruck: Wagner, 1947), 324.

68. diPauli, Vienna Diary, ff. 123v–124, and 121v.

69. Ibid., f. 125, 127v, 128.

70. Ibid., f. 124v.

CHAPTER SEVEN

1. Viktor Bibl, *Kaiser Franz. Der letzte Römisch-Deutsche Kaiser* (Leipzig and Vienna: Johannes Gunther, 1937; reprinted 1958), 82.

2. Robert Murray Keith, *Memoirs and Correspondence (Official and Familiar) of Sir Robert Murray Keith . . .* (London: Henry Colburn, 1849), 2:504.

3. KFA, alt 125, neu 123, No. 6, no folio numbers.

4. SRP Index, 1791, entries under "Weinen," "Eisack," and "Roveredo" referring to SRP No. 1161; also see SRP, 1791, No. 1161. Also see Hermann Ignatz Bidermann, *Die Italiäner im Tirolischen Provinzial-Verbande* (Innsbruck: Wagner, 1874), 184–85.

5. SRP, 1791, No. 3170; also see SRP Index, listings under "Tirol" referring to SRP No. 2130; and SRP, 1791, No. 2130.

6. Joseph Egger, *Geschichte Tirols* (Innsbruck: Wagner, 1876–80), 3:156. On the election see KFA, alt 125, neu 123, No. 9. Within two years Count Spaur too would be dead, and the Tyrolean Estates would have to choose yet another *Landeshauptmann*. See SRP, 1793, No. 4314.

7. For a more detailed discussion of the proceedings of the small *Ausschuss*, see Egger, *Geschichte*, 3:156–58.

8. Ibid. Also see Helmut Reinalter, *Aufklärung—Absolutismus—Reaktion. Die Geschichte Tirols in der 2. Hälfte des 18. Jahrhunderts* (Vienna: A. Schendl, 1974), 134–35; and Bidermann, *Italiäner*, 184–85.

9. See SRP, 1791, No. 4623, as well as Egger, *Geschichte*, 3:158–59, and Bidermann, *Italiäner*, 185.

10. Innsbruck, Statth. Archiv, Landschaftl. Akten von 1791, as cited by Bidermann, *Italiäner*, 186 (this archive has since been renamed the Landesregierungsarchiv). The Collegiate Abbey of Arco was immatriculated by a document (*Weisung*) from the land marshal's office of 10 January 1792. The city of Arco was not immatriculated until 1797.

11. Bidermann, *Italiäner*, 186; also see Ferdinandeum, Dip. 1242/2, No. 1 concerning the 1792 *Ausschüsse*.

12. SRP, 1792, No. 1082; also see references to this SRP in SRP Index, 1792, entries under "Stände" and "Verordneten."

13. Bidermann, *Italiäner*, 187.

14. Franz Kolb, *Das Tiroler Volk in seinem Freiheitskampf 1796–1797* (Innsbruck, Vienna and Munich: Tyrolia, 1957), 99–100.

15. See *Justizfache*, Franz's reign, 332, No. 1223, 24 March 1816.

16. Otto Stolz, "Das Land Tirol als politischer Körper," in *Tirol, Land und Natur, Volk und Geschichte, Geistiges Leben* (Munich, 1933), 1:372; on this constitution see Joseph Egger, *Die Tiroler und Vorarlberger* (Vienna: K. Prochaska, 1882), 145–47; Hermann Gsteu, "Geschichte des Tiroler Landtages von 1816–1848," *Tiroler Heimat* 8 (1927): 85–86, 164–67; Josef Streiter, *Studien eines Tirolers, Erste Abtheilung* (Leipzig: Weit & Comp., 1862), 53–57.

17. Martha Hämmerle, "Der Staatsrat Kaiser Leopold II.," (Vienna diss., 1939), 131–34, 141–43 on Leopold's economic policies.

18. See SRP, 1791, No. 1860.

19. SRP Index, 1791, entries listed under "Eisack" and "Weinen" referring to SRP No. 1161; also see SRP, 1791, No. 1161. For the political content of the 18 March report, see the discussion above on "Seat and Vote."

20. KFA, alt 125, neu 123, No. 6, n.f. For the political requests in the 21 March petition, see above under "Seat and Vote."

21. Tiroler Landesarchiv, Provinciale 11302/1513, den 8 Juli 1791, Quarto 7³–v, 2. Abtheilung, 8. Punkt. Also see SRP Index, 1791, entries under "Tirol" referring to SRP, 1791, No. 2130; and SRP, 1791, No. 2130.

22. On the first decree see *Leopold Laws*, vol. 4, No. 785, 289; also see HHStA, Staatsrat Patente und Zirkularien, Karton 31 (1791), f. 546 for a copy of this law, as issued by the Inner Austrian *Gubernium* at Graz on 24 August. The decree was valid in Lower Austria, Bohemia, Austria above the Enns, Inner Austria, Galicia, and Anterior Austria. On the second decree, see *Leopold Laws*, vol. 4, No. 931, 570–71; also see No. 961, 608–9.

23. *Franz Laws*, vol. 1, 291, Hofdekret vom 30. Junius [1792], section 7; an "Allerhöchste Verordnung" issued 10 July in Linz and announcing this decree can be found in HHStA, Staatsrat Patente und Zirkularien, Karton 32 (1792); also see Franz Laws, vol. 2, 149, No. 16.

24. Leopold had dissolved Joseph's *Vereinigte Hofstelle* so that the chancel-leries, *Oberste Justizstelle, Hofkammer,* and others reported directly to the ruler again; Francis now created a *Directorium*, reinstating an intermediary between all the *Hofstellen* on the one hand and the *Staatsrat* and himself on the other; all reports to the *Staatsrat* would now come through and from the *Directorium*.

25. SRP, 1793, No. 1704, Point 9; on grain import and export, see Franz Laws, vol. 2, 147, No. 13, 12 April 1793.

26. SRP, 1793, No. 4037.

27. SRP, 1794, No. 860.

28. SRP, 1794, No. 3888.

29. "Allerunterthänigste Note" of 24 November 1794; see KFA, alt 94, neu 102, Konvolut 2, No. 3888 (apparently a reference to the SRP number), no folio numbers.

30. His emphasis. HHStA, Staatsrat Patente und Zirkularien, Karton 35 (1793 and 1794), 22/11, 1793.

31. *Franz Laws*, vol. 3, Juli-Dez. 1793, 126–27, section 14 (or No. 13 in the 1817 edition). Also see HHStA, Staatsrat Patente und Zirkularien, Karton 35 (1793 and 1794), 31/12, 1793.

32. *Franz Laws*, vol. 5, 147–49, No. 48.

33. Leopold restored the universities at Innsbruck and Graz and the others that Joseph II had demoted to lyceums.

34. HHStA, Staatsrat Patente und Zirkularien, Karton 31 (1791), 70, No. 110; also see *Justizfache*, Leopold's reign, 15 April 1791, No. 131, 28.

35. *Leopold Laws*, vol. 4, No. 775, 275–76. This decree was proclaimed in Tyrol on 30 August; see HHStA, Staatsrat Patente und Zirkularien, Karton 31, f. 551.

36. *Justizfache*, Franz's reign, 25 April 1796, 7, No. 294.

37. Ettore Zucchelli, *Il Ginnasio di Rovereto in duecentocinquant'anni di vita (1672–1922)* (Rovereto: Ugo Grandi, 1923), 50–51.

38. *Leopold Laws*, vol. 3, 302, No. 545, first point. The published collection of Leopold's laws incorrectly dates this decree as being issued on 6 April and proclaimed in Tyrol on 15 March, clearly an error. The *Justizfache* collection dates the decree 1 April. A copy of the decree as published in Tyrol and dated 17 May is in HHStA, Staatsrat Patente und Zirkularien, Karton 31, 1791, f. 293. Also see SRP, 1792, No. 5875.

CONCLUSION

1. Béla K. Király, *Hungary in the Late Eighteenth Century. The Decline of Enlightened Despotism* (New York and London: Columbia University Press, 1969),

196–211; and Adam Wandruszka, *Leopold II. Erzherzog von Osterreich, Grossherzog von Toskana, König von Ungarn u. Böhmen, Römischer Kaiser* (Vienna and Munich: Herold, 1965), 2: 281–84.

2. Transylvania was organized not into Estates, but into nations—the Magyars, the Szeklers (cousins of the Magyars), and the Saxons (primarily German-speaking descendants of a large twelfth-century Rhineland migration). Each nation had one vote in the Diet, and unanimity was required for acceptance of any law. The four "received" religions in the Grand Principality were Roman Catholic, Reformed (Calvinist), Evangelical (Lutheran), and Unitarian. The overwhelmingly Orthodox Romanians belonged to none of these groups and were therefore excluded from political participation.

3. Keith Hitchins, *The Rumanian National Movement in Transylvania, 1780–1849* (Cambridge, Mass.: Harvard University Press, 1961), 115.

4. Leopold's note to the Hungarian Chancellor, Count Pálffy, 10 June 1790, as quoted in I. Lupaş, "Die politischen Bestrebungen der Rumänen Siebenbürgens in den Jahren 1790–1792," in I. Lupaş, *Zur Geschichte der Rumänen. Aufsätze und Vorträge* (Sibiu: Krafft & Drotleff, 1943), 455, n. 2.

5. Lupaş, "Die politische Bestrebungen," 461.

6. Ibid., 459, 461; Hitchins, *Rumanian National Movement*, 126. Also see Etienne Pascu, "Memoirs et protestations des Roumains de Transylvanie et de Hongrie de 1790 à 1892," *Revue de Transylvanie* (1939), 328–44; D. Prodan, *Supplex Libellus Valachorum. The Political Struggle of the Romanians in Transylvania During the 18th Century* (Bucharest: Publishing House of the Socialist Republic of Romania, 1971).

7. Leopold II was not the first Habsburg to use the Transylvanian Romanians as an *instrumentum regni*; for information about the relations of the Habsburgs to these Romanians through the reign of Joseph II, see Mathias Bernath, *Habsburg und die Anfänge der rumänischen Nationsbildung* (No. 15 of Studien zur Geschichte Osteuropas/Studies in East European History/Études d'Histoire de l'Europe Orientale) (Leiden: E. J. Brill, 1972). I am grateful to Marc Raeff for this reference.

8. See Ferdinand Zieglauer, *Die politische Reformbewegung in Siebenbürgen zur Zeit Josefs II. und Leopold's II.* Neue Ausgabe. (Vienna: Carl Graeser, 1885), 163.

9. As quoted in Luis Sand, "Welschtirols Recht zeugt für Südtirol," in *Südtirol. Land europäischer Bewährung, Kanonikus Michael Gamper zum 70. Geburtstag*, ed. F. H. Reidl (Innsbruck: Wagner, 1955), 114. The large Italian population in present-day Bolzano is the result primarily of policies of the Fascist regime in the 1930s.

10. Ibid.

BIBLIOGRAPHY

Archives and Archival Funds

VIENNA

Haus-, Hof- und Staatsarchiv:
Kaiser Franz Akten
Vertrauliche Akten
Nachlass Kolowrat
Staatsrat Protocolle
Staatsrat Indexen
Staatsrat Patente u. Zirkularien
Familiensammelbände
Kabinetskanzleyakten

Hofkammerarchiv:
Camerale

Kriegsarchiv:
Hofkriegsrat Protocolle
Tirol Militärcommando

Allgemeines Verwaltungsarchiv
Hofkanzlei Akten
Pergen-Akten Index

INNSBRUCK

Landesmuseum Ferdinandeum, Bibliothek:
Dipauliana, FB

Tiroler Landesarchiv:
Provinciale

ROVERETO

Biblioteca Civica Girolamo Tartarotti:
Manoscritti della Biblioteca
Archivi del'Accademia degli Agiati

TRENTO

Biblioteca Comunale di Trento:
Manoscritti

Published Collections of Austrian Laws, 1740–1848

Franz Laws   *Sr. k. k. Majestät Ferdinand des Ersten politische Gesetze und Verordnungen für sämmtliche Provinzen des Oesterreichischen Kaiserstaates, mit Ausnahme von Ungarn and Siebenbürgen (1792–1848).* vols. 1–63 of 74 vols. Vienna: Hof- und Staats-Aerarial-Druckerei, 1806–48.

OR

Sr. k. k. Majestät Franz des Zweyten politische Gesetze und Verordnungen für die oesterreichischen, böhmischen und galizischen Erbländer (1792–1805). 25 vols. in 12. Vienna: Staatsdruckerey, 1806–17.

Joseph Laws   *Handbuch aller unter der Regierung des Kaisers Joseph des II. für die k. k. Erbländer ergangenen Verordnungen und Gesetze.* 18 vols. Vienna: J. G. Moesle, 1784–90.

---

*For reasons unclear, the Library of Congress and other libraries in the United States have cataloged this collection only under Ferdinand's name. However, volumes 1–63 are Franz's laws; volumes 64–74 are Ferdinand's laws.

BIBLIOGRAPHY

Justizfache   *Gesetze und Verordnungen in Justizfache für die deutschen Staaten der Österreichischen Monarchie (1780–1848).* Different places of publication and publishers, 1780–1854.

Leopold Laws   *Sammlung der Gesetze, welche unter der glorreichsten Regierung des Königs Leopolds II., in den sämmentlichen k. Erblanden erschienen sind, in einer chronologischen Ordnung.* 5 vols. Vienna: J. G. Moesle, 1794–96.

Maria Theresa Laws   *Sammlung aller k. k. Verordnungen und Gesetze vom Jahr 1740 bis 1780 . . . ein Hilfs- und Ergänzungsbuch zu dem Handbuche aller unter der Regierung des Kaisers Joseph des II. . . .* 9 vols. Vienna: J. G. Mössle, 1786–87.

Other Published Works

Abafi, Ludwig. *Geschichte der Freimaurerei in Österreich-Ungarn.* 5 vols. Budapest: Martin Bagó and Sohn, 1890–99.

Adler, Sigmund. "Die politische Gesetzgebung in ihren geschichtlichen Beziehungen zum allgemeinen bürgerlichen Gesetzbuche." In *Festschrift zur Jahrhundertfeier des Allgemeinen Bürgerlichen Gesetzbuches—1 Juni 1911,* Pt. 1, 83–145. Vienna: Manz, 1911.

_____. *Die Unterrichtsverfassung Kaiser Leopolds II. und die finanzielle Fundierung der österreichischen Universitäten nach den Anträgen Martinis.* Vienna and Leipzig: Franz Deuticke, 1917.

Aggiunte e Correzioni alle Biografie dei Soci contenute nelle Memorie dell'I.R. Accademia de Scienze lettere ed arti degli Agiati in Rovereto già pubblicate nel 1903 per commemorare il suo 150° anno di vita. Rovereto: Ugo Grandi, 1905.

Alcock, Antony Evelyn. *The History of the South Tyrol Question.* London: Joseph, 1970.

Ambrosi, Francesco. *Commentari della storia trentina con un'appendice di notizie e documenti.* 2 vols. Rovereto: V. Sottochiesa, 1877.

_____. *Scrittori ed Artisti Trentini.* 2nd ed., 1894. Reprinted Bologna: Forni, n.d.

d'Ancona, Alessandro. "Saggio di una bibliografia ragionata dei viaggi e delle descrizioni d'Italia e dei costumi ital. in lingua straniera." Appendix in Allessandro d'Ancona, ed., *Giornale del viaggio di M. De Montaigne.* Lapi: Città di Castello, 1889.

"Andreas Aloys von diPauli." *Taschenbuch für die vaterländische Geschichte,* 30 (1841): 404–46. (In new series, vol. 12.)

Andreis, Girolamo. *Origine e progressi del commercio di Rovereto.* Rovereto: L. Marchesani, 1839.

Arneth, Alfred, ed. *Briefe der Kaiserin Maria Theresia an ihre Kinder und Freunde.* 4 vols. Vienna: Wilhelm Braumüller, 1881.

BIBLIOGRAPHY

_____. *Joseph II. und Leopold von Toscana. Ihr Briefwechsel von 1781 bis 1790.* 2 vols. Vienna: Wilhelm Braumüller, 1872.

_____. *Maria Theresia und Joseph II. Ihre Correspondenz sammt Briefen Joseph's an seinen Bruder Leopold.* 3 vols. Vienna: 1867–68.

Baldauf, Anton. *Beiträge zur Handels- und Zollpolitik Österreichs in der zweiten Hälfte des XVIII. Jahrhunderts insbesondere unter Joseph II.* Halle: C. A. Kaemmerer, 1898.

Baltl, Hermann. *Österreichische Rechtsgeschichte.* Graz: Leykam, 1972.

Barbacovi, Francesco Vigilio. *Memorie storiche della Città e del Territorio di Trento.* 2 vols. Trento: Monauni, 1821–24.

Beer, Adolf. "Die Finanzverwaltung Oesterreichs 1749–1816." *Mitteilungen des Instituts für Österreichische Geschichtsforschung* 15 (1894): 237–366.

_____, ed. *Leopold II., Franz II., und Catherina, Ihre Correspondenz.* Leipzig: Duncker & Humblot, 1874.

_____. "Die österreichische Handelspolitik unter Maria Theresia und Josef II." *Archiv für Österreichische Geschichte* 86 (1899): 1–204. Also published separately by Carl Gerold's Sohn, Vienna, 1898.

_____. "Die Zollpolitik und die Schaffung eines einheitlichen Zollgebietes unter Maria Theresia." *Mitteilungen des Instituts für Österreichische Geschichtsforschung* 14 (1893): 237–326.

Beidtel, Ignaz. *Geschichte der österreichischen Staatsverwaltung 1740–1848.* 2 vols. Innsbruck: Wagner, 1896–98.

Beiträge zur Geschichte Tirols. Festgabe des Landes Tirol zum 11. österreichischen Historikertag in Innsbruck vom 5. bis 8. Okt. 1971. Innsbruck: Kulturabteilung der Tiroler Landesregierung, [1971].

Benedikt, Heinrich. *Kaiseradler über den Apennin. Die Österreicher in Italien 1700 bis 1866.* Vienna and Munich: Verlag Herold, 1964.

Benvenuti, Sergio. "Notizie sulla vita dello storico Carlo Rosmini con un saggio di lettere inedite." *Studi trentini di scienze storiche* 48 (1969): 264–306.

Bertanza, Giovanni. *Storia di Rovereto.* 2nd ed., augmented and enlarged. Rovereto: Grigoletti, 1904.

Bettanini, Anatalone. "Clementino Vannetti." *Atti,* Series 3, 11 (Rovereto, 1905): 255–62.

_____. "Saibante-Vannetti Bianca Laura." *Atti,* Series 3, 6 (Rovereto, 1900): 107–43.

Bibl, Viktor. *Kaiser Franz. Der letzte Römisch-Deutsche Kaiser.* Leipzig and Vienna: Johannes Günther, 1937; repr. 1958.

_____. *Der Zerfall Österreichs. Kaiser Franz und sein Erbe.* Vienna, Berlin, Leipzig, and Munich: Rikola, 1922.

Bibliografia storica nazionale. Giunta centrale per gli studi storici. Bari: Gius. Laterza & Figli, 1958.

Bidermann, Hermann Ignaz. *Geschichte der österreichischen Gesammt-Staats-Idee*

BIBLIOGRAPHY

1526–1804. 2 Parts. Innsbruck: Wagner, 1867–89. (Part 3 was planned but not published.)

_____. *Die Italiäner im Tirolischen Provinzial-Verbande*. Innsbruck: Wagner, 1874.

_____. "Die Nationalitäten in Tirol." *Forschungen zur Deutschen Landes- und Volkskunde*, 1 (Stuttgart: J. Engelhorn, 1886): 390–475.

_____. *Zur Geschichte der Aufklärung in Tirol*. Innsbruck: Franz. I. Gassner, 1868.

Biedermannschronik. See Rautenstrauch, Johann.

Binder, Josef Koloman and Hugo Suchomel. "Zur Lebensgeschichte des Hofrates Franz Georg Edler von Keess." In *Festschrift zur Jahrhundertfeier des Allgemeinen Bürgerlichen Gesetzbuches—1. Juni 1911*, Part 1, 355–77. Vienna: Manz, 1911.

"Biographie. Franz Josef Reichsgraf von Enzenberg." *Carinthia* 62 (5) (1872): 129–41.

Bittner, Ludwig. *Gesamtinventar des Wiener Haus-, Hof- und Staats-archivs*. 5 vols. Vienna: A. Holzhausens Nachfolger, 1936–40.

de Blainville, Monsieur. *Travels through Holland, Germany, Switzerland, But especially Italy: by the Late Monsieur de Blainville, Sometime Secretary to the Embassy of the States-General, at the Court of Spain*. 3 vols. Trans. from the original manuscript by the late Dr. Turnbull, Mr. Guthrie, Mr. Lockman, and the editor. London: John Noon, 1757.

Block, Mathilde de. *Südtirol*. Groningen and Jakarta: J. B. Wolters, 1954.

Borghetti, Giuseppi. *Trento italiano*. Florence, 1903.

Bozner Bürgerbuch, 1551–1806. Schlern-Schriften, vols. 153–54. Innsbruck: Wagner, 1956.

Breval, John. *Remarks On several Parts of Europe: Relating chiefly to the History, Antiquities and Geography, of those Countries Through which the Author has travel'd; as France, the Low Countries, Lorrain, Alsatia, Germany, Savoy, Tyrol, Switzerland, Italy, and Spain*. 2 vols. London: Printed for Bernard Lintot, 1726 and 1738.

Broll, Enrico. "Carlo Antonio Pilati (28 decembre 1733–27 ottobre 1802)." *Archivio Trentino*, 17 (1902): 197–206.

Bücking, Jürgen. *Kultur und Gesellschaft in Tirol um 1600. Des Hippolytus Guarinonius' "Grewel der Verwüstung Menschlichen Geschlechts" (1610) als kulturgeschichtliche Quelle des frühen 17. Jahrhunderts*. Historische Studien, No. 401. Lübeck and Hamburg, 1968.

Bundsmann, Anton. *Die Entwicklung der politischen Verwaltung in Tirol und Vorarlberg seit Maria Theresia bis 1918*. Dornbirn, 1961.

Cambrey, [Jacques]. *Voyage pittoresque en Suisse et en Italie*. 2 vols. Paris: Chez H. J. Jansen, An IX de la République [1801].

Canali, Guido. "I trasporti sull'Adige da Bronzolo a Venezia." *Archivio per l'Alto Adige*, 24 (1929): 277–402.

Carbognin, Maurizio. "La formazione del nuovo catastro trentino del secolo XVIII." *Studi trentini di scienze storiche*, 52 (1973): 70–116.

BIBLIOGRAPHY

Carlen, Louis and Steinegger, Fritz, eds. *Festschrift Nikolas Grass zum 60. Geburtstag*. 2 vols. Vol. 1: *Abendländische und Deutsche Rechtsgeschichte, Geschichte und Rechte der Kirche, Geschichte und Recht Österreichs;* Vol. 2: *Aus Geschichte und Recht der Almen, Kultur- und Kunstgeschichte, Volkstum, Wissenschaftsgeschichte, aus der Sippen- und Familiengeschichte des Jubilars*. Innsbruck: Wagner, 1974–75.

Carli, Ferruccio de. *Lodovico Antonio Muratori. La sua vita la sua opera e la sua epoca*. Florence: Macri, 1955.

Carteggio fra Girolamo Tiraboschi e Clementino Vannetti (1776–93). Edited by G. Cavazzuti and F. Pasini. Supplement IV to *Pro Cultura*. Rivista bimestrale di Studi Trentini. Modena: Giovanni Ferraguti, 1912.

Chiaramonti, Giambattista. *La Vita del cavaliere Giuseppe Valeriano Vannetti roveretano signore di Villanuova fondatore della Imperiale Regia Accademia degli Agiati di Roveredo*. Brescia: Giammaria Rizzardi, 1766.

Chini, Giuseppe. *I Filatoi di Rovereto Sacco e Lizzana*. Rovereto: Mercurio, 1912.

Chiusole, Adamo. *Notizie antiche e moderne della Valle Lagarina e degli uomini illustri della medesima. In supplemento alle Memorie Antiche di Rovereto del chiarissimo Tartarotti*. Verona: L'Erede Marlo, 1787.

Ciccolini, Giovanni. "Contributo alla storia dell'industrie di Val Lagarina fra il 1806 e il 1813." *Atti*, Series 4, 2 (1913): 269–78.

Cobelli, Ruggero. *Cenni storici e statistici sulla bachicoltura nel Trentino*. Rovereto: V. Sottochiesa, 1872.

Cole, John W. *Estate Inheritance in the Italian Alps*. Research Reports No. 10, Department of Anthropology, University of Massachusetts, Amherst, December 1971.

Cole, John W. and Eric R. Wolf. *The Hidden Frontier: Ecology and Ethnicity in an Alpine Valley*. New York and London: Academic Press, Harcourt Brace Jovanovich, 1974.

Costisella, Giuseppe. "La discendenza di Giuseppe Benedetto Vannetti (dal 1760 al 1795)." *Studi trentini di scienze storiche*, 54 (1975): 154–181.

Coulon, Karl. "Mathias Wilhelm Edler von Haan. Ein Lebensbild." In *Festschrift zur Jahrhundertfeier des Allgemeinen Bürgerlichen Gesetzbuches*. Pt. 1, 33–82. Vienna: Manz, 1911.

Cristani di Rallo, Nicolò de. *Breve Descrizione della Pretura de Roveredo del 1766 composta . . . dall'illustrissimo Signore N. de C. de R. Consigliere della Reggenza dell'Austria Superiore Vice Capitano del Circolo di Roveredo a Commissario ai Confini d'Italia*. Translated from the German into Italian. Rovereto: G. Grigoletti, 1893.

Cristellotti, G. *Il Teatro sociale di Rovereto un secolo addietro. Dalle cronache cittadine*. Rovereto: Tipografia Roveretana, 1884.

Deambrosis, Marcella. "Filogiansenisti, anticuriali e giacobini nella seconda metà del settecento nel Trentino." *Rassegna storica del Risorgimento*, 48 (January–March 1961): 79–90.

BIBLIOGRAPHY

Degara, Eliodoro. *Cronaca di Arco dell'Arciprete Mons. Eliodoro Degara dall'anno 1771 al 1879 con aggiunte e complementi.* Arco: C. Emmert, 1905.

[diPauli, Andreas Alois]. "Anton Roschmann und seine Schriften." *Beiträge zur Geschichte, Statistik, Naturkunde und Kunst von Tirol und Vorarlberg,* 2 (Innsbruck, 1826): 1–184.

diPauli, Andreas A. "Der Freiherr Joseph von Sperges." *Neue Zeitschrift des Ferdinandeums für Tirol und Vorarlberg,* Series 2, 3 (1837): 1–57.

Dizionario biografico degli Italiani. Rome: Società Grafica Romana, 1964.

Dopsch, Alphons and Ernst Schwind, eds. *Ausgewählte Urkunden zur Verfassungs-Geschichte der deutsch-österreichischen Erblande im Mittelalter.* Innsbruck: Wagner, 1895.

Dörrenhaus, Fritz. *Das deutsche Land an der Etsch. Eine geographische Landeskunde.* Innsbruck: Tyrolia, 1933.

Dörrer, Fridolin. "Probleme rund um die theresianische Kreiseinteilung Tirols." In *Beiträge zur geschichtlichen Landeskunde Tirols. Festschrift zum 60. Geburtstag von Prof. Dr. Franz Huter,* 57–85. Schlern-Schriften, vol. 207. Innsbruck: Wagner, 1959.

––––––. "Die Verwaltungs-Kreise in Tirol und Vorarlberg (1754–1860)." In *Festschrift für Univ.-Prof. Dr. Franz Huter anlässlich der Vollendung des 70. Lebensjahres,* 25–68 plus 6 maps. Edited by Ernst Troger and Georg Zwanowetz. Tiroler Wirtschaftsstudien, No. 26 (Neue Beiträge zur Geschichtlichen Landeskunde Tirols, Pt. 1). Innsbruck and Munich: Wagner, 1969.

Durig, Joseph. *Ueber die staatsrechtlichen Beziehungen des italienischen Landestheiles von Tirol zu Deutschland und Tirol.* Jahres-Bericht der k.k. Ober-Realschule zu Innsbruck, Studienjahr 1863–64, 3–30. Innsbruck: Wagner, 1864.

Egger, Joseph. *Geschichte Tirols.* 3 vols. Innsbruck: Wagner, 1872–80.

––––––. *Die Tiroler und Vorarlberger.* Die Völker Oesterreich-Ungarns, vol. 4. Vienna: K. Prochaska, 1882.

Emer, Dario. "Accademie ed Accademici nel Trentino. L'Accademia degli Accessi in Trento." *Archivio Trentino,* 11 (1893): 45–67.

––––––. "Accademie e Accademici nel Trentino. L'Accademia degli Agiati di Rovereto." *Archivio Trentino,* 12 (1895): 129–97 and 13 (1896): 177–209.

Enzenberg, Sighard. *Schloss Tratzberg. Ein Beitrag zur Kulturgeschichte Tirols.* Schlern-Schriften, vol. 183. Innsbruck: Wagner, 1958.

Enzenberg, Sighard and Otto Preuschl-Haldenburg. "Franz I. Joseph Graf Enzenberg." *Carinthia I,* 153 (1963): 555–71.

Erläuterungen zum historischen Atlas der österreichischen Alpenländer. Issued by the Österreichische Akademie der Wissenschaften. Part 1 (vols. 1–4 and Nachtrag): Die Landgerichtskarte, 1910–58; Part 2 (vols. 1–9), 1940–57; Ergänzungsheft, 1959.

Ewaldt, H. "Das Innsbrucker Generalseminar. Ein Beitrag zur Geschichte der Universität Innsbruck in den Jahren 1783–1790." Ph.D. Diss., University of Innsbruck, 1951.

BIBLIOGRAPHY

Ferrari, Giacomo Gotifredo. *Aneddoti piacevoli e interessanti occorsi nella vita di Giacomo Gotifredo Ferrari, da Rovereto.* . . . S. Di Giacomo, ed. London: the author, 1830. Reissued 1920.

Festgabe für Hans Kramer. Franz Huter, ed. Innsbruck and Vienna: Tyrolia, 1966.

Festi, Cesare di. "Studenti trentini alle università italiane." *Archivio storico per Trieste, l'Istria e il Trentino,* 4: 36–63.

Filzi, G. B. *Annali del Ginnasio di Rovereto.* Rovereto, 1904.

Fiorio, Livio. "Rovereto ricorda W. A. Mozart 1756–1956." *Atti,* Series 5, 5 (1956): 5–34.

Fournier, August. "Eine amtliche Handlungsreise nach Italien im Jahre 1754. Ein neuer Beitrag zur Geschichte der österreichischen Commercialpolitik." *Archiv für Österreichische Geschichte,* 73 (1888): 223–74.

_____. *Historische Studien und Skizzen.* 3 vols. Prague: F. Tempsky; and Leipzig: G. Freytag, 1885–1912.

Francovich, Carlo. *Albori socialisti nel risorgimento. Contributo allo studio delle società segrete (1776–1835).* Florence: Felice Le Monier, 1962.

Franz Laws. See "Published Collections of Austrian Laws."

Garampi, Giuseppe. *Viaggio in Germania, Baviera, Svizzera, Olanda e Francia compiuto negli anni 1761–1763.* Edited by Gregorio Palmieri. Rome: Tipografia Vaticana, 1889.

Garms-Cornides, Elisabeth. "Marginalien des 18. Jahrhunderts zu zwei Biographien des Grafen Karl Firmian." *Mitteilungen des Österreichischen Staatsarchivs,* 23 (1970): 128–46.

Die gefürstete Grafschaft Tirol. Historisch, statistisch und topographisch beschreiben. Innsbruck: Wagner, 1827.

Ghisalberti, Alberto M. *Gli albori del risorgimento italiano (1700–1815).* Rome: Paolo Cremonese, 1931.

[Goldegg, Franz]. *Journal des offenen Tiroler Landtages zu Innsbruck 1790. Aus den Papieren eines Zeitgenossen.* [Hugo R. Goldegg, ed.] Bozen: J. Eberle, 1861.

Granichstaedten-Czerva, Rudolf. *Altinnsbrucker Stadthäuser und ihre Besitzer.* 4 vols. Vienna: Sensen-Verlag, 1962–66.

_____. *Andreas Hofers alte Garde.* Innsbruck: Der Vereinsbuchhandlung und Buchdruckerei, 1932.

_____. *Beiträge zur Familiengeschichte Tirols.* I: *Nordtiroler Familien.* II: *Tiroler Amtswalter 1486–1953.* Mit einem Anhang über Ständische Einrichtungen. Schlern-Schriften, vol. 131. Innsbruck: Wagner, 1954.

_____. *Bibliographische Quellen zur Tiroler Familienforschung (Tiroler Bauern, Bürger, Edelleute).* Görlitz: C. A. Starke, 1939.

_____. *Bozener Kaufherren (1550–1850). Ihre Geschichte und ihre Familien.* Görlitz: C. A. Starke, 1941.

_____. *Die Entstehung der Tiroler Landesverfassung (1790–1861).* Innsbruck, Vienna, Munich and Bozen: Tyrolia, 1922.

BIBLIOGRAPHY

————. *Innsbrucker Theresianisten. (Die Theresianische Ritter-Akademie zu Innsbruck).* Innsbruck: Albert Ditterich, 1951.

————. "Tiroler in wissenschaftlichen Akademien." *Der Schlern,* 39 (April 1965): 131–34.

Grass, Nikolaus. "Alm um Landstände Tirol." *Ancien pays et assemblées d'états/ Landen en Standen,* 32 (Louvain, 1964; published by Section Belge de la Commission Internationale pour l'Histoire des Assemblées d'États, Brussels): 137–89.

————. "Aus der Geschichte der Landstände Tirols." In *Studies presented to the International Commission for the History of Representative and Parliamentary Institutions,* vol. 24: *Album Helen Maud Cam,* 297–324. Louvain: Publications Universitairès and Paris: Éditions Béatrice-Nauwelaerts, 1961.

————. "Benediktinische Geschichtswissenschaft und die Anfänge des Instituts für österreichische Geschichtsforschung." *Mitteilungen des Instituts für österreichische Geschichtsforschung,* 68 (1960): 470–84.

————. "Die Innsbrucker Gelehrten Akademie des 18. Jahrhunderts und das Stift Wilten." *Tiroler Heimatblätter,* 23 (1948): 13–19.

————. *Österreichische Historiker-Biographien,* Series 1. Innsbruck, 1957.

Gschliesser, Oswald. "Die zivilen und militärischen Repräsentanten kaiserlicher Macht in Tirol." In O. Gschliesser, *Tirol-Österreich. Gesammelte Aufsätze zu deren Geschichte,* 139–44. Schlern-Schriften, vol. 238. Innsbruck: Wagner, 1965. (Article reprinted from *Tiroler Nachrichten,* 28 September 1963, 6.)

————. "Zur Geschichte des stehenden Heeres in Tirol bis zur bayrischen Besetzung (1805)." In *Festschrift zu Ehren Hofrat Prof. Dr. Otto Stolz,* 229–49. Veröffentlichungen des Museums Ferdinandeum, vol. 31. Innsbruck: Wagner, 1951.

Gsteu, Hermann. "Geschichte des Tiroler Landtages von 1816–1848." *Tiroler Heimat,* 8 (1927): 77–170.

Guem, Otto. "Die Entwicklung der Landgerichte in Südtirol und im Trentino." *Der Schlern,* 36 (November/December 1962): 336–39.

Haidacher, Anton. "Die Reise des päpstlichen Archivpräfekten Giuseppe Garampi durch Tirol (1761)." *Tiroler Heimat. Jahrbuch für Geschichte und Volkskunde,* 29/30 (1965–66): 87–89.

————. "Der Tiroler Gubernialpräsident Kassian Ignaz Graf Enzenberg und die staatliche Priestererziehung. Ein Beitrag zur Genesis des josephinischen Generalseminars." In *Beiträge zur geschichtlichen Landeskunde Tirols. Festschrift für Univ. Prof. Dr. Franz Huter,* 119–44. Schlern-Schriften, vol. 207. Innsbruck: Wagner, 1959.

Hämmerle, Martha. "Der Staatsrat Kaiser Leopold II." Ph.D. Diss. University of Vienna, 1939.

Hassinger, Herbert. "Der Aussenhandel der Habsburgermonarchie in der zweiten Hälfte des 18. Jahrhunderts." In *Die wirtschaftliche Situation in Deutschland*

BIBLIOGRAPHY

und Österreich um die Wende vom 18. zum 19. Jahrhundert, 61–98. Edited by Friedrich Lütge. Stuttgart: Gustav Fischer, 1964.

Hefner, Otto Titan, ed. *Stammbuch des blühenden und abgestorbenen Adels in Deutschland*. Regensburg: Verlag Georg Joseph Manz, 1860.

Hellbling, Ernst C. *Österreichische Verfassungs- und Verwaltungsgeschichte*. Vienna: Springer-Verlag, 1956.

Heufler, Ludwig. *Österreich und seine Kronländer; ein geographischer Versuch*. 4 vols. in 1. Vienna: L. Grund, 1854–56.

Hirn, Ferdinand. *Geschichte Tirols von 1809–1814*. Innsbruck: Heinrich Schwick, 1913.

Hirn, Josef. *Aus Bozens Franzosenzeit*. Beiträge zur Neueren Geschichte Österreichs, 5 (November 1910): 67–156. Vienna: J. Wiener, 1910. Reprinted Innsbruck, 1910.

—————. *Erzherzog Ferdinand II. von Tirol. Geschichte seiner Regierung und seiner Länder*. 2 vols. Innsbruck: Wagner, 1885.

Hitchins, Keith. *The Rumanian National Movement in Transylvania, 1780–1849*. Cambridge, MA: Harvard University Press, 1969.

Hochenegg, Hans. *Der Adel im Leben Tirols. Eine soziologische Studie*. Veröffentlichungen der Universität Innsbruck, No. 70 (Studien zur Rechts-, Wirtschafts- und Kulturgeschichte, No. 8.) Introduction by Nikolaus Grass. Innsbruck: Kommissionsverlag der Österreichischen Kommissionsbuchhandlung, 1971.

Hock, Carl and Hermann Ignaz Bidermann. *Der österreichische Staatsrat, (1760–1848)*. Vienna: Wilhelm Braumüller, 1879.

Hölzl, Sebastian. "Studien zum Pflichtsschulwesen in Tirol 1774–1806. Zum 200-Jahres-Jubiläum der Mariatheresianischen 'Schulordnung.' " *Tiroler Heimat*, 38 (1974): 91–138; 39 (1975): 43–90; and 40 (1976): 51–92.

Hoeniger, Karl Theodor. "Origini e sviluppi dell'economica industriale nell'Alto Adige fino al 1918." In *L'Economia industriale della Regione Trentino-Alto Adige*, 2:213–63. Edited by Umberto Toschi. Trento: Arti Grafiche "Saturnia," 1956.

Hofer, Johannes. "Zur Geschichte des Toleranzpatentes Josefs II. in Tirol." *Historisches Jahrbuch der Görres-Gesellschaft* 47 (1927): 500–525.

Hohenbühel, Ludwig, named Heufler zu Rasen. *Beiträge zur Geschichte des Tiroler Adels*. Vienna: Carl Gerold's Sohn, 1891.

Hollerweger, Hans. "Die Zustände in Tirol am Ende der Regierungszeit Joseph II. Drei Dokumente aus dem Verwaltungsarchiv." *Mitteilungen des Österreichischen Staatsarchiv*, 29 (1968): 123–41.

Honold, Walter, *Die Meraner Artikel. Eine Untersuchung der politischen Ideen der tiroler Bauernerhebung des Jahres 1525*. Tübingen: Albert Becht, 1936.

Hormayr, J. *Das Land Tirol und der Tiroler Krieg von 1809*. Leipzig, 1845.

Huber, Alfons. *Die Politik Kaiser Josephs II. beurtheilt von seinem Bruder Leopold von Toscana*. Rede bei Gelegenheit der feierlichen Kundmachung der Preisaufgaben. Innsbruck: Wagner, 1877.

BIBLIOGRAPHY

Huter, Franz. *Alpenländer mit Südtirol.* Stuttgart: Alfred Kröner, 1966.

―――, ed. *Festgabe für Hans Kramer.* Innsbruck and Vienna: Tyrolia, 1966.

―――. "Die historische Entwicklung Tirols." In *Alpenländer mit Südtirol.* 429–40.

―――, ed. *Südtirol. Eine Frage des europäischen Gewissens.* Munich: R. Oldenbourg, 1965.

Hyrtl, Jacob A. F., ed. *Die fürstlichen, gräflichen und freiherrlichen Familien des österreichischen Kaiserstaates.* Mittheilungen über ihren Ursprung, Adel, Geschlechtsfolge und Wappen. Vienna: Schaumburg, 1851.

Inglis, Henry D. *The Tyrol; with a Glance at Bavaria.* 2 vols. London: Whittaker, Treacher, & Co. 1834.

Joseph Laws. See "Published Collections of Austrian Laws."
Justizfache. See "Published Collections of Austrian Laws."

Keith, Robert Murray. *Memoirs and Correspondence (Official and Familiar) of Sir Robert Murray Keith, K.B., Envoy Extraordinary and Minister Plenipotentiary at the Courts of Dresden, Copenhagen, and Vienna, from 1769 to 1792.* 2 vols. London: Henry Colburn, 1849.

Kerner, Robert Joseph. *Bohemia in the Eighteenth Century. A Study in Political, Economic, and Social History with Special Reference to the Reign of Leopold II, 1790–1792.* New York: Macmillan, 1932.

Keul, Michael. *Staatliche Gewerbepolitik in Tirol (1648–1740). Ein Beitrag zur Geschichte des Widerstreites zwischen merkantilistischer Idee und liberalistischer Praxis.* Tiroler Wirtschaftsstudien, No. 8. Innsbruck: Wagner, 1960.

Király, Béla K. *Hungary in the Late Eighteenth Century: the Decline of Enlightened Despotism.* New York & London: Columbia University Press, 1969.

Klaar, Karl. "Andreas diPauli." In *Tiroler Ehrenkranz,* 165–66. Edited by Alois Lanner. Innsbruck: Tyrolia, 1925.

Kneschke, Ernst Heinrich, ed. *Neues allgemeines Deutsches Adels-Lexicon.* 9 vols. 1859–70. Reprinted Leipzig: Degener & Co., 1930.

Kolb, Franz. *Das Tiroler Volk in seinem Freitheitskampf 1796–1797.* Innsbruck, Vienna, and Munich: Tyrolia, 1957.

"Kotzebue über Tirol in seinen 'Erinnerungen von einer Reise aus Liefland nach Rom und Neapel,' Mit Anmerkungen von einem Tiroler." *Der Sammler für Geschichte und Statistik von Tirol,* 1 (Innsbruck, 1807): 47–87.

Kramer, Hans. "Landrichter Franz Michael Senn von Pfunds, ein Bauervertreter Tirols." *Festgabe für Hermann Wopfner. Tiroler Heimat,* 19 (1955): 135–49.

―――. "Die Zollreform an der Südgrenze Tirols 1777–1785." In *Festschrift Hans v. Voltelini zum siebzigsten Geburtstage, 31. Juli 1932,* 239–65. Veröffentlichungen des Museum Ferdinandeum, no. 12. Innsbruck: Wagner, 1932.

Krones, Franz. *Handbuch der Geschichte Österreichs.* 5 vols. Berlin: Theobald Grieben, 1876–79.

BIBLIOGRAPHY

Ladurner, Justinian. "Die Landeshauptleute von Tirol." *Archiv für Geschichte und Altertumskunde Tirols,* 2 (1865): 1–40.

LaLande, Joseph Jérôme Le François. *Voyage en Italie,* contenant l'Histoire & les Anecdotes les plus singulieres de l'Italie, & sa description; les Usages, le Gouvernement, le Commerce, la Litterature, les Arts, l'Histoire Naturelle, & les Ouvrages de Peinture, Sculpture & Architecture, & les Plans de toutes le grand villes d'Italie. 2nd ed. 9 vols. Paris: Desaint, 1786.

Largaiolii, Filippo. *Bibliografia del Trentino (1475–1903).* 2nd ed. Trento: G. Zippel, 1904.

Lechthaler, Alois. *Von Lehrerbildnern, Zöglingen und Lehrern des Innsbrucker Pädagogiums und seiner Vorgänger. Zur Zweihundertjahrfeier im Jahr 1967.* Schlern-Schriften, vol. 244. Innsbruck: Wagner, 1966.

Leopold Laws. See "Published Collections of Austrian Laws."

Leupold, Karl Friedrich Beniamin. *Allgemeines Adels-Archiv der österreichischen Monarchie.* 4 vols. Vienna: Franz Anton Hofmeister, 1789–92.

Levy, Miriam J. "Leopold II and the 1790 Italian Movement in Tyrol: A Case Study in the Politics of the Habsburg Monarchy." Ph.D. Diss., Columbia University, 1982.

Lupaș, I. "Die politischen Bestrebungen der Rumänen Siebenbürgens in den Jahren 1790–1792." In I. Lupaș, *Zur Geschichte der Rumänen. Aufsätze und Vorträge,* 451–77. Sibiu: Druck Krafft & Drotleff, 1943.

Luschin von Ebengreuth, Arnold. *Grundriss der österreichischen Reichsgeschichte.* Bamberg: C. C. Buchner, 1899.

Maasburg, M. Friedrich. *Geschichte der obersten Justizstelle in Wien (1749–1848).* Prague: Carl Bellmann, 1892.

Macartney, C. A. *The Habsburg Empire 1790–1918.* New York: Macmillan, 1969.

Mages von Kompillan, Alois. *Die Justizverwaltung in Tirol und Vorarlberg in den letzten hundert Jahren. Festschrift zur Eröffnung des neuen Justizgebäudes in Innsbruck.* Innsbruck: Wagner, 1887.

[Manfroni, M.] *L'Accademia di Rovereto dal 1750 al 1880.* Rovereto: Giorgio Grigoletti, 1882.

Manzi, Alberto. "Clementino Vannetti tra i comici. L'Origine di un Sonnetto celebre (Dalle 'Memorie' inedite di A. Morrocchesi)." *Nuova Antologia,* Series 7, 353 (February 1931): 449–72.

Marchetti, Livio. *Il Trentino nel Risorgimento.* 2 vols. Biblioteca storica del Risorgimento italiano, Series 7, nos. 4–5. Milan, Rome, and Naples: D. A. di Albrighi-Segati, 1913.

Maria Theresa Laws. See "Published Collections of Austrian Laws."

Marschlins, Meta von Salis. "Ein genialer Abenteurer." 68. *Jahresbericht der Historisch-Antiquarischen Gesellschaft von Graubünden* Jg. 1938 (Chur, 1939): 124–60.

Mascher, Hubert. "Tirol während des österreichischen Erbfolgekrieges in den Jahren 1740–1748." Ph.D. Diss. University of Innsbruck, 1956.

BIBLIOGRAPHY

Mayer, Matthias. *Der mittelalterliche Weinbau im Nordtiroler Unterlande.* Schlern-Schriften, vol. 95. Innsbruck: Wagner, 1952.

Mayer, Theodor. "Über die Grundlagen der Freiheit der Bauern in Tirol und in der Schweizer Eidgenossenschaft." In *Beiträge zur geschichtlichen Landeskunde Tirols. Festschrift für Universitäts-Professor Dr. Franz Huter anlässlich der Vollendung des 60. Lebensjahres,* 231–40. Schlern-Schriften, vol. 207. Innsbruck: Wagner, 1959.

Mayr, Michael. "Die Entwicklung der nationalen Verhältnisse in Welschtirol." *Zeitschrift des Deutschen und Österreichischen Alpenvereins,* 48 (1917): 59 ff.

————. *Der italienische Irredentismus. Sein Entstehen und seine Entwicklung, vornehmlich in Tirol.* Innsbruck: Tyrolia, 1917.

————. *Die politischen Beziehungen Deutschtirols zum italienischen Landestheile. Eine geschichtliche-staatsrechtliche Studie.* Innsbruck: Marianische Vereinsbuchdruckerei, 1901.

————. "Welschtirol in seiner geschichtlichen Entwicklung." *Zeitschrift des Deutschen und Österreichischen Alpenvereins* 38 (1907): 63–92.

Mazzei, Philip. *Memoirs of the Life and Perigrinations of the Florentine Philip Mazzei 1730–1816.* Translated by Howard R. Marraro. New York: Columbia University Press, 1942.

Megerle von Mühlfeld, Johann Georg. *Österreichisches Adels-Lexikon des achtzehnten u. neunzehnten Jahrhunderts enthaltend alle von 1701 bis 1820 von den Souveränen Österreichs wegen ihrer Verdienste um den Kaiserstaat, in die verschiedene Grade des deutscherblandischen oder Reichs-Adels, erhobenen Personen.* Vienna: Mörschner und Jasper, 1823.

————. *Ergänzungsband zu dem Österreichischen Adels-Lexikon . . . 1701 bis 1820 . . .* Vienna: Mörschner und Jasper, 1824.

Memorie della i. r. accademia di scienze, lettere, ed arti degli Agiati in Rovereto pubblicate per commemorare il suo centocinquantesimo anno di vita. Rovereto: G. Grigoletti, 1903.

[Meneghelli, Antonio] "Del Rosmini e delle sue opere." In *Opere dell'Abate Antonio Meneghelli,* 2:183–228. Padua: Minerva, 1830–31.

Mercey, Frédéric. *Le Tyrol et le Nord de l'Italie. Esquisses de Moeurs, Anecdotes, Paysages, Chants populaires, Croquis historiques, statistique, etc. dans ces Contrées en 1830.* 2 vols. Paris: Auguste Auffray, 1833.

Misson, Maximilien. *Voyage d'Italie.* Édition augmentée de Remarques nouvelles & interessantes. 4 vols. Amsterdam-Paris: 1743.

Mitrofanov, Paul. *Joseph II. Seine politische und kulturelle Tätigkeit.* Translated from the Russian by V. von Demelič. Introduction by Hans Schlitter. 2 vols. Vienna and Leipzig: C. W. Stern, 1910.

[Münter, Friedrich]. *Aus den Tagebüchern Friedrich Münters.* 3 vols. [Frederik Münter et Mindeskrift, vols. 2–4]. Øjvind Andreasen, ed. Translated from the Danish into German. Copenhagen and Leipzig: P. Haase & Søn. Otto Harrasowitz, 1937.

BIBLIOGRAPHY

Natali, Giulio. *Il Settecento*. Storia Letteraria d'Italia. Edited by A. Belloni et al. Vol. 8. Milan: Francesco Vallardi, 1929.

Nicolai, Friedrich. *Beschreibung einer Reise durch Deutschland und die Schweiz, im Jahre 1781. Nebst Bemerkungen über Belehrsamkeit, Industrie, Religion und Sitten*. Vol. 3. Berlin and Stettin, 1784.

Noether, Emiliana Pasca. *The Seeds of Italian Nationalism 1700–1815*. 1951. Reprinted New York: AMS Press, 1969.

Noyer-Weidner, Alfred. *Die Aufklärung in Oberitalien*. Münchner Romanistische Arbeiten, vol. 11. Munich: Max Hueber Verlag, 1957.

Nugent, Thomas. *The Grand Tour; Or, A Journey through the Netherlands, Germany, Italy, and France*. 4 vols. 3rd ed. London: Printed for J. Rivington and Sons, et al., in the Strand, 1778.

Oberhummer, Hermann. *Die Angehörigen der Wiener Polizeidirektion (1754–1900). Ein Nachtrag zur Geschichte der Wiener Polizei*. Vienna: Gerold, 1937.

Owen, John. *Letters on Holland, France, Switzerland, Germany and Italy*. 2 vols. London 1796.

Pascher, Franz. "Joseph Freiherr von Sperges auf Palenz und Reisdorf 1725–1791." *Österreich in Geschichte und Literatur*, 10 (1966): 539–49.

Pascu, Etienne. "Memoirs et protestations des Roumains de Transylvanie et de Hongrie de 1791 à 1892." *Revue de Transylvanie*, 3 (1939): 328–53.

Pasini, Ferdinando. "Un cronista delle invasioni francesi nel Trentino (1796–98) (Giambattista Socrella)." *Tridentum* 3 (1900): 298–330.

———. "Memorie originali. Di alcuni giudizi di Clementino Vannetti sulla letterature contemporanea." *Tridentum* 4 (1901): 433–57; 5 (1902): 57–85.

———. "Memorie originali. Un professore trentino all'università d'Innsbruck nel secolo passato (Giambattista Graser). (Un particolare curioso spigolato dai carteggi delle nostre biblioteche)." *Tridentum*, 2 (1899): 277–85, 323.

Perdolli, I. "Barone Giovanni Todeschi e l'invasione francese a Rovereto del 1796." *Atti*, Series 3, 8 (1902): 243–305.

Pedrolli, Savino. "Un capitolo di storia roveretana (1770–1801)." *Atti*, Series 3, 9 (April–June, 1903): 149–81.

———. "Frammenti di storia roveretana." *Atti*, Series 3, 11 (1905): 3–35.

———. "I manoscritti del Barone G. B. Todeschi." *Atti*, Series 3, 16 (1909): 3–26.

Pedrotti, Pietro. *Il Risorgimento nel Trentino*. Trento: A.N.I.F., Gruppo provinciale fascista della scuola, 1928.

Perini, Carlo, compiler. "L'Accademia degli Accessi." In *Cenni Storici, Statistici e Biografici. Scelti dai Manoscritti della Collezione Mazzetti*, 1, 11–19; 2, 192–6. Trento: Giovanni Seiser, 1863.

Perini, Quintilio. "La Famiglia Betta di Tierno, Chizzola, Brentonico e Rovereto." *Atti*, Series 3, 10 (1904): 95–120.

———. "La Famiglia Carpentari de Mittenberg di Rovereto." *Giornale Araldico-*

BIBLIOGRAPHY

Storico-Genealogico, 2 (1913; published Rome, 1914): 5–12.

———. "La Famiglia Saibante di Verona e Rovereto." *Atti*, Series 3, 12 (1906): 49–84.

Pettenegg, Eduard Gaston, ed. *Ludwig und Karl, Grafen und Herren von Zinzendorf. Minister unter Maria Theresia, Josef II., Leopold II. und Franz I. Ihre Selbstbiographien, nebst einer kurzen Geschichte des Hauses Zinzendorf.* Vienna: Wilhelm Braumüller, 1879.

[Pilati, Giuseppe.] *Cenni su la Vita e su le opere di Carlo Antonio Pilati stessi per la prima volta coll'aiuto di documenti da un trentino.* Rovereto: V. Sottochiesa, 1784.

Pizzini, Pasquale, compiler. *Indici analitici delle riviste Archivio Trentino (1882–1914), Tridentum (1898–1913), Pro Cultura (1910–14), Archivio Storico per Trieste, l'Istria e il Trentino (1881–98).* Collana di Monografie edita dalla Società di Studi Trentini di Scienze Storiche, vol. 27. Trento: Società di Studi Trentini di Scienze Storiche, 1976.

Postinger, Carlo Teodoro. *Clementino Vannetti. Cultore delle belle arti.* Rovereto: Carlo Tomasi, 1896.

———. "Delle Costituzioini e del Governo dell'I.R. Accademia di Scienze Lettere ed Arti degli Agiati in Rovereto." *Atti*, Series 3, 4 (1898): 97 ff.

Preradovich, Nikolaus. "Tiroler Edelleute als österreichische Kirchenfürsten des 18. Jahrhunderts." *Der Schlern*, 31 (March–April 1957): 116–20.

Přibram, Karl. *Geschichte der österreichischen Gewerbepolitik von 1749–1860.* Leipzig: Duncker & Humblot, 1907.

Probst, Jakob. "Beiträge zu Geschichte der Gymnasien in Tirol." *Zeitschrift des Ferdinandeums für Geschichte Tirol und Vorarlberg, Series 3, 7 (1858): entire volume.*

———, ed. *Geschichte der Universität in Innsbruck seit ihrer Entstehung bis zum Jahre 1860.* Innsbruck: Wagner, 1869.

Rapp, Ludwig. *Freimaurer in Tirol. Historische Skizze.* Innsbruck: Wagner, 1867.

[Rautenstrauch, Johann]. *Oesterreichische Biedermannskronik.* Freiheitsburg [Salzburg]: Gebrüder Redlich, 1784.

Ravanelli, Cesare. "Memorie originale. Un interdetto per una polemica. Contributi per una storia de Girolamo Tartarotti e i suoi tempi." *Tridentum*, 5 (1902): 289–330.

Reinalter, Helmut. *Aufklärung—Absolutismus—Reaktion. Die Geschichte Tirols in der 2. Hälfte des 18. Jahrhunderts.* Vienna: A. Schendl, 1974.

———. "Franz von Gumer—Ein Tiroler Freimaurer." In *Alpenregion und Österreich. Geschichtliche Spezialitäten. Festgabe zum 70. Geburtstag von Hans Kramer,* 117–33. Innsbruck: Verlag Thauerdruck, 1976.

———. "Freimaurer in Tirol." *Das Fenster. Tiroler Kulturzeitschrift,* 12 (1973): 1169–73.

Reinöhl, Fritz. *Geschichte der k. u. k. Kabinettskanzlei.* Mitteilungen des österreichischen Staatsarchivs. Ergänzungsband, 7. Vienna: Ferdinand Berger, 1963.

BIBLIOGRAPHY

Reitböck, Frida. "Die kulturellen und sozial Reformen unter der Regierung der Kaiserin Maria Theresia in Tirol." Ph.D. Diss. University of Innsbruck, 1943.

Ri, Giuseppe Dal. *Notizie intorno all'Industria ed al Commercio del Principato di Trento dal sacro Concilio (1545) fino alla Secolarizzazione (1803)*. Programma della I. R. Scuola Commerciale di Trento alla fine dell'anno scolastico 1887–88. Trento, 1888.

Ricuperati, Giuseppe. "Zeitschriften und Gesellschaften im Italien der Reformen." Enzyklopädie und Aufklärung in den Zeitschriften der zweiten Hälfte des 18. Jahrhunderts. In Friedrich Engel-Janosi, Grete Klingenstein and Heinrich Lutz, eds., *Formen der europäischen Aufklärung*, 190–223. Wiener Beiträge zur Geschichte der Neuzeit, vol. 3. Munich: R. Oldenbourg, 1976.

Riedl, Franz Hieronymus, ed. *Südtirol, Land europäischer Bewährung*. Innsbruck: Wagner, 1955.

Rigati, Maria. *Un illuminista trentino: Carlantonio Pilati*. Florence: Vallecchi, 1923.

Rigotti, Adriano. "Francesco Giuseppe Frisinghelli d'Isera, prete letterato e poeta (1690–1758)." *Studi Trentini di scienze storiche*, 53 (1974): 30–59, 127–45.

Rizzoli, Giulio. *Il Trentino nella sua condizione politica dei secoli XVIII e XIX*. Feltre: G. Sanussi & Co., 1903.

Rosmini, Carlo. *Memorie intorno alla vita e agli scritti di Clemente Baroni Cavalcabò*. Rovereto: Luigi Marchesani, 1798.

Rossi, Fausta Regina. "Adamo Chiusole, Scrittore d'Arte e Pittore 1729–1787." *Studi Trentini di scienze storiche*, 19 (1938): 63–109.

Rota, Ettore, *Il problema italiano dal 1700 al 1815 (L'Idea unitaria)*. Milan: Istituto per gli Studi di Politica internazionale, n.d.

Sand, Luis. "Welschtirols Recht zeugt für Südtirol." In *Südtirol. Land europäischer Bewährung. Kanonikus Michael Gamper zum 70. Geburtstag*, 111–22. Schlern-Schriften, vol. 140. Innsbruck: Wagner, 1955.

Schaff, Ulrich G. "Die Tätigkeit und der Einfluss der Tiroler Landstände in der Regierungszeit Kaiser Karl VI. (1714–40)." Ph.D. Diss. University of Innsbruck, 1953.

Schlesinger, Eugen. *Johann Rautenstrauch (1746–1801). Biographischer Beitrag zur Geschichte der Aufklärung in Oesterreich*. Vienna: Stein & Steiner, 1897.

Schletterer, Joseph. "Gedächtnissrede auf Sr. Exz. Andreas Alois Di Pauli." *Neue Zeitschrift des Ferdinandeums für Tirol und Vorarlberg*, 6 (1840): 1–43.

Schlitter, Hanns, ed. *Briefe der Erzherzogin Marie Christine Statthalterin der Niederlande an Leopold II*. Fontes Rerum Austriacarum. Oesterreichische Geschichts-Quellen. Zweite Abtheilung. Diplomataria et Acta, vol. 48, first half. Vienna: Carl Gerold's Sohn, 1896.

Schneller, Christian. *Skizzen und Culturbilder aus Tirol*. Innsbruck: Wagner, 1877.

———. *Südtirolische Landschaften. Zweite Reihe. Das Lagerthal—La Valle Lagarina*. Innsbruck: Wagner, 1900.

BIBLIOGRAPHY

Schreiber, Walter. "Zur Lage des bäuerlichen Besitzstandes in Südtirol und im Trentino. Ein Beitrag zur Kulturgeographie der beiden Gebiete." *Tiroler Heimat* 12 (1948): 93–112.

Segarizzi, Arnaldo, "Professori e scolari trentini nello studio di Padova." *Archivio Trentino*, 29 (1914): 158–200 and 5–51.

Sòriga, Renato. *Le Societa segrete, l'emigrazione politica e i primi moti per l'indipendenza*. Collezione Storica del Risorgimento Italiano, vol. 29, Series 1. Modena: Società Tipografica Modenese, 1942.

Staffler, Richard. "Rosenkreuzer in Bozen." *Der Schlern*, 24 (January 1950): 51–57.

————. "Die Speditionskompagnie von Sacco." *Der Schlern*, 23 (September-October 1949): 371–75.

————. "Zur Geschichte des Südtiroler Weinhandels." *Der Schlern*, 33 (May-June 1959): 216–19; 33 (July-August 1959): 313–21.

Steinacker, Harold. "Staatswerdung und politische Willensbildung im Alpenraum und Tirols Mittelstellung zwischen westlichen und östlichen Alpenländern." In *Beiträge zur Geschichte und Heimatkunde Tirols. Festschrift zu Ehren Hermann Wopfners*, 1:271–316. Schlern-Schriften, vol. 52. Innsbruck: Wagner, 1947.

Stella, Aldo. "Riforme trentine dei Vescovi Sizzo e Vigilio di Thun (1764–1784)." *Archivio Veneto*, Anno 85, Series 5, 54 (1954): 80–112.

Stolz, Otto. *Die Ausbreitung des Deutschtums in Südtirol im Lichte der Urkunden*. 4 vols. Leipzig, Munich, and Berlin: Institut für Sozialforschung in den Alpenländern an der Universität Innsbruck und der Stiftung für deutsche Volks- und Kulturbodenforschung Leipzig; R. Oldenbourg, 1927–34.

————. "Die Bestätigung der alten Tiroler Landesfreiheiten durch die Landfürsten." In *Beiträge zur Geschichte und Heimatkunde Tirols. Festschrift zu Ehren Hermann Wopfners*, 1:317–27. Schlern-Schriften, vol. 52. Innsbruck: Wagner, 1947.

————. "Geschichte der Gerichte Deutschtirols." *Archiv für Österreichische Geschichte* 102 (1912): 83–334.

————. *Geschichte des Landes Tirol*. Innsbruck: Tyrolia, 1955.

————. *Geschichte des Zollwesens, Verkehrs und Handels in Tirol und Vorarlberg von den Anfängen bis ins XX. Jahrhundert*. Innsbruck: Wagner, 1953.

————. *Geschichtliche Beschreibung der ober- und vorderösterreichischen Lande*. Karlsruhe: Südwestdeutsche Druck- und Verlags-Gesellschaft, 1943.

————. *Grundriss der österreichische Verfassungs- und Verwaltungsgeschichte*. Innsbruck and Vienna: Tyrolia, 1951.

————. "Handel und Gewerbe, Märkte und Städte." In *Tirol, Land und Natur, Volk und Geschichte, Geistiges Leben*, 1:305–36. Munich: Hauptausschuss des Deutschen und Österreichischen Alpenvereins, 1933.

————. "Kirche, Schulwesen und Wissenschaft." In *Tirol, Land und Natur, Volk und Geschichte, Geistiges Leben*, 1:472–84. Munich: Hauptausschuss des Deutschen und Österreichischen Alpenvereins, 1933.

————. "Das Land Tirol als politischer Körper," in *Tirol, Land und Natur, Volk und*

BIBLIOGRAPHY

Geschichte, Geistiges Leben, 1:337–89. Munich: Hauptausschuss des Deutschen und Österreichischen Alpenvereins, 1933.

———. "Die Landstandschaft der Bauern in Tirol." *Historische Vierteljahrschrift*, 28 (1933): 699–736; 29 (1934): 109–44.

———. *Politisch-historische Landesbeschreibung von Tirol*. Part 1: Nordtirol, in *Archiv für Österreichische Geschichte*, 107 (1923–26); Part 2: *Politisch-historische Landesbeschreibung von Südtirol*, in Schlern-Schriften, vol. 40. Innsbruck, 1931.

———. *Quellen zur Geschichte des Zollwesens und Handelsverkehres in Tirol und Vorarlberg vom 13. bis 18. Jahrhundert*. Deutsche Handelsakten des mittelalters und der Neuzeit, vol. 10. Wiesbaden: F. Steiner, 1955.

———. *Rechtsgeschichte des Bauernstandes und der Landeswirtschaft in Tirol und Vorarlberg*. Bozen: Verlag Ferrari-Auer, 1949.

———. "Salurns Stellung in der Geschichte Tirols." In *Salurner Büchl. Beiträge zur Heimatkunde von Salurn und Umgebung*, 23–27. Schlern-Schriften, vol. 155. Innsbruck: Wagner, 1956.

———. "Weingülten und Weinbau in Nordost-Tirol." In *Tirolensia; zum 80. Geburtstag Konrad Fischnalers*, 194–203. Innsbruck: Wagner, 1935.

———. "Zur Geschichte der Landwirtschaft in Tirol." *Tiroler Heimat*, new series, 3 (1930): 93–139.

———. "Zur Geschichte des Weinbaues in Tirol." *Der Schlern*, 22 (September 1948): 330–37.

Streiter, Josef. *Studien eines Tirolers. Erste Abtheilung*. Leipzig: Veit, 1862.

Suster, G. "Introduzione della 'steura' e dell dazio sul vino." *Archivio Trentino* 27 (1912): 36–38.

T., B. "Una questione per una carta geografica." *Archivio storico lombardo*. Series 2, vol. 1, Anno 9 (Milan, 1884): 533–47.

Thomas, Giovanna. "Tartarotti e le streghe." *Atti*, Series 6, 4 (1964): 43–58.

Tremel, Ferdinand. *Wirtschafts- und Sozialgeschichte Österreichs*. Vienna: Franz Deuticke, 1969.

Trentini, Ferruccio. "Duecent'anni di vita dell'accademia degli Agiati." *Atti*, Series 5, 1 (1952): 5–27.

———. "La figura e l'opera di Girolamo Tartarotti nel bicentenario della morte." *Atti*, Series 6, 2 (1960): 41–66.

Tuma-Holzer, Irene and Josef Jacob Holzer. "Die 'Accademia degli Agiati' von Rovereto. Aspekte ihrer Tätigkeit im Zeitalter der Aufklärung." *Österreich in Geschichte und Literatur* 21 (1977): 353–63.

Vehse, Eduard. *Geschichte des östreichischen Hofs und Adels und der östreichischen Diplomatie*. In Vehse, *Geschichte der Deutschen Höfe seit der Reformation*, vol. 8. Hamburg: Hoffmann und Campe, 1852.

Venturi, Franco. "Carlantonio Pilati." In *Illuministi Italiani*. Vol. 3: *Riformatori Lomardi Piemontesi e Toscani*, 563–640. Edited by Franco Venturi. La Letteratura Italiana. Storia e Testi, vol. 46. Milan and Naples: Riccardo Ricciardi [1958].

————. "Da illuminista a illuminato: Carlo Pilati." In *La Cultura illuministica in Italia*, 233 ff. Edited by Mario Fubini. Torino, 1957.

————. *Italy and the Enlightenment. Studies in a Cosmopolitan Century*. Introduction and edited by Stuart Woolf. Translated by Susan Corsi. London: Longman Group, 1972.

Vittori, Vittore. *Clementino Vannetti. Studio del secolo passato*. Florence: Tipografia Elzeviriana, 1899.

Voltelini, Hans. "Ein Antrag des Bischofs von Trient auf Säcularizierung und Einverleibung seines Fürstentums in die Grafschaft Tirol vom Jahre 1781–82." *Veröffentlichungen des Museums Ferdinandeum*, Jg. 1936, no. 16, (Innsbruck, 1938): 387–412.

————. *Erläuterungen zum historischen Atlas der österreichischen Alpenländer*. Abteilung 1, Part 3: Die Landgerichtskarte, "Das welsche Südtirol," 95–261. Vienna: Adolf Holzhausen, 1919.

————. "Die territoriale Entwicklung der südlichen Landschaften Österreich-Ungarns im Mittelalter und in der Neuzeit und die Entstehung der heutigen Südgrenze Österreichs." *Mitteilungen der k. k. Geographischen Gesellschaft in Wien*, 89 (1916): 481–519.

————. "Zur Geschichte des ehelichen Güterrechts in Tirol." In *Festgaben zu Ehren Max Budinger*, 331–64. Innsbruck: Wagner, 1898.

Walter, Friedrich. *Österreichische Verfassungs- und Verwaltungsgeschichte von 1500–1955*. Aus dem Nachlass Friedrich Walter. Edited by Adam Wandruszka. Vienna, Cologne, and Graz: Verlag Herman Böhlaus Nachf., 1972.

————. *Die österreichische Zentralverwaltung*. II. Abteilung: *Von der Vereinigung der österreichischen und böhmischen Hofkanzlei bis zur Einrichtung der Ministerialverfassung (1749–1848)*. Veröffentlichungen der Kommission für Neuere Geschichte Österreichs, vols. 35, 42, 43. Vienna: Adolf Holzhausens Nachfolger, 1950, 1956.

————. "Zur Wirtschaftslage Tirols um 1770." *Tiroler Wirtschaft in Vergangenheit und Gegenwart. Festgabe zur 100-Jahrfeier der Tiroler Handelskammer*. Vol. 1: Beiträge zur Wirtschafts- und Sozialgeschichte Tirols, 257–79. Edited by Herman Gerhardinger and Franz Huter. Schlern-Schriften, vol. 77. Innsbruck: Wagner, 1951.

Wandruszka, Adam. *Leopold II. Erzherzog von Österreich, Grossherzog von Toskana, König von Ungarn u. Böhmen, Römischer Kaiser*. 2 vols. Vienna and Munich: Herold, 1965.

————. "Leopold II., die 'Welschen Confinen' und die Stände Tirols." *Mitteilungen des Österreichischen Staatsarchivs*, 31 (1978): 154–60.

————. *Österreich und Italien im 18. Jahrhundert*. Österreich Archiv. Vienna: Verlag für Geschichte und Politik, 1963.

BIBLIOGRAPHY

_____. "Die Persönlichkeit Kaiser Leopolds II." *Historische Zeitschrift* 192 (1961): 295–317.

Wangermann, Ernst. *The Austrian Achievement 1700–1800*. New York: Harcourt Brace Jovanovich, Inc., 1973.

_____. *From Joseph II to the Jacobin Trials: Government Policy and Public Opinion in the Habsburg Dominions in the Period of the French Revolution*. London: Oxford University Press, 1969.

Waring, George, Jr. *Tyrol and the Skirt of the Alps*. New York: Harper and Brothers, 1880.

Weber, Beda. *Das Land Tirol*. 3 vols. Innsbruck: Wagner, 1837–38.

Weigend, Guido Gustav. *The Cultural Pattern of South Tyrol*. Chicago: University of Chicago, 1949.

Werunsky, Emil. *Österreichische Reichs- und Rechtsgeschichte. Ein Lehr- und Handbuch*. Vienna: Manz, 1894–1938.

Wesener, Gunter. *Geschichte des Erbrechtes in Österreich seit der Rezeption*. Graz and Cologne: Hermann Böhlaus Nachf., 1957.

Widmoser, Eduard. "Volkskundliches in Wolkensteins 'Tirolischer Chronik.'" In *Volkskundliche Studien aus dem Institut für Volkskunde der Universität Innsbruck. Zum 50.Geburtstag von Karl Ilg*, 141–56. Edited by Dietmar Assmann. Schlern-Schriften, vol. 237. Innsbruck: Wagner, 1964.

Wolf, Adam, ed. *Leopold II. und Marie Christine. Ihr Briefwechsel (1781–1792)*. Vienna: Carl Gerold's Sohn, 1867.

_____. *Marie Christine, Erzherzogin von Oesterreich*. 2 vols. Vienna: Carl Gerold's Sohn, 1863.

Wolf, Eric R. "Cultural Dissonance in the Italian Alps." *Comparative Studies in Society and History. An International Quarterly*, 5 (The Hague: Mouton & Co., October 1962–July 1963): 1–14.

_____. "The Inheritance of Land among Bavarian and Tyrolese Peasants." *Anthropologia*, 12 (1970): 99–114.

Wolfsgruber, Cölestin. *Franz I. Kaiser von Österreich*. 2 vols. Vienna & Leipzig: Wilhelm Braumüller, 1899.

Wolkenstein, Marx Sittich. *Landesbeschreibung von Südtirol, verfasst um 1600, erstmals aus den Handschriften herausgegeben von einer Arbeitsgemeinschaft von Innsbrucker Historikern. Festgabe zu Hermann Wopfners sechzigstem Lebensjahr*. Schlern-Schriften, vol. 34. Innsbruck: Wagner, 1936.

Wopfner, Hermann. *Von der Ehre und Freiheit des Tiroler Bauernstandes*. Innsbruck: Mar. Vereinsbuchhandlung und Buchdruckerei, 1934.

_____. "Zur Geschichte des bäuerlichen Hausgewerbes in Tirol." In *Tiroler Wirtschaft in Vergangenheit und Gegenwart. Festgabe zur 100-Jahrfeier der Tiroler Handelskammer*. Vol. 1: *Beiträge zur Wirtschafts- und Sozialgeschichte Tirols*, 203–32. Schlern-Schriften, vol. 77. Innsbruck: Wagner, 1951.

Wretschko, Alfred. "Die Frage der Landstandschaft der Universität Innsbruck." *Zeitschrift der Savigny-Stiftung für Rechtsgeschichte* Germanistische Abt., 61 (Innsbruck, 1920): 40–74.

BIBLIOGRAPHY

———. "Die Geschichte der Juristischen Fakultät an der Universität Innsbruck 1671–1904." In *Beiträge zur Rechtsgeschichte Tirols. Festschrift zum 27. Deutschen Juristentage*, 101–72. Innsbruck: Wagner, 1904.

———. "Zur Geschichte der Tiroler Landesfreiheiten." In *Festschrift zu Ehren Emil von Ottenthals*, 309–34. Innsbruck: Wagner, 1925.

Wurzbach, Constantin. *Biographisches Lexikon des Kaiserthums Österreichs, enthaltend die Lebensskizzen derjenigen Personen, welche seit 1750 in den österreichischen Kronländern gelebt und gewirkt haben*. 60 vols. Vienna: Zamarksi, 1856–91.

Zieger, Antonio. *Bagliori unitari ed aspirazioni nazionali (1751–1797)*. Milano: Pallade, 1933.

———. *I Franchi muratori del Trentino*. Trento: Tipografia Editrice Mutilati e Invalidi, 1925.

———. "Penombre Massoniche settecentesche." *Archivio per l'Alto Adige*, 12 (1934): 315 ff.

———. "Storia dell'Alto Adige." In *L'Alto Adige nel passato e nel presente. Studi raccolti da Carlo Battisti*, 97–112. Edited by Carlo Battisti. Florence: Istituto di Studi per L'Alto Adige, 1963.

———. *Storia del Trentino e dell'Alto Adige*. Trento: G. B. Monaui, [1926].

Zieglauer, Ferdinand. *Die politische Reformbewegung in Siebenbürgen zur Zeit Josefs II. und Leopold's II*. New edition. Vienna: Carl Graeser, 1885.

Zlabinger, Eleonore. *Lodovico Antonio Muratori und Österreich*. Veröffentlichungen der Universität Innsbruck, No. 53 (Studien zur Rechts-, Wirtschafts- und Kulturgeschichte, edited by Nikolaus Grass, vol. 6). Innsbruck: Im Kommissionsverlag der österreichischen Kommissionsbuchhandlung, 1970.

Zotti, Raffaele da Sacco. *Storia della Valle Lagarina*. 2 vols. 1862–63. Reprinted Bologna: Forni, n.d.

Zucchelli, Ettore. "Da Clementino Vannetti a Carlo Rosmini." In *omaggio a Clementino Vannetti*. Supplemento to the *Messaggero*, XXV May 1908, Numero unico., 7.

———. *Il Ginnasio di Rovereto in duecentocinquant'anni di vita (1672–1922)*. Annuario del R. Ginnasio-Liceo "Vittorio Emanuele III" di Rovereto, new series, Anno IV, scholastic year 1921–22. Rovereto: Ugo Grandi, 1923.

———. "Iacopo Tartarotti (1708–1787)." *LVI Annuario dell'i.r. Ginnasio superiore di Rovereto*, scholastic year 1907–1908 (Rovereto, 1908), 5–65.

INDEX

INDEX

INDEX